Praise for
THE RESISTANCE

"*The Resistance* is life-changing—and one of the most important books you'll ever give away. Fr. John Riccardo speaks directly to the struggles of our time and the deepest needs of our hearts."
—Lisa Brenninkmeyer,
founder and CEO of Walking with Purpose

"Fr. Riccardo preaches the gospel in a way that is astonishingly both new and old. This book is a gift."
—Patrick Lencioni, author of *The Advantage*

"Like St. Francis of Assisi or St. Therese of Lisieux, Fr. Riccardo captures the gospel in a way that is both timeless and completely new. *The Resistance* is another example of his life-changing presentation of what Jesus has done for us, and the battle He is calling us to wake up and fight."
—Fr. Mike Schmitz, host of the *Bible in a Year* podcast

"There is a greatness in you beyond your imagining. No matter where you are in believing this is true, let yourself be amazed through *The Resistance.* Fr. Riccardo's powerful witness and wisdom draw us into the story of a God who pursues, rescues, and restores not just in the past but also today in our times."
—Mother Gloria Therese Laven, O.C.D., superior general of Carmelite Sisters of the Most Sacred Heart of Los Angeles

"Don't resist the chance to be a part of the resistance—the resistance that can and will change the world one person, one family at a time. That's the straightforward and loving message in this beautifully written book."

—Teresa Tomeo, host of *Catholic Connection*

"Fr. Riccardo has a singular gift for presenting the gospel for what it truly is: astonishingly good news. With pastoral warmth, theological depth, and captivating storytelling, he helps us see the drama of salvation history not as an abstract idea, but as the most genuine account of our lives."

—Msgr. James Patrick Shea,
president of the University of Mary

ALSO BY FR. JOHN RICCARDO

Heaven Starts Now: Becoming a Saint Day by Day
Rerouting: Finding Our Way Back to God and His Church
Rescued: The Unexpected and Extraordinary News of the Gospel
Learning to Trust from Mary: Meditations on the Rosary
Unshakeable Hope in the Midst of the Storm

THE RESISTANCE

THE RESISTANCE

God's Plan for Renewing the Human Family

FR. JOHN RICCARDO

IMAGE

Image
An imprint of the Penguin Random House Christian Publishing Group,
a division of Penguin Random House LLC
1745 Broadway, New York, NY 10019
imagecatholicbooks.com
penguinrandomhouse.com

Italics in Scripture quotations reflect the author's added emphasis.

LIBRARY OF CONGRESS CATALOGING-IN-PUBLICATION DATA
Names: Riccardo, John author
Title: The resistance / John Riccardo.
Description: New York, NY : Image, 2026 | Includes bibliographical references.
Identifiers: LCCN 2026015981 (print) | LCCN 2026015982 (ebook) | ISBN 9798217153077 hardcover | ISBN 9798217153084 ebook
Subjects: LCSH: Christian life—Catholic authors
Classification: LCC BX2350.3 .R53 2026 (print) | LCC BX2350.3 (ebook)
LC record available at https://lccn.loc.gov/2026015981
LC ebook record available at https://lccn.loc.gov/2026015982

Printed in the United States of America

1st Printing

The authorized representative in the EU for product safety and compliance is Penguin Random House Ireland, Morrison Chambers, 32 Nassau Street, Dublin D02 YH68, Ireland. https://eu-contact.penguin.ie

BOOKMAKING TEAM: Production editors: Jocelyn Kiker, Helen Macdonald • Managing editor: Julia Wallace • Production manager: Maggie Hart • Copy editor: Laura Barker • Proofreaders: JoLeigh Buchanan, Rachel Kirsch

Book design by Diane Hobbing

For details on special quantity discounts for bulk purchases,
contact specialmarketscms@penguinrandomhouse.com.

In loving memory of John and Thelma Riccardo

Can the prey be taken from the mighty,
　　or the captives of a tyrant be rescued?
For thus says the LORD:
　　"Even the captives of the mighty shall be taken,
　　　　and the prey of the tyrant be rescued,
　　for I will contend with those who contend
　　　　　　with you,
　　　　and I will save your children. . . .
　　Then all flesh shall know
　　　　that I am the LORD your Savior,
　　　　and your Redeemer, the Mighty One of Jacob."

—ISAIAH 49:24–26

When a strong man, fully armed, guards his own palace, his goods are safe; but when one stronger than he attacks him and overcomes him, he takes away his armor in which he trusted and divides his spoil.

—LUKE 11:21–22

One of the things that surprised me when I first read the New Testament seriously was that it talked so much about a Dark Power in the universe—a mighty evil spirit who was held to be the Power behind death and disease, and sin. The difference is that Christianity thinks this Dark Power was created by God, and was good when he was created, and went wrong. Christianity agrees with Dualism that this universe is at war. But it does not think this is a war between independent powers. It thinks it is a civil war, a rebellion, and that we are living in a part of the universe occupied by the rebel.

Enemy-occupied territory—that is what this world

is. Christianity is the story of how the rightful king has landed, you might say landed in disguise, and is calling us all to take part in a great campaign of sabotage.

—C. S. Lewis

Be sober-minded; be watchful. Your adversary the devil prowls around like a roaring lion, seeking someone to devour. Resist him, firm in your faith.

—1 Peter 5:8–9

CONTENTS

PREFACE

"WHY HAVE I NEVER HEARD THIS BEFORE?" SHE SAID TO ME, TEARS streaming down her cheeks.

Her tone was somewhere between sad and downright angry. From outward appearances, she looked like she had everything: twenty-eight years old, breathtakingly beautiful, a great job. In reality, her life was an absolute mess.

She belongs to what is sometimes called the New Great Depression. Whereas the first Great Depression was economic, this new one we're living through has to do with mental health: sadness, loneliness, depression, anxiety, fear, and despair.

So, what moved her to tears? Why had she literally collapsed to the floor as I spoke to her? What's the remedy for people like her and other members of the New Great Depression? For that matter, what's the remedy for all of us, since deep down we are all restless for the same thing?

God. God is the remedy. Not the God you might think you know: The one who's spying on you, just waiting to catch you doing wrong. The distant God who is deaf to your cries. The God of philosophers. The God you might have walked away from in your teens or twenties. No—the God who reveals Himself in Scripture. The God who, above all, reveals Himself in the person of Jesus.

I believe that these are urgent, though not desperate, times.

People everywhere are longing for unity and yet divided and often prone to demonizing the other. While this is happening, churches are emptying. Oh, some stories are being told of a sort of movement taking place among young people, especially young men, of how they're being drawn to Christianity. But these stories are far outweighed by the massive numbers of those who are leaving churches. According to one study, 89 percent of those baptized Catholic no longer go to church on Sunday. Other Christian communities are seeing similar trends.

And yet.

The human person—every human person—longs for the same thing. Love. To be loved and to love. Life without love is meaningless. We all know this deep down. The core of the gospel message is the life-changing, life-saving, wondrous and explosive news that you are loved. And not just loved by anyone but by the Creator of a universe. A God who is infinitely happy, good beyond all telling, and faithful even when we are not. And you and I are not loved as a reward for good behavior. We are not loved because of some great accomplishment. We are loved just because.

This book is an urgent appeal to those of you like that young woman, who are anxious and afraid, angry, depressed, or perhaps just flat-out bored despite all you might have. The truths on the pages that follow—that you matter, that you're worth fighting for, that you're worth dying for, that you are far, far, far more important than you ever dared to dream or imagine—will change your life.

But not just *your* life. Faith is personal, but it's not private. It's meant to be shared. God's desire—His purpose in creating anything, but especially in creating us—His longing even at this very moment is to gather all His children together. The world is crying for what only God can do, even if it doesn't know this. Even if it doesn't believe this.

You and I have been destined by God to live at this very moment in history, with all that's going on around us, to bring hope, to share with others this remarkable, life-changing, and life-saving news. We've also been destined by God to get involved in every dimension of life, every sphere of human activity, to make it ever more human, ever more in accord with how the good God created it to be.

Each one of us longs to know the real God, to know that this God sees us, that we matter to Him, that we're worth fighting for to Him, that we're loved by Him. And that we were born for a purpose, a mission, one that is far nobler than we might imagine. That's the gospel. The core of it anyway.

And I don't think most people have ever heard it, whether they go to church every week or they have never thought of setting foot in one. That's why I'm writing this. This book is for you. It's for everybody.

INTRODUCTION

WHY STORIES MATTER

I ONCE HEARD A MAN SAY, "EVERY PRIEST ONLY HAS ONE HOMILY." I'm not honestly sure if he meant that as an insult or a compliment, but I think he's right. In other words, one core message shows up virtually every Sunday, week after week.

My one homily is the cross. One of my earliest childhood memories is noticing the crucifix that still hangs behind the altar in the church where I grew up. It wasn't the pain and suffering of the man on the cross that I noticed as a young boy, though. It was the love that was visible. Somehow, in a way I can't adequately explain, I knew that what I was looking at was real, true, happened for me, and would forever mark me. Somehow, I knew that the man on the cross was doing that for me, that He loved me. And that my life, if it was to have any real integrity, had to be a response to Him.

For most of my life, even over the course of many years when I deliberately wandered far from God in my daily choices, I have returned again and again to Jesus on the cross, and to the extraordinary love shown there. It's the reason for hope. Not just for me, but for all of us. And I'm painfully aware, as a Catholic priest who has sat with, prayed with, and cried with thousands of people, that this world is aching for tangible, concrete reasons to hope. This is why the cross has been at the center of my life and my preaching and teaching.

Just as priests, at least many of us, only have one homily, I think you could make the argument that Jesus only had one homily too. His one homily was the Father. Jesus speaks explicitly about God the Father more than 180 times in the Gospels. If I were to title Jesus's homily, I think it would be something like this: "You're wrong about Him." I can hear Jesus say about God the Father, "You think you know Him, but you don't. You think He's like *this,* but He's not. And I have come to make Him known, to show you that He's a good Father—kind, gracious, merciful, patient, faithful to His promises—and that you can trust Him like you can no one else."

In the prologue of his gospel, Saint John writes, "No one has ever seen God; the only God, who is at the Father's side, he has made him known" (John 1:18). Jesus, John says, "has made [the Father] known." The Greek word He uses there, *exegesato,* means "to explain, describe, or interpret." In His words, life, and above all in His going to the cross for us, Jesus has exegeted—made known—the Father. Saint Paul, a contemporary of John, says that Jesus is "the image of the invisible God" (Colossians 1:15). In other words, Jesus is the physical representation of God. Jesus does what He sees the Father doing; He says what He hears the Father say (see John 5:19; 12:49). To see Jesus is to see the Father (see John 14:9). Jesus tells us that He is "the way, and the truth, and the life" (John 14:6). The way *where*? To the Father. The truth about what or *who*? The Father. *Whose* life? The Father's.

This revelation of God is immensely important in every age but perhaps especially so in ours. We live in a culture increasingly riddled with loneliness, anxiety, fear, depression, and hopelessness. Are we just thrown into existence? Is life, as Shakespeare's

Macbeth declares, "a tale told by an idiot full of sound and fury,"[1] or is there a good author of this story we call human history in general and our lives in particular? I believe there is indeed a good author. But this author, God, is terribly misunderstood, often ignored, rejected, and in fact considered by many the enemy of our freedom and happiness.

I think it's safe to say that every one of us has a distorted image of God in one way or another. I believe that God wants to heal this in me and in you. He wants us to know who He is, and in knowing who He is, to come to know who we are. But it can't stop there. As we come to experience the love of God, that He sees us, cares for us, thinks we're worth fighting and dying for, He wants to use us to bring hope into a restless world. God's desire, in fact, is nothing less than to renew the entire human family and to transform it into His family. This is the reason He made us, made anything at all.

This book is about trying to make sense of really big questions. It's about proposing a way of seeing not just some things but, well, everything. It's about offering a vision that I believe both makes the most sense out of life and gives us hope that our lives are far more important than we have ever imagined.

So let's begin with an image that I've found particularly useful. Imagine, if you will, that it is 1944, and you and I are living in France. Four years ago, our country was invaded by a tyrannical, megalomaniacal, demonic dictator the likes of which the world has never before seen. In the years since, we've lost houses, villages have been destroyed, and cities have been reduced to ruin. We've lost loved ones too. More than four hundred thousand ordinary civilians are dead in a country of just under forty-two million people. Neighbors, friends, and family have been imprisoned, sent off to concentration camps, or executed publicly in the streets—or have simply disappeared. Every day and everywhere we hear jackboots marching all around us. Huge swastika flags hang from the Hôtel de Ville in Paris and fly atop the Eiffel Tower. During the day we are subject to an ever-increasing number of police-state regulations, including being forbidden to go anywhere without permission and without our identification papers. At night, we have to abide by a curfew. We have to close our shutters and turn off every light to prevent Allied aircraft from using city lights for navigation. And as if all of this weren't horrific enough, "the alien presence," explains historian Ian Ousby, "increasingly hated and feared in private, could seem so permanent that, in the public places where daily life went on, it was taken for granted."[2] Brutality and oppression now define our lives. Worst of all, we've become used to it. We have come to accept (if we think about it at all anymore) that nothing is likely to change because clearly nobody is stronger than this "alien presence," this occupying army. Hope is gone.

Then one day, as some of us are sitting around a coffee table, the newsboy throws in the newspaper. I open it, and there in bold, big, beautiful letters reads the headline ALLIES INVADE NORMANDY! You can't see the headline, however. And so, with no expectation of anything other than more bad news, with no expectation of anything encouraging whatsoever, you ask me what's in the news. I raise my eyes to you and answer in a dry, monotone voice, "Eh, nothing, really. Same old same old. Oh," I continue, "it appears the Allies have landed at Normandy."

Do you think I would read that headline that way? Not a chance! The Allies landed at Normandy and I'm not out-of-my-mind ecstatic about that? This was not just *news* for the people of France on June 6, 1944. This was *extraordinary* news! News that changed *everything* for them. Somebody had come to fight for them, to do something about the condition they were in because of that "alien presence" and that occupying army. Hope had returned!

Let's look at this situation from a slightly different perspective. Imagine that you are teaching freshman history in high school. Because the students are young, their tests are simple. In fact, they're multiple choice—with pictures. The test offers a picture of soldiers landing at Normandy with the question, "Why are they there?" To make it easy, there's even a date under the picture: "June 6, 1944." The multiple-choice answers are:

A. The beaches in France are spectacular.
B. The Mona Lisa is amazing.
C. The coffee in downtown Paris is second to none.
D. To fight!

Even the freshmen get this one right! It's "D." The soldiers are there to fight, obviously.

Here's the problem. Every year in December we routinely set up manger scenes in our churches and sometimes in our homes. A little baby is lying in the straw, with a woman and an older-looking man beside Him. They, in turn, are surrounded by shepherds, sheep, donkeys, and cows—not to mention three wildly dressed men kneeling there with strange-looking hats on their heads and gifts in their hands. Why is that child there? What has He come to do? Do people know? I honestly don't think most people do.

I would argue that just as quickly, just as obviously, and just as clearly as we can answer why the Allies were landing at Normandy on June 6, 1944, we should be able to answer the question, "Why is Jesus lying there in the manger?"

Can you answer that question? Do you know why Jesus is

there? Has He simply come to tell stories? Did He come to perform some miracles? Is His purpose just to tell us to be kind and love one another? Or has He, like the Allies, come to fight? And if He's come to fight, who has He come to fight against and who has He come to fight for?

Which brings us to the importance of stories. Stories are remarkably powerful. They can shape who we are and how we think about reality. Annie Murphy Paul, an acclaimed science writer, points out, for example, that reading great works of literature "enlarges and improves us as human beings. Brain science shows this claim is truer than we imagined."[3] In other words, it is possible for stories to change not just our perspective; they can also change us physiologically. Rod Dreher, author of the book *How Dante Can Save Your Life,* makes a similar argument:

> Neuroscientists have found that the telling of a story, no matter how simple, lights up parts of our brains that lie dormant when we process language. In fact, research has shown that the brain reacts to stories in the same way it responds to actual events. When a story fully enters into your imagination, it is as if you experience it yourself. The more vivid and sensual the descriptions within a story, the more powerfully its lessons, moral and otherwise, lodge in the brain.[4]

Over the next several chapters, I am going to propose a story. I will not worry about trying to convince anybody of anything. That is not my task; it belongs to another. I just want to propose a story, or maybe repropose one.

Every one of us, without exception, sees reality through "lenses." Some of us are conscious of this and some of us are not. Here's an image I find helpful in explaining this. I wear eyeglasses.

Eyeglasses are an easy way for me to think about what are called "worldviews." Worldviews, like eyeglasses, "are that *through* which, not *at* which, a society or an individual normally looks." Worldviews are "the basic stuff of human existence . . . the blueprint for how one should live in [the world], and above all the sense of identity and place which enables human beings to be what they are."[5] These "lenses" are "a largely unconscious but generally coherent set of presuppositions and beliefs that every person has."[6]

All of us have these "presuppositions and beliefs"; all of us "wear eyeglasses." Our worldviews become clear in our "religious viewpoints, political allegiances, or moral practices." They impact "how [we] see the world, [our] place in it, and the personal standards to which [we] hold [ourselves]. . . . How [we] answer the important questions of existence will inform how [we] behave in [our] day-to-day existence."[7] Finally, all worldviews "claim to be public and comprehensive. They must therefore offer some account, along with everything else, of what the adherents of other worldviews are 'really' doing. . . . The question is, whose account of everybody else makes most sense?"[8] And which account of reality leads to hope?

Dreher makes a connection between the importance of stories and worldviews:

> Stories tell us how to think and what to do. They teach us what to love, what to fear, what to hope for, and whom to trust. . . . They tell us where we came from, where we stand, where we are going. Stories impose order on chaos. From grand cosmic myths to intimate family tales, it is in stories that we find meaning, purpose, and the truths by which we live. . . .
>
> Our choices often emerge from how we feel about the information we take in and how the stories we have

> accepted as truthful accounts of reality train our emotions to engage and interpret the world.[9]

That is to say, we all see reality in a particular way. Dreher goes on:

> If we don't understand ourselves as part of a greater story . . . we will have no idea what we are supposed to do with our lives. In our modern world, we have lost the story that for centuries gave most people in our culture a way to make sense of their lives: the biblical narrative.[10]

In other words, much of the world, for the better part of the last fifteen hundred years or so, has understood reality as being shaped by a common story. We've seen reality through a particular set of lenses. Again, people may or may not have been conscious of that. Regardless, that story, the biblical narrative, shaped most of daily life: education, architecture, music, morality, politics, art, and more. Today, however, we live in a time and place where new lenses have been given to us, and new stories are shaping how we understand reality.

It has been noted that the Church has existed in two different eras: a Christendom era and an apostolic era. In the Christendom era, the story, the worldview, that shaped the culture was deeply influenced by Christianity. Those categories of life we mentioned above—education, entertainment, art, politics, law, architecture, family life—were all influenced by a biblical way of seeing. Even if people didn't know it, they were looking through lenses that had been shaped by a Christian worldview. That worldview proposed that there was a good God, who freely and lovingly brought all of creation into being. Again, this is not to say that everybody back then was aspiring to be a saint—clearly many of them weren't! But still the culture was shaped by a Christian worldview.[11]

We are no longer living in a culture like that—and we haven't been for some time. That should be pretty obvious.

Here's an example. In the 1950s, the top-rated television show was *Life Is Worth Living,* which featured Bishop Fulton J. Sheen, a Roman Catholic bishop. Sheen could and did compete with the likes of Milton Berle and Lucille Ball, the most popular personalities on the air at the time. In fact, Sheen went head-to-head with Berle on Tuesday nights for several years, and the bishop won an Emmy in 1953 for "Most Outstanding Personality." When asked how he felt about losing to a bishop, Berle quipped, "He's got better writers—Matthew, Mark, Luke, and John."

Ponder that for a moment. A Roman Catholic bishop winning an Emmy? The most popular show on television centering on what the Catholic Church teaches? Another actor referencing four names—Matthew, Mark, Luke, and John—and everybody knowing who they were? All of these are instances of Christendom.

However, by 1974, just twenty years after winning an Emmy, the same bishop declared that Christendom was dying. Sheen said, "The economic, political, social life as inspired by Christian principles, that is finished. We've seen it die. Look at the symptoms: the breakup of the family, divorce, abortion, immorality, general dishonesty."[12] He was calling attention to the fact that our culture was shifting into new ways of thinking and seeing. In this new era, the one we are currently living in, the worldviews, the eyeglasses, the lenses that most people are looking through have been shaped by a story that is very different from the biblical narrative.

Dreher puts this transition we're living in and through this way: "In our secular age, we no longer believe we're part of any universal story. We are free to choose our own narratives, which means we can follow our hearts. . . . *If it feels good, do it; if it feels right, believe it.* . . . This is how many people think today."[13] It may be how you're living right now. It's certainly how I lived for a long time when I was younger.

I grew up in a family where God was very much a part of our daily life. In our home I experienced the normalcy of faith. My mom and dad were successful people who, in the eyes of the world, had everything you could want in life. They had a happy marriage, lived in a big house, were professionally successful, made good money, took fun vacations, and were athletic and downright fun to be around. To this day, some fifty years later, childhood friends regularly tell me how much they loved being at our house—not because of the stuff we had but because of the people my parents were and how they made my friends feel.

At the clear center of my parents' life was God. They went to Mass, read the Bible daily, and modeled a life of prayer. I remember seeing my father on his knees at the side of his bed every night. He prayed in a way that was, again, normal. And attractive. Together with my mom, he didn't offer formal and rote prayers very often, though there's nothing wrong with those. Rather, he prayed as though he was having a conversation with God. And he didn't just do this at the end of the day or before meals; he prayed when someone got hurt in our backyard playing basketball, or when a friend came over and mentioned his dad had lost his job. My parents and my sisters and brother were daily models for me of people who saw *all* of reality through a Christian worldview. They were joyful, hopeful, and fun people to be around.

And yet . . .

Though I couldn't deny the happiness of my parents' lives,

and though I knew it wasn't because of their wealth or status but because of their faith in God, I resisted living that way. To me, their way seemed like less, not more. And so, despite their example, I set out to indulge every appetite I had. All the while, though, that crucifix that hung in our church was present in my mind. More specifically, the love I somehow knew God had for me, the love on display on that crucifix, was present in my mind. I tried to assuage my conscience by telling myself that one day, much, much later in life, I would come back to God and ask Him to forgive me. This way, I told myself, I could have the best of both worlds: live it up now and go to heaven later.

The problem was, though, that I wasn't living it up. I was trying to convince myself that I was living it up. Oh sure, I was happy some of the time, but I wasn't what I would call joyful. And I certainly wasn't peaceful. I'd look at myself in the mirror late at night, or early in the morning, and know I wasn't living the way I was supposed to be living. But instead of changing, I did more and more in an attempt to numb the pain I was feeling internally, or did various things to distract myself from seriously thinking about the big questions in life.

This was my life for a long time. Dreher's words fittingly describe where I found myself: "When you are the captain of your own soul, though, and have cast aside all the maritime charts showing you the safe route through dark waters, navigating only by your own stars, it's easy to make a shipwreck of your life. You wake up one day and wonder, *Where am I? How did I get here? How do I get home?*"[14] I could have written those words. Maybe those words describe where you are at this very moment, or maybe they call to mind a moment in your life when you woke up suddenly feeling lost.

David Duval was the world's number one golfer before Tiger Woods began to dominate the sport in the early 2000s. Duval won The Open Championship, or what's often (wrongly) called "The British Open," in 2001. The Open is one of professional golf's four major tournaments. For many golfers, winning The Open would represent the crowning achievement of a life's work. But Duval went into a tailspin shortly after his victory. Once the top-ranked golfer on the professional tour, he fell to number 434 in the official world ranking by 2004. You see, his whole life had been geared toward achieving a victory like The Open Championship, but that accomplishment, great as it was, didn't actually satisfy him. On the plane ride home from England, the Claret Jug right next to him, Duval reportedly said, "Is that all there is?" As much as he loved golf, and as good as he was at it, he realized it was just a game. He wanted more.

Perhaps surprisingly, many of us find ourselves lost and in trouble not so much when our prayers go unanswered but when we actually *get* the answers to our prayers. We pray for "X" to happen. Then "X" happens and we ask ourselves, "Okay, that was great, but is that it? Why am I still restless? Why am I still hungry?" For Duval, winning was good; it just wasn't enough. His life became a "shipwreck." So did mine.

Why is all of this so important? It's important because this is the story many of us are living right now. Casting aside all "the maritime charts," believing what we want to believe, thinking what we want to think, doing what we want to do, is leading a lot of people toward shipwreck and pain. I know this as a priest. I know this as a counselor. I know this as a pastor. I know it as someone who talks to people all around the country and the world. I hear it from other priests, from faithful churchgoers, and from people who have never stepped inside a church in their lives.

Evidence of the shipwrecks can be found all around us. For me, it all hit home a few years back when I happened across a column written by Mitch Albom, titled "Why Is Living Shorter, Dying Sooner a New Trend?" Albom wrote this article right before Holy Week in 2019, and it rocked my world. Albom detailed how sociologists the year before had noted the startling trend that life expectancy in the United States had declined for a third consecutive year.[15] Just think about that for a moment. In the United States of America, with everything that we have—all our wealth, all our technology, all our healthcare—life expectancy was *falling*. The last time life expectancy declined three years in a row was 1918. What was happening in 1918? World War I and the Spanish flu. Despite the political football the COVID-19 pandemic often became, there's no denying that what we lived through was terrible for many people. I had a brutally severe case myself and more or less lost six weeks of my life. One of my dearest friends died. The pandemic caused countless lives to be turned upside down. But as terrible as all of that was, the Spanish flu was horrific in a way beyond comparison. Fifty million people died from the Spanish flu at a time when the world's overall population was just 1.8 billion.[16]

Why is life expectancy in the United States falling? We are not in the middle of a world war, and in 2019 there was no pandemic. Life expectancy is falling because of what are called "deaths of despair." We're literally losing the will to live. Nobody is killing us; we're killing ourselves.

In his article, Albom identified three primary "deaths of despair." The first is suicide. Probably everyone reading this has been deeply impacted by the traumatic choice of a loved one taking his or her life. The suicide rate in our country is almost literally off the charts. Over the last twenty years it's gone up 30 percent in the United States overall. It's up 40 percent in rural America. It's up 50 percent among women. In 2022, one-third of teenage girls seriously considered taking their lives. The statistic, though, that utterly breaks my heart is this one: In the United States of America, suicide is the second leading cause of death *among children ages ten to fourteen.*

I, too, have been profoundly struck by this trauma. A brother-in-law of mine took his life beside a statue of the Sacred Heart. He had struggled for a long time with an addiction to crack cocaine and felt utterly impotent to beat it. The note he left behind simply said, "Jesus, I'm so tired of fighting." An uncle ended his life in his garage with the car running. A frightening number of friends' sons have taken their lives. As a priest, I can't even begin to add up all the people I have buried who left this life this way. If you're someone, a mom or dad especially, who has lost a loved one to suicide, I pray that even now the Lord will reach into your heart as only He can, assure you of His goodness, His mercy, His gentleness, and His kindness, and give you hope even as He stitches up the enormous and unspeakable wound that I know is inside you.

The second "death of despair" Albom mentions is alcoholism. Over the last twenty years, deaths from alcohol-related liver disease have tripled. The biggest increase is among twenty-five- to thirty-four-year-olds, especially men, but women are rapidly gaining.

The third and final "death of despair" is related to the opioid crisis. Despite the United States constituting just 5 percent of the world's population, we consume 80 percent of the world's opioids. As Albom says, that's simply "insane."

Now, there are no simple explanations or simple solutions for all of this. But I would argue the core problem is that, as the Creator gets pushed farther and farther and farther off the stage, the creature made in His image loses any sense of purpose and meaning.

More and more people are describing our age as the "new

great depression." As just one example, an ongoing study over the last thirty-five years has polled nearly fifty thousand eighth, tenth, and twelfth graders from across the country. The study presents a series of statements to these students, who are asked to respond either yes or no. One statement is: "I can't do anything right." Another reads: "My life is not useful." A third says: "I do not enjoy my life." When they first began this study, roughly 20 percent of the young people answered yes to these three statements. Now, almost 50 percent say yes. Please look at the statements again. Nearly 50 percent of eighth, tenth, and twelfth graders responded yes to "I do not enjoy my life." These are future leaders. These are future parents. These are our neighbors. These are our kids. And this is the culture we're living in right now.

It's not just youth, though, who are experiencing the New Great Depression. The mental health crisis is an epidemic and it's growing. One in four American adults takes a psychiatric drug on a daily basis. American adults lead the world in taking antidepressants, with more than 10 percent doing so. On May 3, 2023, the U.S. Department of Health and Human Services announced, "Today, United States Surgeon General Dr. Vivek Murthy released a new Surgeon General Advisory calling attention to the public health crisis of loneliness, isolation, and lack of connection in our country. Even before the onset of the COVID-19 pandemic, approximately half of U.S. adults reported experiencing measurable levels of loneliness. Disconnection fundamentally affects our mental, physical, and societal health."[17]

When I first came across that long-range study of American teenagers, one line in particular struck me. Commenting on the results, and especially on the increase in depression among our youth, Professor Jean Twenge observed, "Depression isn't just about emotions. It's about cognition, it's about thinking, *it's about how you see the world*" (italics mine).[18]

As you read this book right now, how do you see the world? What are the lenses you're looking through? Are you calm right now or stressed? Peaceful or restless?

But what if there's another story? What if there's another set of lenses? Another way of seeing? Another way of thinking?

Maybe you've watched the streaming series called *The Man in the High Castle*? It's based on a science fiction novel published in 1962 by Philip K. Dick. The story is downright bizarre, but a scene from the first season is one of the most powerful examples I've ever come across to show what can happen when another story is presented to us.

For those unfamiliar with the book or the show, the premise of *The Man in the High Castle* is that the Allies lost World War II, and the United States was divided between Nazi Germany and the Empire of Japan. From the Rocky Mountains east, Germany is in control, and from the Rocky Mountains west, Japan rules. The American people of the 1960s are living under oppression, systematic torture, slavery, and mass executions. Fear, anxiety, and despair are rampant.

In the first episode of the series, a woman named Juliana, who turns out to be the lead character in the story, is given a package by her sister, Trudy. Trudy belongs to an American resistance movement, and she's executed in the street shortly after she makes the handoff. The package turns out to be a reel of film. Juliana takes the reel home and watches it on an old-fashioned movie projector. We see her watching the reel, visibly stunned and bewildered by what she's looking at. Several times she shakes her head as if to ask herself, "What is this?" The reel finally ends, and she goes back to the projector and rewinds it so she can watch it again. Again it ends and again she rewinds it. She watches the film again, it ends, and again she rewinds it. She does this over and over and over. And as she watches this reel on repeat, her countenance is radically transformed. When she first sits down to watch, she's a woman riddled with fear, anxiety, and despair. As she continues to watch, she's drawn into what she's looking at but is obviously in disbelief. Her disbelief soon changes to confusion. By the time she watches it for the umpteenth time, she begins to smile and to weep with joy. Initially, we don't see what she's watching, but eventually we discover that the film shows scenes of the Allies landing at Normandy, bombs falling on Berlin, and the unconditional surrender of Japan.

As she watches the film the final time, her boyfriend, Frank, walks into the apartment. "What is this?" he asks.

"It's newsreel film," Juliana replies.

"Yeah, I see that," Frank answers.

In an exasperated and exuberant tone she says, "It shows us winning the war!"

Frank tells her, "But we didn't win the war."

She answers, "That's what they told us."

That's what they told us.

I would like to suggest that a lot of us are like Juliana. We're "watching a reel," if you will. We're looking at life through certain lenses. We have a story that is shaping how we think, how we see, and it goes something like this: God is not real, or even if He is real, He's utterly irrelevant. He's distant. He's not involved. In short, the "reel" is telling us that even if God exists, He doesn't care. He's not faithful. He's not good. And you can't trust Him.

But what if there's another "reel"? What if there's another story? What if there's something that we can know, and that we can share with others, that can have the same impact on us that the reel of film had on Juliana?

My experience is that a lot of people's impression of Christianity is something like, "I tried that (or I grew up that way), and it offered me nothing. I'm moving on." The problem is that they mistakenly think Christianity is just a bunch of rules to obey, a set of assertions, a lifestyle choice. But it's not! At the heart of Christianity is the revelation and announcement that God is real, that He's good, He is love, and He cares for us and all of creation far more than we could ever dare to imagine.

This revelation and announcement is the gospel. *Gospel* is a Greek word that literally is translated as "good news." The word, however, wasn't something unique to Christians or to the Jewish people. It was a common word, a word with political overtones. The separation of politics and religion is a rather new phenomenon in human history. There was no such split for the Jewish people. And there was no such split for the Roman Empire either. As New Testament scholar Michael Gorman writes,

> In Paul's day the word "gospel" did not refer to a kind of writing but to a piece of news—good news. It was a term known both in the Jewish community and in the wider Greco-Roman world.
>
> Jews who knew the text of [Isaiah] 40–66 would have associated the announcement of good news with the onset of God's presence, salvation, and reign. They would have understood this in social and political as well as "spiritual" terms; God's salvation would bring not only the renewal of the people's hearts, but also the liberation of Israel from foreign oppression, the establishment of God's *shalom,* and blessings to the poor.
>
> For non-Jews, the word *euangelion* and related terms had a variety of connotations. Perhaps the most important was the use of "good news" to refer to the arrival of an emperor and his benefactions. . . . [T]he sentiment expressed in the famous calendrical inscription of 9 BC found in Priene (near Ephesus) and else-

> where was taken for granted: "Caesar [Augustus] through his appearance . . . has exceeded the hopes of all former good messages [*euangelia*], surpassing not only the benefactors who came before him, but also leaving no hope that anyone in the future would surpass him, and since for the world the birthday of the god was the beginning of his good messages [*euangelion*]."[19]

In a letter to the Christian Church in the very heart of the Roman Empire, Saint Paul writes that the Christian gospel is "power" (Romans 1:16). The Greek word translated here as "power" is *dunamis.* This is the same word from which we get the word *dynamite.* In other words, the gospel isn't *news,* let alone *ordinary* news, any more than the Allies landing at Normandy was news. That was extraordinary, explosive, life-changing news! It changed everything for the people living under Nazi occupation.

The gospel is better than that. Infinitely better. Because there is a tyrant worse than Adolf Hitler and an occupying force worse than the Nazis, and there's a good God who is better than the Allies.

In my estimation, the single most urgent task in the Church right now is a compelling and attractive proclamation of the gospel. Why? For the simple reason that I don't think most people have ever heard it. Fleming Rutledge, an author, pastor, and preacher, wrote a spectacular book called *The Crucifixion: Understanding the Death of Jesus Christ.* In it she writes, "In the final analysis, specialized theological knowledge can take us only so far; we need to know the *story.*"[20] If you work in the Church, if you follow the Church, you probably know that conversations within often remain at somewhat academic levels. These conversations are important, to be sure. But I couldn't agree more with

Rutledge. More than anything else right now, we need to know and preach "the story."

Rutledge and I are not the only ones who feel this way. Pope John Paul II, in a 1979 letter, described "the story" as "the initial ardent proclamation by which a person is one day overwhelmed and brought to the decision to entrust himself to Jesus Christ by faith."[21]

I would humbly invite you to go to any Catholic or Protestant assembly this Sunday and gently ask everyone there two questions. First: "How many people here have been *overwhelmed* by the gospel?" How many hands do you think would go up? Ten? Twenty, maybe? Second question: "How many people here have made the decision to entrust *everything* to Jesus in faith? Time. Body. Family. Children. Career. Reputation. Sexuality. Finances. Everything." How many hands do you think would go up? Two, maybe? Frankly, I'm not even sure my hand would go up! Why? Again, I just don't think most people have heard the gospel. Not in a concise and compelling way.

A particular challenge for Catholics is the Lectionary that we read from at Mass each day. Now, don't get me wrong. The Lectionary is an amazing gift for Catholics, as it exposes people to a wide selection of the Bible over the course of three years. But the Lectionary presupposes a person knows the Bible. How many of us really know the Bible?

What about you? Have you been overwhelmed by the gospel? What does it even mean to be overwhelmed? Well, think of it this way: Have you been stunned by the reality of what God has done for you? How many of us walk into a church, look at the crucifix, and suddenly fall to our knees in thanksgiving and adoration? Shouldn't we immediately collapse when we see what God has done for us? Probably. But many people quite sincerely don't know what God has done for us.

So what's "the story"? Well, the way I break the story open is by posing four questions for us to consider. The first question is, "Why is there something rather than nothing?" The second is, "Why is everything so obviously messed up?" The third is, "What, if anything, has God done about it?" The fourth is, "If He's done anything about it, how should I respond?" For each of these questions, I like to propose a single word: *created, captured, rescued,* and *response.* I think that these four questions and these four words can be a helpful way for us to wrap our minds around "the story" and better understand the gospel. Now, behind each of those four questions and four words stand stacks of books that we could spend the rest of our lives reading. But if we can start with these questions, know these answers, and find a way to compellingly communicate them to others, we'll know and be able to share "the story." And that will change our lives and potentially the lives of countless people all around us living in this New Great Depression.

As powerful as the scene from *The Man in the High Castle* may be, it's just a work of fiction. So let me offer another one that is true. Actually, I already shared it, at least the ending of it, at the start of this book.

This might come as a surprise to you, but people rarely call a priest and say, "Hey, Father, do you have some time for me to come in and tell you how great my life is going?" We just don't get calls like that. Priests are something like trauma doctors. We live most of our days in the midst of people's pain. Quite candidly, it gets a little overwhelming some days.

"You don't know me," the woman on the phone said, "but I was told I should come and speak with you. Do you have time to meet me?"

"Sure," I answered. "How about we meet out at the church?" She said that would be fine.

I arrived early and waited for my mystery caller to walk in. After some time, a young, stunningly attractive woman walked into the church. I asked if I could help her. It quickly became clear that this was the woman who had called me and wanted to meet. She sat down and I asked her what it was I could do for her. She told me that she was twenty-eight and had a high-profile, high-paying job. Through tears she told me that her life was "a nightmare."

When she finished telling me about her situation, I asked her gently how it was that she would like me to try to help her. She told me.

"Okay," I said. "I'll try my best. But before I do that, can I take five minutes and tell you how I see the world? Because if I don't tell you how I see things, I'm afraid that nothing I say after will make any sense." She said yes and in doing so gave me permission to share the gospel with her. Over the next five minutes I walked her through the four questions and four words I mentioned above: *created, captured, rescued,* and *response.* I offered her, if you will, the "lenses," the worldview, that I wear.

When I finished, she was literally on the floor, curled up in a ball, sobbing. Now, however, they were tears of joy and not sadness. After several minutes, she looked up at me, wiping the tears from her eyes. Right after she asked me why she had never heard this before, she added, "Father, that's not the God I knew growing up."

That woman represents for me many of the people living in our culture today. Some of us are looking through lenses right now that are causing us incredible anxiety, tremendous fear, and all too often hopelessness. All I did for that woman was offer another way of seeing. She came in as a woman who, despite all that she had, was on the verge of taking her own life. She left with hope, smiling, crying tears of joy, knowing that her life mattered and that in God's eyes she was worth fighting for.

N. T. Wright suggests, "This . . . is how stories work. They invite listeners into a new world, and encourage them to make that world their own, to see their ordinary world from now on through this lens, within this grid."[22]

So let me end this introduction with a few questions that might be worth considering as we embark on this journey:

- How do you see the world right now?
- Do you feel all alone—as if no one sees you and all you're going through?
- Are you filled with anxiety, fear, or sadness?
- What is your image of God?
- Where did that image of God come from?
- Is He harsh, cruel, demanding, and distant, or is He a loving Father who is intimately concerned for and about you?

THE RESISTANCE

CHAPTER 1

THE SPLENDOR OF CREATION

IT WAS JUST BEFORE 8 A.M. CENTRAL TIME ON SEPTEMBER 11, 2001. I was in Chicago Midway International Airport, on my way to Minneapolis to meet a friend, Father Eric. We were then going to drive to his home in La Crosse, Wisconsin, to lead a men's retreat.

A group of us were in line, waiting to show our tickets to the gate agent and board the plane. It was a typical Tuesday morning, so we thought. No sound could be heard from the television mounted on the wall nearby. The talking heads on the screen were discussing who knows what, when suddenly the scene changed and we were looking at the morning skyline in New York. I'll never forget what we saw next. As we stood there, a plane flew into the World Trade Center. We all froze in disbelief. Then, within a matter of seconds, Midway Airport turned into bedlam. Police emerged out of nowhere and flooded the terminal. Some people didn't seem able to move, others were screaming. Some were crying, some were shouting, others were running aimlessly, desperately looking for the nearest exit. Two policemen approached the crowd I was in, hurried us out of the airport, and ushered us onto buses and hotel shuttles.

I ended up on a shuttle with a number of pilots and flight attendants. They simply stared at one another, silent and frightened. The shuttle stopped in front of a downtown hotel, and we all got out. The driver headed back to Midway for more passengers. I sat in the hotel lobby for the next four and a half hours, waiting for my friend to make the drive down from La Crosse. The lobby was filled with people, yet eerily silent. Everyone was glued to the television as we watched everything play out in real time. Much as my parents and their generation never forgot the events at Pearl Harbor on December 7, 1941, I will never forget September 11, 2001. I'll never forget how I felt. I'll never forget the faces of the people all around me. I'll never forget the dread of what might happen next. I'll never forget the Chicago skies devoid of planes and jet trails as the day went on.

Late that night, after Father Eric came to get me and we finally made it up to La Crosse, we celebrated Mass. Much like the Jewish people have a blessing for virtually every conceivable occasion, the Catholic Church has a Mass for pretty much every situation you can imagine. There's even a Mass that can be celebrated in a time of war. We chose that, since the details of the terrorist attacks were still coming to light and nobody really knew for sure what was going on. We had only been priests for a little over five years at that time. I remember looking at him as we were setting everything up and asking, "Eric, did you ever in your life think we would be celebrating a Mass in the time of war?"

While I sat for many hours in the hotel lobby, waiting for Father Eric to come get me, I saw the towers come crashing down. I saw the terrified crowds of New Yorkers running down the streets, vainly trying to escape the massive cloud of smoke and debris chasing them from the wreckage. Many of my shell-shocked companions were sobbing uncontrollably. It was all so horrific. The reporters on the televisions had to be shell-shocked too. They were trying their best to appear composed in the midst of all the confusion and anger. At a certain point, one of the newscasters we were watching suddenly became even more visibly distraught. He seemed to be getting new information from the voice in his earpiece. He turned away from the camera, looked offstage, and grabbed a piece of paper with an update from his producer. As he read it, his head slumped down for a quick moment before he regained his composure. "We're just learning the origin and destination of these planes. Two of them fly regularly from Boston to Los Angeles." And then he said something that I'll never forget. Staring straight into the camera, with an almost reverent tone, he said, "I'll bet there were some *important* people on that plane."

Excuse me? "*Some* important people?" Everybody on those planes wasn't important? Did he mean athletes, actors and actresses, politicians, and even people in the media like him? The moms and dads, farmers, engineers, physicians, nurses, and teachers—he didn't mean to imply that they were really not of any consequence, did he? There were *some* important people. Can you imagine the gall of someone saying something like that? I'll come back to his comment shortly.

In this chapter, we want to address the first of the four big questions that make up "the story": "Why is there something rather than nothing?" Needless to say, this is a massive question. Some years ago, I was leading a retreat for students at Dowling Catholic High School in Des Moines, Iowa. During a break after a presentation on this same question, a young student walked up to me and said, "Father, I'm going to have to ask my friends what that talk was about, because after you posed that question, all I could do was think about *it.* In fact, my head's been kind of exploding ever since."

"Why is there something rather than nothing?" is a philosophical question. Science, for all its greatness, can't answer this. Despite what some of us may have heard, science does not pose a threat to faith. In fact, it can and often does stir deeper faith.

Science is useful in answering the question "How?" but it is unable to answer the question "Why?" And "Why?" is the deeper question. The story I'm proposing, the biblical story, has an answer for why there's something rather than nothing: because someone created it.

Pause for a moment and ask God—even if you're not totally convinced He's real or listening—to give you a gift. As we examine each of the four words mentioned in the introduction (*created, captured, rescued,* and *response*), we will return to this same practice. God, as we will see, is a most generous giver. He loves to give gifts. The very specific gift we want to ask Him for now is the gift of wonder or awe. Sometimes when we pray, it's enough just to be in God's presence, much like there are times with loved ones and friends when it's enough simply to be in their company; there is no need for words. At other times, however, it's good to not only talk but also to be specific, or intentional, about what's on our minds—again, just like with friends. This is one of those times.

If you've never prayed, that's fine. Our prayer could go something like this:

> *Lord God, I ask that in a way only You can, You would move in my mind and imagination, and that You will fill me with a brand-new, or at least a deeper, sense of wonder and awe as I contemplate the universe that You have brought into being.*

As you're doing this, know that I have also prayed as I wrote this that God would do in you what He did in that woman who came to visit me, the one who, through tears, said, "That's not the God I knew growing up." I pray especially that God will bring you a tangible peace that goes beyond all understanding. For there isn't one of us who isn't anxious or concerned or maybe even fearful about something. It could be our health or the health of a loved one. It could be a difficult situation at work that seems beyond any hope of resolution. It could be something going on in the news right now, either at home or abroad. So I pray that God will replace any fear or anxiety or worry with a newfound childlike trust as we reflect together on the wonder of His creation, and most especially the wonder of the creation that is you.

As we ask the question, "Why is there something rather than nothing?" we will consider three things. First, we will touch quickly on how we are supposed to read and understand the opening eleven chapters of Genesis, the first book of the Bible. Second, we will make some important observations about the absolute uniqueness of the biblical accounts of creation, especially as found in the first three chapters of Genesis. Third, I'd like to draw our attention to just one verse in one of the creation accounts in Genesis—a verse that has over time become one of my favorite passages in the entire Bible.

Before we do any of that, allow me to make a few preliminary remarks. First, and obviously, we're twenty-first-century people. The Bible, however, wasn't written in a time like ours, so it can be difficult to enter into its worldview. Second, we're likely from the West or have been deeply influenced by Western thought. Most of us don't see the world the way the Middle East sees the world. When you combine these two things—reading ancient Middle Eastern texts with a twenty-first-century Western mindset—wholesale confusion can result at times.

Another reason many people find reading the Bible challenging is that the Bible is not a book. It's a library. Just as a public library contains different genres like contemporary fiction, classics, biographies, romance, histories, and "how to" books, Scripture has numerous sections and shelves. Those shelves hold historical narrative, poetry, apocalyptic literature, and even a love song right smack in the middle. Precisely because the Bible contains so many different literary styles throughout, we have to be mindful when we're reading it. There's no catalog number system like in the library to point the way, so we need to ask, for any given book of the Bible, "What genre am I reading?"

Now I'm very mindful that Christians can and do approach Scripture in different ways, depending on the tradition from which they come. In what follows, I am approaching the Bible as a Catholic, and so I will at times draw on Catholic teachings regarding Scripture. Even if you're not Catholic, though, or even Christian, I pray that what I share will be helpful.

One of the first things I often encourage people to do when they start to read the Bible more seriously is to read a document called *Dei Verbum* (Latin for "Word of God"). You can find this easily online or in the introduction of most Catholic Bibles. *Dei Verbum* is short, easy to read, and super helpful for understanding how to read Scripture, especially the Old Testament. I find paragraphs 11 and 12 particularly helpful. First, it affirms that God is the author of Scripture:

> For holy mother Church . . . holds that the books of both the Old and New Testaments in their entirety, with all their parts, are sacred and canonical because written under the inspiration of the Holy Spirit, they have God as their author and have been handed on as such to the Church herself.

Next, pay close attention to these points that immediately follow:

> In composing the sacred books, God chose men and while employed by Him they made use of their powers

> and abilities, so that with Him acting in them and through them, they, as true authors, consigned to writing everything and only those things which He wanted. . . .
>
> However, since God speaks in Sacred Scripture through men in human fashion, the interpreter of Sacred Scripture, in order to see clearly what God wanted to communicate to us, should carefully investigate what meaning the sacred writers really intended, and what God wanted to manifest by means of their words.[1]

Here, the Church is insisting that Scripture needs to be "carefully" investigated. In other words, when we read the Bible, we not only have to be on guard against the tendency that many of us have developed in our modern age to simply scan the text, but we also should strive to do our best to learn all we can about a particular book or passage. Thankfully, in our times, numerous and accessible resources are available online and for sale that can contribute to our learning.

Finally *Dei Verbum* declares,

> To search out the intention of the sacred writers, attention should be given, among other things, to "literary forms." For truth is set forth and expressed differently in texts which are variously historical, prophetic, poetic, or of other forms of discourse. The interpreter must investigate what meaning the sacred writer intended to express and actually expressed in particular circumstances by using contemporary literary forms in accordance with the situation of his own time and culture. For the correct understanding of what the sacred author wanted to assert, due attention must be paid to

> the customary and characteristic styles of feeling, speaking and narrating which prevailed at the time of the sacred writer, and to the patterns men normally employed at that period in their everyday dealings with one another.[2]

Prayerfully reading Scripture, in sum, takes effort. That doesn't mean you need a doctorate in theology to be able to read it, though sometimes it might feel as if you do! We just need to pay attention to what we're reading, being mindful that it was authored in a particular time and place very different from our own, using a variety of literary forms. This is perhaps especially true when we get to the first few chapters of the first book: Genesis.

What style of writing, what genre are we reading when we open the Bible and read those first eleven chapters? A wise mentor of mine, an excellent Scripture scholar, frequently reminded me that perhaps the best way to approach Genesis 1–11 was to read those chapters as inspired poetry. Now, I was an English major in college, so when I hear the word *poetry,* I'm on board, ready to analyze, discuss, and go the whole nerdy nine yards. But maybe when you hear the word *poetry,* you think, *Sheesh, why should I waste my time with this? I hate poetry.* Stay with me. When you grasp what I mean by *poetry,* it will change everything.

I find that some people, often engineers and mathematicians, recoil at the suggestion that poetry can be true. Sometimes this is because we tend to equate truth with cold, hard, scientific facts. But to think that way is terribly reductive. If the only truth is that which is made up of repeatable scientific data, and if the world is understandable only through solvable mathematical formulas, how do we prove intangibles like love? Is love mathematically or scientifically provable? Imagine expressing your love using only objective, mathematical, or scientific terms. It might sound like this: "I am experiencing something in relation to you that is characterized by feelings of warmth, closeness, and affection. As a human being, I am programmed to live in community, and it's in my DNA to form attachments to other people. I sense such an attachment to you. Various hormones are involved as well, and I may occasionally act in a way that seems contrary to reason, perhaps even responding with giddiness. I believe the term for this is *love.*" Think that will win the heart of the man or woman you love? I doubt it. As we get deeper and deeper into Scripture, we'll find that the Bible is more like a love letter from God to the whole human person than a scientific lab report detailing results. And that's part of the beauty of the Word of God.

Poetry is a remarkable way of speaking to the whole human person that a scientific formula cannot match. It communicates truths to us in language that speaks to the whole human person: mind, heart, soul, and imagination. As important as science is—and again, the Church has tremendous respect for science because it helps us understand truth—it has limits. Science can't answer the most important question of the universe: *Why?* Only the author of the universe can tell us why there is something rather than nothing. And He does that. And the answer leads us to, or should lead us to, amazement, wonder, and peace.

Another way we might approach the initial chapters of Genesis is through the genre of myth. When we moderns hear that word, we tend to think it means "untrue." Myths can make us think of a cyclops or a centaur, and of those we rightly scoff, "None of that stuff is true." But that's not what I mean when I use the word *myth* here. Much like poetry, myths attempt to describe reality in its entirety.

Mythic language, for authors like C. S. Lewis, is how we explain certain realities that simply defy explanation in ordinary language. We use myths to make us think about and understand deep truths that otherwise cannot be understood. Through grand stories, myths communicate grand truths to their listeners or readers. They communicate truth in a genre that penetrates far deeper than science.

We need to keep all of this in mind as we approach the first few chapters of Genesis, especially the stories of the Creation and the Fall, because they are not presented as cold, hard, scientific facts. As a result, many people, both in and outside the Church, often think—or maybe even fear—that to believe the Bible means we have to check our intelligence at the door. "How am I supposed to believe," they often ask, "stories about a world created in seven literal days, a woman made from a man's rib, and a talking snake? Or that eating some fruit led to the downfall of the entire human race? Are you Christians crazy or just stupid?"

We're not crazy, we're not stupid, and we can all relax because we're not taking those stories literally either. When we read the Bible, we find that *Scripture itself* tells us not to read these chapters literally. Let's repeat that: We do not read everything in the Bible literally. A literal interpretation applies, of course, to many stories and events in the Bible, most especially—though not only—in the Gospels. We need to be mindful, however, of the genre being employed before we determine whether or not a biblical text is meant to be taken literally, and the genre of Genesis 1–11 is poetry. Remember what *Dei Verbum* said:

> To search out the intention of the sacred writers, attention should be given, among other things, to "literary forms." For truth is set forth and expressed differently in texts which are variously historical, prophetic, poetic, or of other forms of discourse.[3]

From within this literary form found in Genesis, the material itself practically screams, "Don't read this literally!" Let's look at two cases that prove the point.

First, do you know how many versions of the creation story are in the book of Genesis? Two. One is in the first chapter; the other is in the second. There are two distinct stories of creation, in consecutive chapters, and they are not identical! It's not as if the divinely inspired writers and editors of Scripture missed this, and they didn't throw in multiple versions just to cover all the bases, hoping we wouldn't notice. More importantly, God, the ultimate author, is revealing to us complementary truths in these two chapters. There are reasons for this complementarity—many reasons, actually. One is to subtly say, "Don't read this literally."

Here's another reality presented in Genesis that seems to caution us against interpreting the story of creation literally:

> God said, "Let there be lights in the firmament of the heavens to separate the day from the night; and let them be for signs and for seasons and for days and years, and let them be lights in the firmament of the heavens to give light upon the earth." And it was so. And God made the two great lights, the greater light to rule the day, and the lesser light to rule the night; he made the stars also. And God set them in the firmament of the heavens to give light upon the earth, to rule over the day and over the night, and to separate the light from the darkness. And God saw that it was good. And there was evening and there was morning, a fourth day. (1:14–19, RSVCE)

As I mentioned earlier, people sometimes challenge the Bible's authority by asking, "Are you guys so stupid that you think the earth was actually created in seven twenty-four-hour days?" Here's one way I often respond: "I'm stupid about plenty of things, but that's not one of them. No, I don't believe the world was created in seven twenty-four-hour days. Actually, the Bible itself tells us that they were not twenty-four-hour days."

"Huh? Where does the Bible say that?" Genesis says that the sun and moon were created on "the fourth day." How, precisely, would we get "a day" without a sun? We wouldn't, and we didn't, because it's impossible. Days, as we know them, did not exist until the sun and moon were created and set in motion. Clearly these are not literal days. The story of what happened on each "day" is another way in which Scripture urges us, in essence, "Don't get lost in the minutiae. Don't focus on what the authors are *not* trying to communicate to you. Focus on the truths that *are* being communicated to you." God is not revealing *how* everything happened. He's revealing *why* it happened. Not understanding that Scripture contains a variety of genres gives rise to fruitless debates about things like creation versus evolution, but there's no need for such debate. The real debate is about creation versus chaos. Either everything that exists is here for a reason, or everything just randomly appeared somehow. If it's the former, let's be serious about trying to find answers. If it's the latter, well, what's the point of anything?

Now that we understand that we need to view the early chapters of Genesis through the lens of inspired poetry, or myth, we need to address a second question: How did the contemporaries of the early Jewish people see the world? Let's compare the first chapters of Genesis with the cosmogonies, or the accounts of the origins of the cosmos, of the ancient Near East.

When I was an undergrad at the University of Michigan, I took a class in mythology—several in fact. I loved these classes, but I didn't love hearing the professors assert that all ancient cultures, including that of the Jewish people, had essentially the same creation stories. I assure you that assertion is absolute rubbish. There is nothing comparable to the stories of creation in Genesis among the stories of their ancient Near East contemporaries. There are similarities in some details, perhaps, but not in terms of worldviews.

Most of these ancient Near Eastern cultures were looking through similar lenses and sharing a similar worldview. These cultures included the Sumerians, the Ugarites, the Akkadians, and the Babylonians. They lived in what we know as modern-day Iran and Iraq. They had a common religious heritage that was polytheistic, meaning they believed in many gods. And while there were significant differences between their creation stories, many of the themes, many of the stories, and in some cases even the gods and goddesses, were shared in common.

Though these cosmogonies offered many different stories of creation, their attempt to address the question "Why is there something rather than nothing?" looked roughly like this: There are many gods. These gods aren't in control but are subject to something greater—often called "the fates"—so they're kind of puny gods. The gods are violent, arbitrary, lustful, greedy, and capricious. The earth came into being either through some violent struggle between the gods or through sexual activity. Human beings, especially men, were made by the gods to be slaves so that the gods could rest and enjoy themselves. Women had even less dignity than men, were considered inferior to men both mentally and physically, and were fashioned more or less for man's (or the gods') sexual pleasure and childbearing. These creation myths present gods who act, well, just like us. They're greedy, lustful, spiteful, angry, and constantly at war with one another. They are often awful and obvious projections of human beings.

In truth, most of the cosmogonies are pornographic, and so

I won't cite them in any detail here. Let's take a look, though, at how one of these stories, *Enuma Elish,* presents the creation of the sky and the earth. This will not only give us a glimpse into their worldview, but it will also serve as a stark contrast to how Genesis speaks about the creation of the earth.

> He shot off an arrow and it tore her interior; it cut through her inward parts, it split her heart. When he had subdued her, he destroyed her life; he cast down her carcass (and) stood upon it. . . . The lord trod upon the hinder part of Tiamat, and with his unsparing club he split (her) skull. He cut the arteries of her blood and caused the north wind to carry (it) to out of the way places. . . . The lord rested, examining her dead body, to divide the abortion (and) to create ingenious things (therewith). He split her open like a mussel into two (parts); half of her he set in place and formed the sky (therewith) as a roof. . . . And a great structure, its counterpart, he established (namely) Esharra (the earth).[4]

Since the gods were always on the lookout for leisure, they decided to make a creature that would take on their labor, leaving them free to loaf, act on their lust, or just hang out. The gods, in short, made man to be a slave (paraphrased from *Atrahasis*):

> The work of God man shall bear. The goddess they called to inquire, the midwife of the gods, the wise Mami. Thou art the mother-womb, the one who creates mankind. Let one god be slain. And let the gods be purified by immersion in his flesh and blood. Let Nintu mix clay, god and man, let them together be smeared with clay.[5]

The conclusion of such myths, at least from a human being's perspective, is that life is meaningless and we have no inherent dignity. How could we? If we were fashioned by the gods to be playthings, those gods will pay attention to us only when they feel the urge to be entertained, much like a child might view ants on a sidewalk through a magnifying glass or demand to be appeased.

When humanity is seen through these lenses, there's no ultimate purpose to marriage, family, sexuality, or work. There's no purpose to friendship. There's no purpose to life. What emotions do you think would predominate in such a worldview? Despair. Meaninglessness. Hopelessness.

What would you do if you saw life through those lenses? How would you choose to live? I'll tell you how I'd live: I'd do all I could to maximize pleasure and to minimize pain. If nothing really matters, I'd feel no shame seeking to exploit other people, knowing that they would be looking to exploit me. It would be every man for himself. Why would anyone waste time being kind or good? If life has no purpose, no meaning, and there are no ultimate consequences, then what else could be the goal except to enjoy yourself? And when that was no longer possible, to just end it.

I don't think it's a stretch to say that the attitude of those living with a typical ancient Near East worldview looks and sounds an awful lot like the attitude of many people living today. Remember, depression isn't just about emotions; it's about thinking. It's about how you see the world. How do you see the world? What lenses are you looking through?

Again, being mindful of the New Great Depression that so many are experiencing right now, let's see what the biblical worldview proposes.

In contrast to their neighbors, the Israelites' worldview revealed this: There's one God. This God is good. He's not controlled by fates or anything above Him. He's not at war with anybody. He's not unhappy, lustful, lonely, or bored. He freely, without any effort, struggle, or sexual activity, creates everything out of nothing. And perhaps most especially, He does it all out of generous love.

Recall the story of creation we looked at in *Enuma Elish.* Let's compare that with what Genesis reveals:

> God said, "Let there be an expanse in the midst of the waters, and let it separate the waters from the waters." And God made the expanse and separated the waters that were under the expanse from the waters that were above the expanse. And it was so. And God called the expanse Heaven. . . .
>
> And God said, "Let the waters under the heavens be gathered together into one place, and let the dry land appear." And it was so. God called the dry land Earth, and the waters that were gathered together he called Seas. And God saw that it was good. (1:6–10)

Unlike other ancient Near East accounts of creation, there's no splitting apart here. There's no abortion. There's no tearing of someone's interior. Apparently, my Greek mythology teacher had never read Genesis, or she would've known that this is nothing at all like the other stories of the ancient Near East.

And, let's not miss this, everything God created was *good.* The Bible doesn't say it once; it says it over and over again—seven times in fact. In other words, matter *matters.* God loves stuff. He loves His creation. It's significant to Him. That's why it should be significant to us. Because God brought it all into existence and with a purpose in mind.

But the highlight of everything that God created is the

human person. You. Me. We're made in His image and in His likeness. We're not made to bear His yoke, we're not made to do His dirty work, we're not made to be slaves or objects to satisfy His lust. We're made for friendship. We're made for love, to be loved and to love—in that order. We're made for communion: communion with God and communion with one another.

Let's now contrast the Babylonian text on the creation of man, mixed with the blood of a slain god, with this account found in Genesis:

> God said, "Let us make man in our image, after our likeness. And let them have dominion over the fish of the sea and over the birds of the heavens and over the livestock and over all the earth and over every creeping thing that creeps on the earth."
>
> So God created man in his own image,
> in the image of God he created him;
> male and female he created them.
>
> And God blessed them. And God said to them, "Be fruitful and multiply and fill the earth and subdue it." (1:26–28)

In this first creation narrative, the human race is created in God's own image and likeness, equally so as male and female. Man and woman are blessed by God and called to generate new life themselves. Finally, human beings are entrusted with the wondrous and glorious task of subduing the earth. Not dominating it, but exercising dominion over it, caring for it, acting as God's agents. That's one of the meanings of being made in His image and likeness. We're supposed to be making God, and His care, and His love, and His kindness, and His generosity, and

His mercy, present on this earth that He made. That's why things like ecology matter.

Unlike the rest of creation, though, the creature made in God's image and likeness is not simply "good." After the creation of man and woman, the first chapter of Genesis concludes: "God saw everything that he had made, and behold, it was *very* good" (verse 31, emphasis added). Stop and rest with that for a moment. You are, in God's eyes, "very good."

Immediately following the creation story in Genesis 1, there's another creation story in Genesis 2—and it's not as though the editors of the Bible missed this! Rather, something complementary is being revealed in this second account of creation, where we read:

> These are the generations
> of the heavens and the earth when they were
>   created,
> in the day that the LORD God made the earth
>   and the heavens.
>
> When no bush of the field was yet in the land and no small plant of the field had yet sprung up—for the LORD God had not caused it to rain on the land, and there was no man to work the ground, and a mist was going up from the land and was watering the whole face of the ground—then the LORD God formed the man of dust from the ground and breathed into his nostrils the breath of life, and the man became a living creature. And the LORD God planted a garden in Eden, in the east, and there he put the man whom he had formed. . . .
>
> The LORD God took the man and put him in the garden of Eden to work it and keep it. And the LORD

> God commanded the man, saying, "You may surely eat of every tree of the garden, but of the tree of the knowledge of good and evil you shall not eat, for in the day that you eat of it you shall surely die."
>
> Then the LORD God said, "It is not good that the man should be alone; I will make him a helper fit for him." Now out of the ground the LORD God had formed every beast of the field and every bird of the heavens and brought them to the man to see what he would call them. And whatever the man called every living creature, that was its name. The man gave names to all livestock and to the birds of the heavens and to every beast of the field. But for Adam there was not found a helper fit for him. So the LORD God caused a deep sleep to fall upon the man, and while he slept took one of his ribs and closed up its place with flesh. And the rib that the LORD God had taken from the man he made into a woman and brought her to the man. Then the man said,
>
> "This at last is bone of my bones
> and flesh of my flesh;
> she shall be called Woman,
> because she was taken out of Man."
>
> Therefore a man shall leave his father and his mother and hold fast to his wife, and they shall become one flesh. And the man and his wife were both naked and were not ashamed. (verses 4–8, 15–25)

This account is clearly different from what we read in Genesis 1, and it easily lends itself to all sorts of confusion, so let's try to glean the key points being revealed to us. First, we see God intimately involved in the creation of man. He gets His hands dirty, if you will, by forming the man from the ground. This reveals something very special about the human being. God personally fashions man, rather than just speaking him into existence. While all of creation is God's handiwork, something is especially significant about us. This is further made clear when God breathes the breath of life into man. God's own breath is now inside of man! Finally, in these first few verses, we watch God place man in a garden, which he is tasked with keeping.

In this garden, a paradisiacal place, thanks to God's gracious provision, man has all he needs for food. However, he doesn't have what he needs for life. God calls his attention to this fact in dramatic fashion by saying, "It is not good that the man should be alone." So far so good. Then, though, comes what sounds like a most offensive statement with regard to women: "I will make him a helper fit for him." Excuse me? "Helper"? Is this how the Bible sees woman? As some sort of domestic servant, or worse? Actually, no, not at all.

The Hebrew word used here that's translated into *helper* in English is found roughly twenty times in the Old Testament. Most of those occasions refer to *divine assistance.* Woman is hardly to be understood as some sort of servant. But for what does the man need help? The answer is this, simple and yet profound: The man needs help to be human. Alone, the man cannot be fully human for the simple reason that, alone, he cannot love and be loved, and life without love is meaningless.

Next comes a somewhat comical, at least as I read it, series of verses. God tells the man that it's not good for him to be alone, and then what does He do? He creates and parades various animals in front of the man. One could mistakenly get the idea that God isn't quite sure what kind of helper the man needs. "Hmm . . . let's try the hippopotamus and see if he does the trick, shall we?

No, not good enough? Shoot. How about the panda? Not quite right either? Nuts. Ah, I know: man's best friend, the dog! Darn, that didn't quite do it." This is, of course, not what's happening. Instead, God is positioning the man to exercise dominion over the other creatures by naming them, and at the same time He is intensifying the hunger within the man for the one who will finally be the right "helper." That one is woman.

As we read on, God causes the man to fall into a dreamlike state and then takes something out of the man and creates his true helper. From this we come to understand that not only is woman made from the same stuff as man, but she's created by God, just as He had personally created man. We see again radical equality here, even though we also see difference. The woman, we should note, comes from the man's side—more specifically, from his rib. This is again beautiful, inspired poetry that reveals not only that she is neither inferior nor superior to him, since she comes neither from his head nor his feet, but more importantly she is intimately tied to love, for the rib guards and protects the man's heart.

We then see something beautiful and moving: After fashioning her, God presents the woman to the man, like a father presents his daughter to a future son-in-law. This is no mere transfer of property rights. This is God saying to the man, "Here she is, My own beloved daughter. Created directly by Me even as I directly created you. Love her!" And now, for the first time in Scripture, the man is quoted as speaking: "This at last is bone of my bones and flesh of my flesh." In other words, "Finally! Here's one who is like me!" Scripture is revealing that the woman is a person absolutely equal in dignity to the man, and yet very different from the man. In this equality and difference we see that only together do man and woman image God.

Finally, we need to call attention to something that is often misunderstood. It would appear from a casual reading that, in naming the woman, the man is exercising dominion over her in the same way that he exercised dominion over the animals by giving them names. However, that's not at all what's happening. Unfortunately, this isn't as clear in our English translations as it is in the original Hebrew.

In English, we read *man* throughout this passage, but in Genesis 2:2, a new word gets introduced in the original Hebrew. Up until that moment, the word *adam* has been used for man. Now, however, when the man speaks, he not only is giving a name to the woman but also is giving a name to himself. A more literal translation would read, "Then the *adam* said, 'This at last is bone of my bones and flesh of my flesh; she shall be called Woman, because she was taken out of *ish*." What's the big deal here? The big deal is this: In naming the woman, the man also gets a new identity and names himself. In other words, he only really comes to know who he is as a result of the woman. As all of this is happening, the man comes to know that he is made for her, made for the woman, made to be in relationship with her, made to love her and to be loved by her. The woman knows this as well, and thus we read a verse that we can only look at from a faraway distance: "The man and his wife were both naked and were not ashamed." That is, there was no lust and no fear of being objectified; no sense of being used or wanting to be used; no dominating and no conniving with being dominated. Each knew that they were made for the other, made to love and be loved by the other. This was truly paradise.

Having looked at the approach we are to bring to the early chapters of Genesis, and at how vastly different those chapters are from the creation stories of the neighbors of ancient Israel, I hope we better understand what is (and is not) being revealed. Now let's take a look at just one verse: Genesis 1:16. Over the past few years, I have found myself lingering over this passage time and time again. I find it to be one of the more humorous, and power-packed, verses in all the Bible.

The verse starts with this: "God made the two great lights, the greater light to rule the day, and the lesser light to rule the night" (RSVCE). These lights, obviously, are the sun and moon. Here comes the humorous and power-packed part, at least to me. As I pray with this verse, I imagine Moses, or whoever is the sacred author, sitting. In his hand is . . . whatever he's writing *with,* and in his lap is . . . whatever he's writing *on.* He's just finished the previous verse. After a reflective pause, he begins writing again and puts down these words: "He made the stars also."

Excuse me? "He made the stars *also*?"

Do you have any idea how many stars there are? Say, "No!" Nobody does.

Astronomers estimate that our galaxy, the Milky Way, contains somewhere between 100 billion and 400 billion stars.[6] The observable universe is made up of roughly 2 *trillion* galaxies. Each one of those galaxies has roughly 100 billion to 400 billion stars in it. The universe in its entirety is approximately 90-plus billion light-years across. How big is that? Well, a light-year is 5.88 trillion miles. That means the universe is 90 billion times 5.88 trillion miles. That's 522 *sextillion* miles across. That's 522,000,000,000,000,000,000,000.

We noted that in this unimaginably vast universe there are 2 trillion galaxies, give or take a few, each containing 100 billion to 400 billion stars. That means there are somewhere between *200 sextillion and 800 sextillion* stars in the universe. "He made the stars also." We should probably pay attention to that, don't you think?

Now, again, I'm an English major. I don't like numbers. I can't understand numbers that large. I was invited some years ago to participate in a men's conference in Worcester, Massachusetts. One of the other invited speakers was a high-energy particle physicist. I'm not sure I even know what that means. He was trying to give all of us some idea of just how big the universe is. He said, "Let me offer you a visual. Imagine the universe is a sandcastle, and every grain of sand is a star. How big would the sandcastle be?" I sat there for a moment, trying to guess the answer. "It would be," he continued, "thirty-five miles high, thirty-five miles wide, and thirty-five miles long." The tallest mountain on the face of the earth is a little bit more than five miles high. The universe, if you made a sandcastle out of it, with every star being a grain of sand, would be thirty-five miles high.

"He made the stars also"!

Many people, I know, love these kinds of numbers. Not being an engineer or math major, I need visuals. So let me offer you another image I've found staggeringly helpful. Our sun in the Milky Way is relatively small in comparison to most of the other stars in the universe. Yet you could fit roughly one million earths inside our sun. The largest star yet found in the universe, at least until somewhat recently, is called Canis Majoris—the Big Dog. Uh, yeah.

Do you know how many earths you can fit inside the Big Dog? Seven *quadrillion.* Read that again please. You can fit seven quadrillion earths inside *one star.*[7]

How big is a quadrillion? Well, let's play a little game in our minds right now. Imagine we ask for four volunteers to help us understand how big numbers are. We ask the first volunteer to count to one million. Do you know how long that would take him? Eleven and a half days. That's doable. It will be boring as can be, but it's doable.

The next volunteer is going to count to one billion. How long will that take this person? Well, I hope she's young, because we won't see her for a while. It will take this person thirty-one and a half years to count to one billion. Start now, we'll hold your dinner. The third volunteer is going to count to one trillion. We'll never see them again. In fact, this person won't finish the job, because it takes thirty-one thousand years to count to one trillion. The last volunteer, well, forget about it. It would take thirty-one million years to count to one quadrillion. And you can fit seven quadrillion earths inside one star.

Remember, there are at least 200 sextillion to 800 sextillion stars in the universe. It takes thirty-one million years to count to one quadrillion. If you wanted to count to one sextillion, you would need to count to one quadrillion one million times.

"He made the stars also."

Let's not forget to mention that, shall we?

And here's the thing that just floors me when I pray with this passage: Speaking about the stars, the book of Isaiah says, "Lift up your eyes on high and see: who created these? He who brings out their host by number, calling them all by name" (40:26). All 200 sextillion to 800 sextillion of them. But majestic as they are, those are just stars. You and I have been created in God's image and likeness, created by Him to be loved and to love. And far more meaningful than God knowing the names of the stars is that He knows your name and mine.

Remember the newscaster on 9/11? "I'll bet there were some important people on that plane." It's a simple fact that virtually every group and every organization has a special interest. Political parties, the Scouts, Kiwanis International, you name it. Everybody's got a special interest. They're always championing and petitioning on behalf of that special interest.

God has a special interest too. Do you know what it is? Do you know *who* it is?

It's *you.*

Not y'all.

It's *you,* by name.

He knows everything about you. Not because He's spying on you through the keyhole. He knows everything about you because He created you out of love, effortlessly, for friendship, for fellowship, to be happy, to know Him, to live—to live forever, actually—to share in His own divine and abundant life.

The simple truth is, there are *no* unimportant persons. God never sees crowds. God sees His children. There's Sue, there's Rob, there's Dom, there's Carol, there's Scott. He loves us. He doesn't want the world to exist without us. He doesn't want the world to exist without you.

Can you imagine if, even for a moment, we had access to all the thoughts, concerns, fears, worries, and more that are going on inside the head of each person we encounter? There isn't one of us that doesn't have countless concerns on our minds. I know I do.

I don't know about you, but when I pray, because I'm so visual, I usually have an image of God in my mind. I'm always trying to picture exactly who I'm talking to. Maybe you do the same thing. Whatever picture you and I have, though, is wrong. My image of God is too small. It's not big enough. Ninety-plus billion light-years across. Ninety billion times 5.88 trillion miles across. Five-hundred-twenty-two sextillion miles across. This is unimaginable power!

If I'm truly honest, when I pray about certain things, I'm usually wondering if God is actually able to do what I'm asking. I think many of us think the same way. Do we have any idea who we're talking to? He can do anything! He simply speaks and a universe beyond comprehension comes into existence. This means He can handle my problems, and yours. He can handle whatever we're anxious about right now. And He's inviting us, at this very moment, as we ponder His majesty and grandeur, to bring those people, those situations, those needs to Him.

God isn't just powerful, though. He created it all out of love. He created you out of love. "I think, therefore I am," said René Descartes, the father of modern philosophy. The truth is something more like, "He—that is, God—loves, therefore I am."

Why is there something rather than nothing? Because God, out of His love, created it all. And out of love He especially created *you*.

CHAPTER 2

THE ONLY ENEMY OF THE HUMAN RACE

I WAS SEXUALLY ABUSED WHEN I WAS A YOUNG BOY. I DON'T REmember how old I was when it started. I don't remember how long it lasted either. I do remember it happened at the hands of multiple people over what I think were multiple years. And I definitely remember very well the day it ended.

As I get older, I find myself talking about my experience more and more. There are two reasons for this. First, every time I do, I find that the trauma loses something of its grip on me. Second, each time I speak about what I went through, inevitably others come forward and tell me something similar happened to them, but most of them have never been able to talk about it.

I was sitting in a small group of people a few years ago, sharing what had happened, and a man I knew rather well froze as he listened. "What did you just say?" he asked. I repeated what I'd gone through, and again he looked at me, his expression somewhere between stunned and sad. "Wait . . . what?!" he stammered. After saying one more time what I had gone through, he began to cry and said, "That happened to me. I'm sixty-five years old now. I've never before told a soul. Thank you for talking about this. But how do you do it?"

Those years of abuse were my personal trauma. Actually, I have experienced many other traumas—some of them self-inflicted. Each one of us, though, has experienced our own trauma.

As a dear friend of mine says, "We all have stuff" (only he didn't say "stuff"). Maybe you, too, were sexually abused. An alarming percentage of people have been scarred in this way, including a staggering number of men. Or you may have gone through another trauma, the likes of which I can't fathom. And here's the thing: Most people would never guess what we've gone through. Even though we've all gone through something, most of the people around us, even those closest to us, have no clue about the pain we've experienced. To protect ourselves, we often become skillfully adept at wearing masks and pretending everything is fine. I know I learned to do that at a young age. Inside me, though, was an indescribable ache, combined with a terrible feeling of being damaged beyond repair that often goes with being sexually abused.

As we continue our way through "the story," we now begin to tackle the second question, "Why is everything so obviously messed up?" The answer to the first question—"Why is there something rather than nothing?"—seen through biblical lenses, proposes something wondrous and comforting: because the one God, who is good, generous, and without rival, brought it all into being out of love. And the creature He especially loves is you and me. The answer proposed to the question we're looking at next, however, is more than just sobering. It's worse than our worst nightmares.

Gospel, we mentioned, means "good news." And as we saw, it's not just news. Rather, the announcement, the proclamation of what God has done for us is life-changing, lifesaving, explosive, and extraordinary news.

By contrast, this second question makes us confront what we might call "the bad news." I find most people, including most priests and pastors, don't spend much if any time on the bad news. And who can blame them! Who wants to preach about nightmarish realities? And yet unless we confront the bad news, the good news is in fact just news.

Father Robert Spitzer, a Jesuit priest and gifted author and speaker, helps us understand why it's so important to tackle the bad news. In a book titled *Christ Versus Satan in Our Daily Lives,* he writes,

> As every prudent person knows, "forewarned is forearmed." If there really is a calculating, dangerous, dark, destructive, and vicious evil force who intends us harm—even eternal harm—then we should want to know about it. If a terrorist is living in our neighborhood, wouldn't we want to swallow the bitter pill of knowing this fact so that we could do something about it, or would we rather pretend that he is not there until he goes away? The devil, like the terrorist, does not go away if we ignore him. Instead, he increases his influence, domain, destructiveness, and malevolent intent to seduce and goad "the unaware" into his eternal darkness. Putting our hands in front of our eyes and insisting, "You can't see me!" is a highly ineffective strategy for contending with a demon of remarkable intelligence and cruelty.[1]

In other words, without understanding the bad news, we will never truly be able to see reality through biblical lenses. In my experience it seems that many of us go through life as if we are living on a stage with only two persons on it: God and us. Accordingly, when something bad happens to us, our response is often to blame God. Sometimes we go so far as to imagine that God is like the bored kid in the neighborhood who once in a while enjoys doing terrible things to bugs with a magnifying glass and sunlight. The biblical lenses, however, offer us a sobering view of reality in which there are three persons on the stage: me (or you), God, and someone else. This chapter and the next are about that someone else.

If we don't make time to consider this, we will never understand why Jesus came and what He did, especially on the cross. We will never be able to understand why it's so reasonable and logical to not only thank Jesus for what He's done for us, but to also entrust ourselves to Him. We will never understand why the gospel is such extraordinary and explosive news. We will never understand why our mission in this life is so important. Again, without the bad news the gospel is more or less just news, and maybe that's a big part of the reason many people find the gospel and Jesus so boring.

Let's go back for a moment to the question we're trying to answer. If I can be candid with you, when reflecting on what happened to me in my youth, I don't typically pose the question as delicately as, "Why is everything so obviously messed up?" I usually say something more like, "What the hell happened to me? And why?!" In my life as a priest that single question—"Why?"—is the one I hear most often. Why do bad things happen, especially to good people? Why do children get abused? Why do people get cancer? Why do wars constantly break out? Why do marriages dissolve? Why, why, why, why, why?

People are sometimes surprised to learn that nobody takes the question of evil as seriously as do the writers of the Bible. Knowing God to be good, faithful, kind, gracious, and more, how can it be that so much is wrong in His creation? The Bible is full of outcries, laments, complaints, and protests about the problem of evil. It's also full of what I like to call "game film."

In sports, once you reach a certain level, coaches and players spend lots of time watching game film of their upcoming opponents. Why? Because they want to be aware of what the other team does well so they can be prepared for and on guard against it. They also want to be aware of what their opponents don't do well so they can exploit the daylights out of their weaknesses. Why? So they can win, right? Well, God wants us to win too. He wants you to win the game of life. The only game that actually matters. Football's fun. I love it. It ultimately doesn't matter. Life matters. And God wants you and me to win.

Reading the Bible is like watching game film. In it, God reveals to us the sobering truth that we have an opponent in the game of life. He reveals to us not just what that enemy did years ago but also what he does now. He reveals our opponent's origin, his strategy, his goal for our lives, and the tactics he deploys against us. And God does this because He wants us to win!

I invite you to watch the game film with me. I warn you in advance that this is sobering stuff. We're going to come face-to-face with the enemy of our race and see how utterly dire the situation of humankind was and would be if God had not done something about this enemy. But we need not be terrified as we do this, because God *has* done something about him. With that, let's say a prayer and begin.

Once again, we're going to ask God for a grace, a gift. The specific grace and gift we want is light. I want you to picture a searchlight, or perhaps something as bright as an aircraft landing light. We're talking some seriously intense wattage! We want to ask God right now to shine intense wattage on the one who, as we'll see, is the only enemy of the human race. We want to ask God to expose him and to give him and his tactics nowhere to hide.

> *God in heaven, creator of the stars, builder of the universe and all that is, both seen and unseen: You are the*

Lover of the human race. We humbly and confidently ask You to shine as only You do, so that everyone reading this might be able to see more clearly the enemy—the real enemy. Expose his nature, his tactics, his goal, and how he seeks to hurt us. As only You can, Lord God, we ask You to do this so that we might grow in freedom, so that we might win the game of life. All this we ask in Jesus's name. Amen.

"The enemy gets a vote" is a phrase that military leaders routinely use. It means you can have the absolutely best plan in place, but once you engage in combat, you'd better not forget that there is an opponent with a mind and a will and a desire to defeat you. Putting on a biblical set of lenses reveals the same thing for us. Before we get into the origin of this enemy, before we talk about why he rebelled against God, before we consider his primary strategy, before we expose his goal for our lives and the tactics he commonly uses against us, let me offer a most important reality that the Bible reveals to us: The enemy is the enemy, period.

The title of this chapter is "The Only Enemy of the Human Race." By this I mean to say that part of seeing reality with a biblical worldview—an increasingly essential part with all that's going on around us—is that no human being is my enemy. Period. The enemy is not another political party. It's not another race. It's not another gender. It's not another economic class. It's not even Ohio State fans. (I'm a University of Michigan grad, so I had to throw that in there.) No human being is my enemy. As a disciple of Jesus, I realize I might be theirs, but no human being is my enemy, nor should any human being be the enemy of any Christian.

This is not at all to say that people don't do wicked things.

They certainly do! But they're not the enemy. They're just rebels. Just as for many years I acted like a rebel, and still do some days, if I'm brutally honest. If we don't know this, or if we forget this, then we will quickly do what we see being done all around us. We'll start blaming people, or categories of people. And then we will demonize them. And when we demonize another human, whether in politics, in communities, in schools, or even in the Church, we will end up seeking to cancel them, silence them, or worse.

We have to stop this.

Who, then, is this enemy, this third person on the stage? Well, he has many names according to the Bible: Satan, the devil, the accuser of our race, the ruler of this world, the prince of the power of the air, and others. In looking at him, we want to be mindful of two common tendencies. These tendencies are well expressed by C. S. Lewis. Born in Belfast, Northern Ireland, Lewis was baptized when he was young but later made a conscious decision to become an atheist. After he fought in World War I, he became a professor at Oxford. There he became good friends with a number of other professors, including J.R.R. Tolkien. Tolkien and these other men were devout Christians, and over many years of friendship, conversation, and argument, they gradually helped Lewis to see the reasonableness and the beauty of faith. Lewis then became one of the most popular Christian speakers and authors of the twentieth century. In his book *The Screwtape Letters,* a book perhaps unmatched in all of literature in its insights into the schemes of Satan and his demons, Lewis writes: "There are two equal and opposite errors into which our race can fall about the devils. One is to disbelieve in their existence. The other is to believe, and to feel an excessive and unhealthy interest in them."[2]

I think Lewis is spot-on. Not long ago I was helping to lead a group of priests on retreat. During a break, after I presented the material we're about to dive into, one of the priests pulled me aside. He was seventy-five years old and had been a priest for fifty years. Sheepishly, he looked at me and said, "Up until now I don't think I've ever even thought about the devil in my life. I *know* I've never preached on him." This priest falls into the first group Lewis describes. He doesn't, or didn't, believe in his existence. There is, though, that second group that Lewis writes about. These people exhibit what seems to be a preoccupation with the devil. This is flat-out dangerous, and so we want to walk the fine line of exposing the enemy, or asking God to expose him, without becoming excessively interested in him. We need to know our opponent, not only because we need to see reality accurately, but also because we want to better understand who Jesus is and what He has done for us.

Who is Satan, the devil, and the other demons that Scripture speaks about? Are they a rival to God? Is life like a Marvel comic book or movie, a celestial duel between a good god and a bad god and we're just pawns in their battle, hoping the good god wins?

Uh, no. There's only one God, and the devil is not him. The one and only God, the one who created the universe and especially us, has no rival. Period. The devil, in short, is a creature. Allow yourself to linger with that for a moment. He's just a creature. A mighty creature, to be sure. An angel, in fact. But he himself didn't exist until God created him. And God created him good, for God only creates good. The *Catechism of the Catholic Church* teaches that "Satan was at first a good angel, made by God."[3] His name was Lucifer, meaning "light bearer." All sorts of traditions surround him, many of which place him closest to the throne of God. This creature was brought into existence by God, knew God, worshiped God, loved God, and received God's love. But the devil and other angels who became demons intentionally chose evil.

The early chapters of Genesis teach us this but in a way that's so subtle sometimes it's missed. The devil is introduced near the start of the story in Genesis 3, where we read, "Now the serpent was more crafty than any other beast of the field that the Lord God had made" (verse 1). The point to note here is that this enemy is a creature. The Lord God *made him.* Scripture is shining a light here, exposing him as just a creature, not a rival to God.

Jesus speaks directly about this third person on the stage. In one place in the gospel of Saint John, Jesus identifies him as "the ruler of this world" (12:31). That's worth mulling for a moment. Jesus, the One through whom and for whom a universe exists that is ninety-plus billion light-years across, identifies someone else as "the ruler of this world." Jesus also reveals that this "ruler" is a murderer and a liar. Saint Paul calls him "the prince of the power of the air" (Ephesians 2:2). In the last book of the Bible, Revelation, he is called "the accuser of our brothers" (12:10). This is our enemy.

If this creature was originally good, then why did he become evil? Why would an angel rebel?

When I first really came to grips with the answer to the question of the devil's rebellion, everything began to change for me. When I was in high school and in college, doing a whole set of things that I shouldn't have been doing, my understanding of my life went something like this: "I'm the captain of my own ship, living for myself right now. I'm the American man, John Wayne riding out into the sunset. Rugged, independent, in need of nothing and no one." I more or less did whatever I wanted whenever I wanted, all the while knowing I should probably not be doing many of these things but thinking, *Heck, there will be time to turn back to God when I'm older.*

In short, I believed I was in control, until I learned why the enemy rebelled. The Wisdom of Solomon in the Old Testament offered me a different way of seeing reality:

> God created man for incorruption
> and made him in the image of his own eternity,
> but through the devil's envy death entered the world,
> and those who belong to his party experience it.
> (2:23–24, RSVCE)

Here, then, we see the biblical explanation for the rebellion of this good angel. We're offered insight into why he became evil. And the *why* has to do with us—you and me. It's personal. The devil's root sin is typically thought to be pride, and it is. But his *motive* for rebelling isn't pride, not according to Scripture. His motive for rebelling is *envy.* This is where everything began to change for me.

What's envy? Envy is a certain sadness over the good fortune of another, the well-being of another. It's considered a deadly sin because it easily and often gives rise to all sorts of other evils. When I'm envious, I'm so sad at what you have that I wish you didn't have it. And this can lead to my taking action to ensure that you no longer have whatever I was envious of, even to the point of taking your life. This is envy.

Who is the devil envious of? Not just God. You. Me. Here is where the lightbulb went on. Scripture is proposing to us that the enemy is envious of the destiny that God has prepared for you and me; he finds it absolutely abhorrent. So he turned evil and turned all his energy toward trying to keep us from the good end for which God created us. Here's how one author explains it:

> The sight of these happy creatures [that's you and me] filled the Devil and his fallen angels with anger and envy. They took thought as to how they might mar God's work and destroy the destiny of this newly created race. They set about to enslave those whom they had been meant to serve and to degrade those who had been assigned such an exalted place into the lowly slime beneath their feet.[4]

There, my friends, is the devil's game: slavery and degradation. With even a cursory glance back at my life in my teens and twenties that's what I find: slavery and degradation. The enemy is literally hell-bent on trying to ruin you and me.

How do the devil and the other fallen angels go about trying to do this? Is there a primary strategy? In fact, there is. Remember, Scripture is game film. And the Bible doesn't only reveal what happened long ago; it reveals what always happens. In other words, in seeing "the plays" the enemy ran against other members of the human family, we gain insight into the plays he is constantly running against us.

The devil's strategy is learned by knowing his names. In Scripture, a person's name reveals his character. It says something about who that individual is and how they act. While a number of names are given to our enemy, two especially stand out. Together, these two names appear more than fifty times in the New Testament—lest we think this part of the story is just some incidental tidbit. These two names are *Satan* and *the devil.*

Satan means "the accuser." This is what he does. He accuses God and he accuses us. The accusation against God is a variation on a constant theme that goes something like this: "God is not good, He's not your loving Father, and you can be happier apart from Him." This is his primary strategy. This was at the heart of his temptation of our first parents in the garden in Genesis 3. And for you and me, too, this accusation is at the heart of every temptation. The enemy relentlessly proposes to our minds a narrative. He's trying to get us to see through a particular set of lenses that distort reality and accuse God of being something other than what He is—good. "No," the accuser says, "God is not your loving Father; He is in fact your adversary. He's holding you down. He's a curtailment on your freedom. He's limiting you. He's not faithful; you can't count on Him." In my mind he often shouts, "Where was this good God when you were getting abused? He wasn't there. He didn't stop it. You were crying out, and where was He? Can't you see, He's not a good Father? Just turn away. All those laws. All those rules. You'd be so much happier apart from Him."

I bought that hook, line, and sinker. Maybe you did too.

Though his primary accusation is against God, this is not to say that the enemy doesn't also accuse us. He does, and it happens oh so frequently. After he seduces us into turning against God, if we should think about turning back, he quickly accuses us, telling us that there is no hope for us, that God will never welcome us back, not after what we have done—whatever it is. Satan, as one person astutely observed, knows our name but he calls us by our sins.

The enemy's other primary name, *the devil,* comes from the Greek word *diabolos* and means "the divider." That doesn't quite catch the sense of the word, though. You can divide things in a neat and tidy way. That's hardly what the devil does. More than divide, he *shreds*; he rips to pieces, or tries to, anyway. Friendships, marriages, families, communities, schools, churches, cities, nations, and the world.

The enemy's ultimate goal, the demons' desired outcome for your life and mine, is nothing less than this: our destruction.

"The thief," Jesus says, "comes only to steal and kill and destroy" (John 10:10). I have finally gotten to the point in my life where I'm painfully aware of this "third person" on the stage. But I've also come to the point where I acknowledge in a most humbling fashion that I can participate all too willingly in my own destruction. When I experience the various temptations that come my way (and I experience them, just like you do—and possibly much worse), it's as if I can see an enemy army. I know they're hostile, they're dangerous, and they want to hurt me. Yet, alarmingly often I simply raise the white flag, say, "Here I am!" and then proceed to walk into the enemy camp knowing full well what I'm doing! I don't know about you, but I am darn well aware when I succumb to temptation, of whatever kind. Why do I do this? Why do so many of us do this? We'll save the answer to that question for the next chapter.

As we continue to put on biblical lenses, we discover that certain tactics are constantly—relentlessly, in fact—employed against us by this accusing and dividing foe. Among these are the following: He lies, he flatters, he tempts, and he discourages.

Let me put all of this together and tell you how the various tactics of hell worked in my life. First, I'll share how the enemy accuses me. I'd like to say how he *accused* me, but I'm now sixty and he continues to do it. Even though my abuse happened decades ago, he still accuses me. He continues to bring to my mind what happened and says things like, "You're damaged goods," "It was your fault," "You enjoyed that," or "You're wrong." Not "bad"—"wrong." As if something is wrong *with* and *in* me.

I didn't tell anybody about my abuse until I was almost fifty years old. And you never would have guessed it. I had become quite skilled at acting a certain way, speaking a certain way, even walking a certain way. These things became my coping mechanisms. I deliberately put walls around myself, walls of self-protection. They were my way of saying to myself, *Don't ever get hurt again. Don't ever let anybody in. The outcome could be too painful.* So I kept everybody out.

By the time I went to seminary to study for the priesthood, I had developed a reputation, among some at least, of being aloof. I was told this over and over again by certain mentors whose responsibility it was to share with me how I was perceived by others. This is part of what's called "formation" in the seminary. And it's painful! It's the experience of having people tell you over and over again all the things that you do that others find annoying, concerning, or inappropriate, and in my case the list was long. In theory, of course, this is all done out of love so that, if and when you are ordained a priest, your behaviors are not obstacles to others hearing the gospel through you.

Anyway, I was repeatedly told in the seminary that I appeared to be apart from and not a part of, that I came off with a sense of superiority—all due to the masks and various coping methods I had developed to help assuage the pain of my childhood trauma. As I heard this feedback, I found myself thinking, *You've gotta be kidding me. You think I'm* aloof? *I think I'm worthless, damaged goods, bad, wrong.* That's where my head was, and I still am prone to think this way.

The enemy also lies to me. He says things like, "You'll never be well. No one will ever love you for who you are. You're not worth loving. Every friend you have will eventually abandon you."

The enemy divides. This is painfully true, especially in my family. My parents never knew what happened to me. They died before I began to speak about it. But just after my father passed away, and before I told my siblings what had happened to me, I found myself at the end of my mom's driveway in an ugly exchange with one of my sisters. It was not exactly the proudest moment of my life. I don't even remember how the conversation started, but at some point, with a look of both sadness and anger, she said to me, "John, you're never here. You are *never* here." And she was right.

A priest is ordained to preach the gospel, to care for people, to be a spiritual father for, in some cases, thousands of people. Before I was ordained, I would spend holidays with my family. Once I was ordained, however, Christmas and Easter and other holidays weren't exactly days off, so I often stopped in briefly, wolfed down some food, told everyone I loved them, and then headed home to go to bed.

But I didn't do this just because I was tired. At a certain point I had made an unconscious decision not to be around the family. I realized this at the end of the driveway when my sister told me I was never around. I knew then that I needed to tell her, and my other sisters and brother, why.

All of us went out to lunch later that week, and I told them about my experience as a child. I acknowledged that I tended to pop in and out of the house and that I regularly used either my busyness or my exhaustion as an excuse to not stay longer. "But those aren't the real reasons I don't stay," I said. "The real reason is because I don't feel safe with you." Even though I was fifty-some years old at the time, I didn't feel safe at home or with them because home was where I got hurt. And they didn't stop it.

Now, they didn't know what was happening to me. And if they had known, I'm sure they would have stopped it. But the enemy had brought division between me and them. He whispered in my ears things like, "Your sisters and brother don't love you. If they did, they would have done something. But they didn't, did they? You can't trust them. They don't care about you." These words look so clearly wrong on paper as I write this, and the now sixty-year-old man knows better, but the four-, five-, and six-year-old boy inside me with all the memories is screaming and wondering where the hell they are! That's how the enemy divided, and divides, me from those who love me.

The enemy also flatters me. Maybe you can relate to this, or maybe you'll find this quite strange, but this is the way he flatters me: "Because of all that happened to you, you can do whatever you want. Okay, not whatever you want, but more or less whatever you want, at least once in a while. After all you went through, God will understand. Don't worry. It's all good." That might not sound like a strong temptation to you. Trust me, it's an amazingly strong temptation for me. In the back of my mind, under the right (wrong?) conditions, I sometimes think, *I'm entitled to that and it's okay.*

The enemy also tempts me. I don't think I need to say anything about this one, right? This one's probably pretty obvious. Temptation comes in lots of different ways for all of us.

Finally, the enemy discourages me. To discourage is to take the heart out of someone, to deflate them, to make them feel defeated. It's a primary tactic of our common enemy. For me, the discouragement usually goes like this: "You will never be well."

The purpose of my sharing all this is to let you see how our enemy works in me so that you can think and pray about how he is trying to work in you. Why? Because God wants us to be free! He wants us to have abundant life! Given that, I invite you to take time to think about the following questions, and not just to think about them but to consider pulling out pen and paper and writing down your answers. This can be immensely helpful.

Where is the enemy accusing me right now?
What lie of the enemy is crippling me right now?
Where is the enemy causing division in my life right now?
Where is the enemy flattering my ego right now?

What temptation is strongest in my life right now?
Where am I most discouraged right now?

O loving, merciful, and all-powerful God, be gracious even now and shine Your light. Expose the enemy and his tactics in our lives. Help us to grow in freedom.

CHAPTER 3

TRAFFICKED

BACK IN MY LATE TWENTIES, I HAD THE OPPORTUNITY TO TAKE AN extended retreat called "The Spiritual Exercises of Saint Ignatius." Ignatius was the founder of the Society of Jesus, a religious order more commonly known as the Jesuits. A Spaniard who lived in the sixteenth century, Ignatius, or Inigo, as he was originally named, grew up with worldly aspirations. Like many young men, both in his time and ours, his desire was for fame, fortune, and women. Though he had been baptized Catholic, faith held no real interest or importance for him. In his twenties he was wounded severely while fighting in a battle. His leg was broken, and he spent several months at his father's estate in bed, immobile. To pass the time, he asked for books about knights, chivalry, and things of that sort. Instead, some family members brought him books on the lives of the saints and the life of Jesus. Disappointed, he began to read them anyway out of boredom.

As he read, Inigo went through a profound conversion. He encountered the explosive news of the gospel, Jesus became real for him, and he came to see that the real heroes weren't the ones living for themselves and trying to leave a mark but those who wanted to do great things for the glory of God. He changed his name from Inigo to Ignatius, after one of the early heroes of the Church, and soon thereafter he began one of the most significant movements in the history of the Church. Within twenty years of his conversion, there were one thousand Jesuits. These men had also encountered the explosive news of the gospel, realized that true hope for the human family was found only in Jesus, and chosen to live sold out for Him. Like their founder, they longed to do great things not for their own notoriety but for God. Everywhere they went they changed the world. And all of this from a vain and wounded man who went from thinking Christianity was about rules and regulations to knowing it was about a relationship with the God who loves and rescues.

Though Ignatius's conversion began while he was convalescing in bed, it significantly deepened through an extended time of prayer. During this time of prayer, Ignatius experienced God teaching him intimately about Himself, His plan for creation, the enemy, what Jesus has done for us, and how he should respond to all of this. Ignatius's early followers were keen for him to pass on what he had learned, so he more or less codified his experience into what is now known as "The Spiritual Exercises of Saint Ignatius." To this day, these are administered by retreat directors across the world. They have exposed tens of millions of men and women to the life-changing news of the gospel and helped them discern how God is inviting them to respond.

The exercises are largely made up of meditations on Bible passages and prayers, all aimed at helping the retreatant come to know God's original plan for creating us, and rousing in the participant a desire to gratefully and joyfully surrender to this good and faithful God. In their fullest form the exercises are completed over the course of thirty consecutive days, with the participant spending hours each day in silent prayer. While the bulk of the meditations, especially in the later weeks, focus on the life of Jesus and how we should respond to all He has done, the most sobering meditation takes place in the first week. The meditation is on hell. And I'll never forget my first encounter with it.

Ignatius encourages the retreatant to use his or her imagination, memory, and senses to engage with whatever passage or scene they're trying to pray with. Blessed—and challenged!—with a vivid imagination, I was able to enter into this meditation rather easily.

I began by meditating on the final judgment, when Jesus will return in glory. As I prayed, I saw what looked like a large auditorium absolutely packed with men, women, and children of all ages and every ethnic background. At the front of the auditorium, Jesus was seated on a majestic throne. The crowd was lined up before Him, and as each person arrived at His throne, I saw Jesus smile and say, "Well done, good and faithful servant! Enter into the joy of your master! Just wait until you see what my Father has prepared for you." This went on for some time, and with each and every person coming to Him, I saw Jesus smile and utter those amazing words, "Well done!"

Until it was my turn.

In my visualized prayer, I was the last person in line. As I moved closer and closer to meeting Jesus, I began to get more and more anxious. Finally, after what seemed like hours, there I was, standing in front of Jesus's throne. As I looked at Him, His head was down. I kept waiting to see the smile and hear words I longed to hear. They never came. Instead, He slowly lifted His head and looked at me with sad eyes. Then, in a heavy-hearted tone of voice, He said, "Depart from me, John, into the fire prepared for the devil and his angels."

And then He rose from His throne and left.

I was all alone.

Immediately, I panicked. Sweat started to pour from my face as I realized I was out of time. The hourglass had finally run out of sand. There was no chance to go to confession. No chance to say, "I'm sorry." Though I had spent much of my life afraid of people since I had a hard time trusting others, I longed to talk with somebody. But there was no one. I began to think that I was about to be utterly alone for eternity. I can't adequately put into words how desperate I felt as I lingered with this scene. I felt sick to my stomach and could taste what seemed like acid in my mouth.

As I continued to pray, however, the scene began to change. I started to hear what sounded like laughter coming from the back of the auditorium. It was faint at first but grew increasingly louder and more hideous. As I continued to stand there, now more afraid than I had ever before been in my life, a creature emerged from the shadows. It was the enemy. He walked up the stairs of the stage on which I was standing. Soon his face was inches from mine. His breath reeked of sulfur, and his eyes were filled with contempt and mockery. Then he spoke to me: "You *fool*! God promised you abundant, joy-filled, unending life. And you put Him off. You told yourself you'd get back to Him later. Well, you're out of time. And now just wait until you see what *I* have waiting for you."

And with that, the bad news we looked at in chapter 2 gets much worse.

Let's pause to remind ourselves why we're thinking about something as truly dire as this. If we don't understand how bad, how horrific, the bad news is, then we will never understand why the gospel is such extraordinary, explosive, and life-changing news. We're still in our question, "Why is everything so obviously messed up?" or, as I put it, "What the hell happened?" The one-word answer to this question is *captured.*

As we have before, let's ask God for a grace. In the last chapter, we prayed for the grace of light. We asked God to help us to see the enemy as he is. We wanted to see his goal for our lives and his tactics—the accusations, the lies, the division, the temptation, and the discouragement. Now, let's ask God for what may sound like a strange gift: despair. That hardly sounds like a grace, right?

But it is! What do I mean by the grace of despair? Simply this: We want God to help us understand how absolutely and utterly hopeless we would be *if* He had not come to our rescue in the person of Jesus. Challenging as it is then, let's pray:

> *O good Father, I ask You to do right now what only You can do. Help us to understand what happened to our human family back at the beginning of history. Help us to know, as we've never known before, how utterly hopeless the human race was before Jesus came, all so we can know why it is so right to praise and to thank and to worship You. All this I ask in Jesus's name. Amen.*

Let's review some key insights from the last chapter. Scripture proposes to us that we have an enemy. This enemy is, like us, a creature. He is an angel, as are all the demons. Though created good, they rebelled against God, driven by envy, and went to war against the creature God loves most. That creature is us. You. Me. Every single human person, for there are no unimportant persons. At the beginning of human history, this envious, hateful, murderous creature, who wants nothing less than to destroy us all, deceived our first parents, Adam and Eve, and this deception is commonly referred to as "the Fall."

Before the Fall our first parents had no experience of anything ever going wrong. They lived in paradise. It was perfect. They never got sick or afraid. They never had any arguments. Nothing ever died. They never even got bitten by a mosquito or had a paper cut. Everything was sheer bliss. Yet despite this, despite the fact that they had absolutely zero experience of evil, the enemy was able to trick them, deceive them, get them to doubt that God is good, and turn them against Him.

What, then, can this enemy do to us? Let me assure you, the accusations he throws my way about God's goodness in view of what happened to me as a child are fierce some days! And I know that so, too, are the ones he throws your way. But he's a liar and a deceiver and a murderer. We need to constantly remember that. His goal is our slavery, degradation, and destruction.

It is often said and taught that the consequence of the Fall is that we were separated from God. This is true. Having said that, I don't know about you, but when I heard that as a teenager, I received it with a resounding yawn. *Who cares? I'm separated from God. What's the big deal about that?*

Here's the big deal. When our first parents fell for the deception of our enemy, when they believed his lie that God was not good, that they could be happier apart from Him, they unknowingly sold our race into slavery to powers that you and I can never defeat. That's the consequence of the Fall. And that's why we're asking God for the grace of despair. We want to understand this more deeply than we ever have before.

The *Catechism of the Catholic Church* teaches: "By our first parents' sin, the devil has acquired a certain *domination*" (emphasis mine).[1] The Latin root of that word *domination* suggests lord, lordship, rule, government, authority, power, control. The devil has acquired a certain and real control over humanity. We have been *captured.* This is the situation of the human race.

What exactly have we been captured by? What are these enslaving powers we cannot defeat? Death and Sin, both of which are best written in capital letters. The writers of Scripture—especially, but not only, Saint Paul—speak of these things as if they're powers, authorities, or governments. In other words, Death isn't just something that happens at the end of your life. It's a power, a government, if you will. And Sin isn't just something that we do or don't do, or say or don't say. It's a power.

In his letter to the Romans, Paul writes, "Just as sin [or Sin] came into the world through one man, and death [or Death] through sin [Sin], and so death [Death] spread to all men. . . . Death reigned" (5:12, 14). The word *came* here could be translated as "invaded." The man Paul is referring to is Adam. The invasion happened at the moment when he, together with his wife, Eve, succumbed to the deception of our enemy, who tricked them into thinking God cannot be trusted.

The enslaving power of Death, Paul says, came through this fateful decision made by our first parents. Then the power of Death *spread* like a deadly virus through and to all of humanity.

It gets worse, though. All of this, Paul goes on to say, results in this desperate situation: "Death reigned." Translated more literally, though it doesn't read well in English, Paul writes something like "Death *kinged.*" It lords its power over the human race, over every single human being. And there's no escape from it.

We all know this is true. We all know it's going to happen to us. In fact, it's the only thing we know for sure is going to happen in our future. It doesn't matter how much money we have, how good our healthcare plan is, or who we know. You and I will die. You and I will go into the ground.

Death is an enslaving power. Fleming Rutledge puts it this way:

> Have you buried someone? If you haven't, you will. You will come to know the cold clasp of death. You will know it in the literal sense, when someone who means the world to you is gone, when you yourself must stare it in the face.[2]

I buried my dad, my brother, and my mom within a relatively short span of time. My dad and my brother died within two months of each other. It felt like getting run over by a truck. Twice. My mom died shortly thereafter. She was the classiest woman I've ever known, and together with my father, she was the hero of my life. I was with her the day she died, though not present when she breathed her last, as I had to leave to celebrate a wedding. My sisters and I were gathered together, praying around her hospital bed. At a certain moment, one of my sisters gently nudged me and said, "Feel her feet!" My mom was starting to get cold from the feet up. It seemed like Death was taking her.

My father had left us a fair amount of money. Our mom had a tremendous doctor. She was blessed with exceptional nursing care around the clock. It didn't matter. Death was taking my mom, almost inch by inch, as she turned colder and colder. It was sobering and terrifying.

And I've never in my life felt more impotent.

Rutledge quotes William Stringfellow, "Death is so great, so aggressive, so pervasive and so militant a power that the only fitting way to speak of death is similar to the way one speaks of God. Death is the living power and presence in this world which feigns to be God."[3] It might be cancer. It might be a bus. It might be a plane crash. It might happen in our sleep. But death is coming.

Death is a power.

What about the power of Sin? I personally think this one is easier to prove, easier to relate to. Can I ask you a question: Have you ever done anything that you *knew* you shouldn't do? Have you ever done anything that you didn't *want* to do? Have you ever done anything that you *hated* doing? And you *still* did it anyway? I do this all the time! Why? Why do we do things that we hate doing? Because Sin is a power. It's not just something that I do or don't do, say or don't say, think or don't think. Sin is a power with which I conspire, with which I cooperate.

Paul, again in his letter to the Romans, underscores the power of Sin when he writes, "I do not understand my own actions. For I do not do what I want, but I do the very thing I hate. . . . For I do not do the good I want, but the evil I do not want is what I keep on doing" (Romans 7:15, 19).

Many years ago I counseled a couple who were going through a most trying time. The husband was addicted to crack cocaine. Crack is something like the ultimate demonic drug. My brother-in-law who took his life was a crack addict. Crack creates a high in your brain that you can never physiologically replicate. The addict *knows* this. But even though the addict knows he or she will never be able to get that initial experience again, they keep hunting for it. And often they'll do reckless things in their vain search.

One particular day this couple walked into my office. The husband sat down, unable to even look at me. As he sat there, slumped over, the wife went into a rage. "Father! I walked into the house and everything was *gone*! He sold our *furniture*! He sold our *car*. He even sold *himself*—all to get another hit!" As she was screaming, I looked over at him and saw that his shoulders were heaving as tears gushed down his face onto the floor. He finally managed to raise his head and said through the tears, "Do you think I *like* this? I *hate* what I'm doing! But I can't get out. I'm stuck! I feel chained. And I don't know what to do."

Sin is a power.

You may not have had an experience as traumatic as that, but we all have the experience of not doing what we want to do, and the very things we hate, we end up doing. How many times do we rehearse a sentence or two in our minds, and then, as they're making their way out of our mouths—even though we *know* they will not be received well—we say the words anyway?

Explaining Paul's words in Romans, Scott Hahn and Curtis Mitch write,

> The controlling metaphor [here] is slavery and freedom. Paul paints a black-or-white picture of the human situation: either one lives in service to sin and remains in spiritual bondage, or one lives in obedience to God and enjoys liberation from sin's captivity. It is a stark either-or: no fence-sitting, no third option.[4]

I didn't realize it when I was younger, but upon reflection I came to realize that this is what I was doing. I was *obeying* Sin. I was in *service* to Sin. I thought I was just doing what I wanted, but I wasn't. I knew that because I didn't like doing what I was doing, even though I often tried to trick myself into thinking that I did.

Here's how another author describes the human predicament:

> No one is capable of being captain of his own soul, master of her own fate. Each of us is worked upon by unconscious impulses of which we are not even aware and over which we have little control. Paul, unlike the typical American, does not think in terms of autonomous human beings. Paul proudly identifies himself as a "slave of Christ" (Gal. 1:10). If the apocalyptic scenario is a picture of true reality, then *no one* is "free" in the domain of this world as it is. Either we must live our lives in the clutches of soul-destroying Powers or we are delivered into "the obedience of faith" (Rom. 1:5; 16:26).[5]

Jesus tells an enigmatic parable in the Gospels. Through this parable He is trying to give us biblical lenses. He's trying to help us understand the hopeless situation of the human race. He's trying to make sure we're watching the right reel. He says, "When a strong man, fully armed, guards his own palace, his goods are safe" (Luke 11:21). Who is the "strong man"? The devil. What's his "palace"? This world. What are "his goods"? You and me. And there's no hope. There's no way out.

While on retreat with a number of college kids years ago, I was breaking open this parable when I felt like the Lord gave me what I think is a striking image to explain what Jesus is saying to us. The image was that of human trafficking. If there's an evil in our world right now that's worse than abortion and human trafficking, I don't know what it is. There are more slaves right now than ever before in the history of the world, both economic slaves and sexual slaves. My home state, Michigan, ranks third in the United States with regard to the number of trafficking victims. I want to encourage you to use your imagination and enter into the scene I'm going to describe, much like Ignatius encourages the retreatants during the spiritual exercises to use their imaginations. For men, we might slightly adapt the image.

If you're somewhat pressed for time right now, then stop reading and come back to this when you know you will have time. Find a place that's quiet, free from distractions, and without screens. Once there, use your imagination and try to see in your mind the following: You've been captured, tied up, and locked away somewhere. No one knows where you are. No one's coming for you. You're in the possession of someone who delights to use you, mock you, humiliate you, and taunt you. And this is your life. It will be your life until he tires of you.

This is the situation of our race.

This is the bad news.

This is the horrific, hellish news.

Thanks be to God, this is not the end of the story. On another retreat I led recently, a gentleman came up to me after a presentation like this chapter and said, "Please tell me we're not stopping here. This is not the end, right?"

"No," I reassured him, "this is not the end. But we need to stay here for a while. It will prepare us for the extraordinary news that is coming."

"Through the devil's envy [D]eath entered the world," we saw earlier, "and those who belong to his party *experience* it" (Wisdom 2:24). It's important to note that *experience* is in the present tense. It's not simply that those who have been sold into slavery will die. Those who are in its possession experience Death *now.* As I look back on my life, especially certain years, that was me. I was like the walking dead. My life wasn't integrated; it was fragmented. Though I tried to put up a good front to everybody, inside I knew better. I knew something was wrong and I was stuck.

This is why we began this chapter asking God for the grace of despair. We were, as a race, utterly hopeless. And we still would be, if God hadn't done something about this.

But He *has.*

CHAPTER 4

RESCUED

IMAGINE A CONVERSATION BETWEEN THE FATHER, THE SON, AND the Holy Spirit.[1] The conversation takes place in heaven right after that disastrous event called "the Fall" that we just looked at. Our first parents, Adam and Eve, unknowingly and unintentionally sold our race into slavery to the powers of Sin, Death, and Satan.

The conversation goes something like this. The Father says about Adam and Eve, "Who will go and get them? Who will bring them back? Who will rescue them? Who will bring them home?" The Son turns toward the Father and says, "I will. I'll go get them. I'll bring them back. I'll rescue them. I'll bring them home." As the Son speaks, the Holy Spirit slowly lowers His head, for He knows what it will cost the Son to go and get our first parents, bring them back, rescue them, and bring them home. The conversation, though, isn't just about Adam and Eve. It's also about you and me. Wherever you find yourself right now, please know this: God *sees* you. You *matter* to Him. He *cares* for you. And He *loves* you. No matter what.

We've finally left behind the bad news. We needed to spend the past two chapters doing what we did because without them the gospel is just ordinary news. But once we understand where we were before the cross and what God has done for us in Jesus, then everything changes.

Our focus turns now to the third question: "What, if

anything, has God done about the mess the world is in?" The word that sums up the answer to this question is *rescued.* In this chapter we're going to concentrate especially on two things. First, we want to have a biblical understanding of why the second person of the Trinity became man. Second, we want to try to better understand what Jesus was doing on the cross.

As we have done before, so again we will begin by asking God for a grace to help us better understand what we're about to read, think about, and pray with. The grace we will pray for is once again light. Whereas before we asked God to shine a light on the enemy so that we could see who he is, his goal, his strategy, and his tactics, now we ask God to shine a light on Jesus. We ask Him to help us see Jesus a bit more clearly.

We all have a distorted image of Jesus. How could we not? It's impossible to fully understand an infinite person with our finite minds. But as we discuss Jesus in this chapter and the next, I pray we will grow profoundly in our understanding of Him. Jesus is so much more than what is commonly understood. Jesus is something like a diamond. By "turning Him," if you will, by looking at Him from different angles, the mystery of who He is becomes clearer, even though we will never fully grasp Him.

> *Jesus, You said that when You were lifted up You would draw all people to Yourself.*[2] *My desire right now is to lift You up in the words that follow. Shine a light in our minds and help us to see You as You are, even just a bit more clearly. As we do so, help us to know God's love for us as never before. Amen.*

Let's return to the house of the trafficker from the imagined scenario in chapter 3. We're captured. There's no way to escape the fiendish grip of the one who has us. No one's coming for us.

We're in utter despair. It's hopeless. This was the situation of the entire human race after the Fall. This was *our* situation.

As Fleming Rutledge puts it, "The clear implication here is that there is no way for the human being to move from the domain of Sin to the domain of God's righteousness unless there is an invasion of the kingdom of Sin from outside."[3] Remember, the domain of Sin—the government, authority, and power of Sin—leads to death. Sin's goal and purpose is death. Your death!

Let's recall C. S. Lewis's words: This world is "enemy-occupied territory." He goes on to say, however, that "Christianity is the story of how the rightful king has landed, you might say landed in disguise."[4] What's the disguise? Flesh. Jesus's flesh—His human nature—is His disguise.[5]

As we ponder Jesus's "landing," there is something we need to understand about the enemy. The proud demonic mind can't fathom the majestic Lord and Creator of all becoming a creature to save creatures. The demonic mind does not love, so the enemy's way of thinking cannot perceive that God would address the human situation by becoming one of us. This is the disguise.[6]

Why, then, did the second person of the Trinity become a man? Why was Jesus lying in the manger? To fight. To liberate. To rescue. And He didn't come to do this so much for "us" as a race, but for you as an individual whom He knows by name.[7] The question discussed within the Trinity after the rebellion of Adam and Eve wasn't, "Who will go and get them?" It was, "Who will go and get Mark? Who will go and get Rachel? Who will go and get John?" And the Son says, "I will. I will go and get Susan. I will bring her back. I'll rescue her. I'll bring her home."

The Incarnation, then, which is to say, the event of God becoming flesh, is the invasion of one kingdom—the kingdom of Sin, the kingdom of Death, and the kingdom of Hell—by a stronger kingdom. That modifier, *stronger,* is very important.

God's kingdom is the stronger kingdom. We don't usually think that way. Many of us tend to think that evil is strong and goodness is weak. But that's not true. It's a lie. It's the wrong film reel. It's a deception of the enemy. Evil is not stronger. Don't fall for the lie. Goodness is stronger. Love is stronger. *God* is stronger.

The First Letter of John tells us, "The reason the Son of God appeared was to destroy the works of the devil" (3:8). We could also translate "to destroy" from the Greek as "to loose" or "to untie" or "to set free from."

Go back to the house of the trafficker or to a prison or a concentration camp. Like the men and women in those hopeless situations, we were all shackled by the powers of Sin and Death. But God didn't create us to be slaves. He didn't create us to be in chains. He didn't create us to die. So God comes "in disguise" to shatter our chains, to loosen our bonds, and to set us free from the powers that we cannot overcome on our own.

We get a hint of why Jesus has come in the first miracle recorded in the gospel of Mark—His driving out a demon. Before Jesus rescues this man from his horrific bondage, the demon inside the man shouts at Jesus, "What have you to do with us, Jesus of Nazareth? Have you come to destroy us?" (1:24). Jesus doesn't answer the question. Instead, He says, "Be silent, and come out of him!" and the demon helplessly departs (1:25). We might imagine this was quite a tussle, but the Greek makes clear that it wasn't a struggle at all. What we translate into English as, "Be silent," is something akin to "Be muzzled!" With a mere word, Jesus muzzles the demon the way a trainer muzzles an animal. In doing so, the demon's question receives its answer: Yes, Jesus has come to destroy the demons.

Now, my experience over the past few years especially is that people are often confused by these exorcism scenes in Scripture. As Jesus drives out the demons, we come across them saying things like, "We know who you are." So do they? Do the demons, does Satan, know who Jesus is? Is He really "in disguise" as Lewis says? The answer is perhaps both yes and no. Clearly, the demons are aware that God has a plan to undo what happened in Eden. They know God has promised that something will happen to crush the serpent's head (see Genesis 3:15). How that will happen, though, and who will do it, is only hinted at.

After all, the demons are only spirits and don't have physical heads, so how can they be "crushed"? The second person of the Trinity is a spirit, too, or was before the Incarnation, so it's not as though the demons could recognize Jesus's face from before. This will come a bit more into focus as we look at what Jesus was doing on the cross, but for now it's important to wrestle a bit with this.

Think for a moment of the Gospel accounts of the temptations of Jesus in the desert. Clearly, the temptations were an attempt to find out who and what Jesus was and had come to do, but they don't reveal any clear answers. As Frank Sheed writes, "It seemed that [Jesus] might very well be [the Messiah], but of him Satan knew no more than he could find in the Old Testament; and that is mysterious darkness shot through with gleams of light, which seem to have a darkness of their own."[8] Messiahs, after all, or at least men claiming to be the Messiah, had come and gone. Several such men had lived (and died) near the time of Jesus. And most importantly *nobody* expected the Messiah to be God. That was unthinkable. God is the thrice holy one, absolutely other. Besides, the Messiah was understood to be a revolutionary, someone who would liberate the Jewish people from their political and military oppressors—the Romans.[9]

In those Gospel temptation accounts, Satan begins his attack with the words, "If You are the son of God" (see Matthew 4:3). Most of us are probably prone to read that as the tempter asking

Jesus whether He is God, but that's not so clear. The expression "son of God" is used in the Old Testament in reference to the angels that didn't fall, the people of Israel, and even various judges.[10] And then there's Jesus's reply to the first temptation. "Man," He says, "shall not live by bread alone" (Matthew 4:4). This answer, as Sheed writes, "contained one word which [the devil] may have been relieved to hear. The word was 'man'—man does not live by bread alone. Christ could not possibly have quoted that text, if it had had no bearing on himself at all. It is the clearest possible statement that he is man. And if man, then presumably *only* man!"[11] After all, God had said through the prophet Hosea, "I am God and not a man" (11:9). Since this is an issue, let me share at length some insights from one scholar I have found most helpful:

> Since Adam's fall, the demons must have suspected that God was preparing something like a major coup. Yet, despite the prophecies, the modalities of this work of redemption largely escaped them—hence the ambiguity of their attitude toward the person of Jesus, as it emerges from the Gospels themselves. On the one hand, the demons manifest a certain knowledge of Jesus' identity, . . . but, on the other hand, they remain undecided since they tempt him and seek to know who he really is. . . .
>
> St. Thomas [Aquinas] turned several times to this question. Relying on an already existing tradition of interpretation, he thinks that the demons effectively knew that Jesus was the Christ, the one sent by God who had been announced by the prophets. On the other hand, they were in doubt and uncertainty as to his deeper identity. Certain signs—the performance of

> miracles—sometimes led them to conjecture and suspect that he was the Son of God in the strong sense, but they were not at all sure of it, especially because of the weaknesses—such as hunger and fatigue—that they observed in him. *The scandal of the Incarnation worked thoroughly against the demons.*
>
> It was only gradually, compelled by events like the Resurrection and Ascension, that the demons were led to recognize the divinity of Jesus Christ.[12]

Jesus came, then, to liberate and to fight. But how did that liberation happen? Where did the fight reach its culmination? These questions lead us to the second part of this chapter: What was Jesus doing on the cross? That's a rather odd question, at least to me. After all, it doesn't look like He's *doing* anything, except dying. But more is happening than meets the eye.

We said earlier that Jesus identifies the enemy as "the ruler of this world." He actually uses this expression twice, in John 12:31 and 14:30—both times shortly before His passion begins. In the latter passage Jesus tells His disciples, "I will no longer talk much with you, for the ruler of this world is coming." He immediately adds though, "He has no power over me" (RSVCE). With these words, Jesus is preparing His followers for what's about to happen. The disciples, of course, only understand later what's actually going on, but Jesus is telling them that, no matter how it appears, He is the one going on the attack. It's as if He's saying to them, "The enemy is coming for Me. But know this: He doesn't have any power over Me. In all that's about to happen, you're going to be utterly scandalized and terrified. But what's about to happen to Me is entirely in My control. No one has power over Me. Regardless of how it looks, I'm in control. I will cast out the 'ruler of this world.' "

What's almost beyond words, however, is the astoundingly creative way Jesus casts him out.

To better grasp this we would do well to think for a moment about the images of Jesus on the cross that we usually see in art or in our churches. They are, in reality, far too sanitized—understandably so! Crucifixion, after all, was a death so horrific that a Roman citizen was exhorted never to look at a man on a cross.[13] Crucifixion was the utmost in degradation and humiliation. Absolutely nothing in our experience is helpful for understanding this, as there is no modern referent—at least not in the Western world. Crucifixion was not only the most brutal deterrent the Romans could employ against those tempted to mess with the empire, but it was also something like ritualized sport. Rutledge, drawing on the work of Joel Green, can help us here:

> Crucifixion was specifically designed to be the ultimate insult to personal dignity, the last word in humiliating and dehumanizing treatment. *Degradation was the whole point.* . . .
>
> Crucifixion . . . was supposed to be seen by as many people as possible. Debasement resulting from public display was a chief feature of the method, along with the prolonging of agony. It was a form of advertisement, or public announcement—this person is the scum of the earth, not fit to live, more an insect than a human being. The crucified wretch was pinned up like a specimen. Crosses were not placed out in the open for convenience or sanitation, but for maximum public exposure. . . .
>
> Crucifixion as a means of execution in the Roman Empire had as *its express purpose* the elimination of victims from consideration as members of the human

> race. It cannot be said too strongly: that was its function. It was meant to indicate to all who might be toying with subversive ideas that crucified persons were *not of the same species* as either the executioners or the spectators and were therefore not only expendable but also deserving of ritualized extermination.[14]

Given this description, how can we ask, "What was Jesus *doing* on the cross?" His body is utterly naked and brutally mangled by the scourging He received from the Roman soldiers. He's nailed to the instrument of torture, every last drop of fluid spilling out of His body, and He's gasping for breath until He can no longer breathe.[15]

And yet . . .

Who is that on the cross? He is the eternal Son of God. He is the one through whom a universe spanning 522 *sextillion miles* came into existence. "All things were made through him, and without him was not any thing made that was made" (John 1:3). How, then, could anyone nail such a person to a cross? Where would you get that nail? God is not subject to some sort of spiritual kryptonite.

There's only one way Jesus can get on the cross.

Only one.

He has to *want* to be there.

Why in the world would He want to be there?

Love.

Love for *you.*

By *name.*

"Who will go and get him? Who will bring him back? Who will rescue him? Who will bring him home?"

"I will."

While many things are happening on the cross, I'm going to

be intentionally provocative and focus on three things in particular.

The first thing Jesus was doing on the cross is showing me how much the Father loves me. This might sound simple, but it's not. It's astounding! In a universe that's ninety-plus billion light-years across, I'm not only seen by God but also loved by Him. And you're not only seen by God but also loved. *This much!* On the cross, the love of God was made manifest, made known, revealed, explained, and broken open (see 1 John 4:9–10).

Remember my contention that Jesus has one homily—the Father? He has come to reveal the Father. And nowhere does this revelation happen more powerfully than on the cross. Jesus was constantly talking about His Father, and the religious leaders often considered His talk to be scandalous. This scandal was epitomized in a lament from the leaders: "This man receives sinners and eats with them" (Luke 15:2). Perhaps nowhere else does Jesus speak about the Father's love as powerfully as in a parable He tells almost immediately after this accusation. Commonly known as the parable of the prodigal son, it's really about the Father. It has been suggested by some that it could be better called the parable of the father who runs. In this moving parable, Jesus paints a word picture about what He has come to do, and at the same time He appeals to the religious leaders to enter into His Father's way of seeing. The parable is found in Luke 15:11–32. There, we read,

> [Jesus] said, "There was a man who had two sons. And the younger of them said to his father, 'Father, give me the share of property that is coming to me.' And he divided his property between them. Not many days later, the younger son gathered all he had and took a journey into a far country, and there he squandered his property in reckless living. And when he had spent every-

thing, a severe famine arose in that country, and he began to be in need. So he went and hired himself out to one of the citizens of that country, who sent him into his fields to feed pigs. And he was longing to be fed with the pods that the pigs ate, and no one gave him anything.

But when he came to himself, he said, 'How many of my father's hired servants have more than enough bread, but I perish here with hunger! I will arise and go to my father, and I will say to him, "Father, I have sinned against heaven and before you. I am no longer worthy to be called your son. Treat me as one of your hired servants."' And he arose and came to his father. But while he was still a long way off, his father saw him and felt compassion, and ran and embraced him and kissed him. And the son said to him, 'Father, I have sinned against heaven and before you. I am no longer worthy to be called your son.' But the father said to his servants, 'Bring quickly the best robe, and put it on him, and put a ring on his hand, and shoes on his feet. And bring the fattened calf and kill it, and let us eat and celebrate. For this my son was dead, and is alive again; he was lost, and is found.' And they began to celebrate.

"Now his older son was in the field, and as he came and drew near to the house, he heard music and dancing. And he called one of the servants and asked what these things meant. And he said to him, 'Your brother has come, and your father has killed the fattened calf, because he has received him back safe and sound.' But he was angry and refused to go in. His father came out and entreated him, but he answered his father, 'Look,

> these many years I have served you, and I never disobeyed your command, yet you never gave me a young goat, that I might celebrate with my friends. But when this son of yours came, who has devoured your property with prostitutes, you killed the fattened calf for him!' And he said to him, 'Son, you are always with me, and all that is mine is yours. It was fitting to celebrate and be glad, for this your brother was dead, and is alive; he was lost, and is found.' "

There is so much in this extraordinary story Jesus tells, but for our purposes let me offer four quick points. First, let's make sure we grasp what the younger son said in asking for his inheritance *while his father was still alive*: "I wish you were dead." Such words from a child cause unimaginable heartache for a parent, and Jesus is inviting us to imagine the Father's "pain" over our rebellion against Him, which He knows will hurt us.

Second, after the son hits rock bottom (a Jewish man feeding pigs—an animal he can't even eat!), he decides to return home. In preparation he carefully crafts a speech to help "grease the skids," if you will, with his rejected and offended father. The speech goes like this: "Father, I have sinned against heaven and before you. I am no longer worthy to be called your son. Treat me as one of your hired servants."

Third, there's a detail many of us probably pass over that is absolutely key to understanding this parable. Jesus says that when the father, an image of our heavenly Father, caught sight of his son on his way home, *he ran.* The Greek phrasing is perhaps better understood as "he raced." *What's the big deal about that?* you might wonder. Well, here's the big deal: In the Middle East at the time of Jesus, men didn't run. Ever. Poor people ran. Slaves ran. Children ran. But not wealthy, dignified men. It was beneath them. Kenneth Bailey, who spent forty years living and teaching in the Middle East, observes,

> It is safe to assume that [this man] has not run anywhere for any purpose for forty years. No villager over the age of twenty-five ever runs. . . . To do so, he must take the front edge of his robes in his hand like a teenager. When he does this, his legs show in what is considered a humiliating posture. All of this is painfully shameful for him.[16]

Your Father, Jesus says, *runs.*

He runs especially because, in the Middle East at the time of Jesus, the townspeople would have started to gather as soon as the rebellious son's arrival became known—to abuse him both verbally and physically. They would then line the street and force the young man to run the gauntlet, subjecting him to all sorts of vile treatment. They would do this because the son had offended not only his father and his family but the entire community. The father knows this, so as soon as he sees his son, he sets off in haste to protect him from the abuse of the townsfolk. When he gets to his son, he covers him in an embrace, as if to say to the townspeople, "If you want to hit him, you have to hit me."

Here's the fourth and final point to note in this passage. Remember, the son had carefully crafted a speech. But he doesn't manage to get it all out. It stops short right after he says, "I am no longer worthy to be called your son." Why does it get interrupted? Some argue that this is because the father cuts him off. Perhaps. Bailey, however, offers another explanation, one very much in keeping with my imagined title of Jesus's one homily. As the son watches his father run, exposing himself to shame with his robe lifted high, welcoming him back with loving and open arms, and protecting him from the abuse of the town, the son is "stunned beyond belief" by this display of his father's love. Utterly overwhelmed, the young man abandons the end of his speech as he sees his father like he never has before and realizes how much he has wounded his father's heart. His image has been shattered.[17]

This is what Jesus was doing on the cross. He was shattering our distorted image of His Father. Truly, the Father's love for you and me is beyond imagining.

The second thing Jesus was doing on the cross is "becoming sin," that is, He's making atonement for us. This, too, can be difficult for us to understand. More than a few of us walk into a church, see Jesus hanging on a cross, and think to ourselves, *I don't think I'm such a bad person that He needed to do that for me.* So let's try to understand this better.

Saint Paul writes, "For our sake [God] made him to be sin who knew no sin" (2 Corinthians 5:21). What in the world does that mean? We are dealing with a profound mystery here. We may be able to scratch the surface, but none of us can conceive what this experience was like for Jesus. On the cross, Jesus was "absorbing" into His body all the sins that have ever been committed. Not just my sins or your sins but the sins of everybody who's ever existed or who will ever exist, from the beginning to the ending of the world.

A wise teacher of mine who was highly gifted in using analogies proposed one about the cross that I've always found helpful. He suggested that a driver slamming on the brakes of a car gives us a helpful image for understanding this aspect of what Jesus was doing on the cross. If you were to watch in slow motion as a car's brakes abruptly engage, you'd see that the first thing the car does is lurch forward. However, before it comes to a standstill, the car also lurches backward. (In fact, the back-and-forth can continue for some time.) Only after this back-and-forth does the vehicle finally come to a rest. Similarly, my teacher explained, on the cross Jesus first "reached forward" and pulled into His body the sins of everybody who would walk the face of the earth in the future. Then He "lurched backward" and pulled into Himself all the sins of those who had lived before He walked the earth. Then He "came to a standstill" and rested on the cross.

This second thing Jesus was doing on the cross calls to mind words that are perhaps familiar to you: "Behold, the Lamb of God, who takes away the sin of the world" (John 1:29). These words were spoken by Jesus's cousin, John the Baptist, just before Jesus entered into His public ministry. But what do the words mean? The image of a lamb would immediately call to mind for John's audience at least three things.

First, they would remind the listeners of words the patriarch Abraham spoke to his beloved son Isaac as they were walking up Mount Moriah. On that soulful walk to the place of sacrifice, Isaac said to Abraham, "'Behold, the fire and the wood, but where is the lamb for a burnt offering?' Abraham answered, 'God will provide for himself the lamb for a burnt offering, my son'" (Genesis 22:7–8). This scene is often referred to as "the Calvary of the Old Testament." Though a real event, it was also a type, or image, of another sacrifice that would take place hundreds of years later on a hill not far from Mount Moriah. Moriah is traditionally identified with the location of the Temple Mount in Jerusalem. The Temple Mount is very close to Calvary, the hill where another beloved son became the long-awaited fulfillment of Abraham's words to Isaac. In Jesus, God had finally provided a lamb.

"Lamb of God" would also call to mind the Passover meal and the liberation of the Jewish people from slavery to Egypt. The night before God dramatically rescued His people, the Israelites were instructed by God, through Moses, to take a lamb, one per household, and slaughter it. Its blood was to be smeared on the lintels and doorposts of their doorways, and its flesh was to be eaten. Like that lamb, Jesus's blood was shed on the wood of the cross. This was just hours after Jesus had told His disciples, while celebrating the Passover, that even as the Israelites had eaten the flesh of the lamb back in Egypt, they were to see in the bread being broken before their eyes His body, which was true food and was to be eaten "in remembrance" of Him (see Luke 22:19; John 6:32).

Finally, to hear Jesus identified as "the lamb of God" would have called to mind the prophecy in Isaiah about the mysterious figure called "the servant of the Lord." This prophecy is one of the most powerful in all the Old Testament for helping us understand the Passion of Jesus and deserves to be quoted in full:

> Behold, my servant shall act wisely;
> he shall be high and lifted up,
> and shall be exalted.
> As many were astonished at you—
> his appearance was so marred, beyond human semblance,
> and his form beyond that of the children of mankind—
> so shall he sprinkle many nations.
> Kings shall shut their mouths because of him,
> for that which has not been told them they see,
> and that which they have not heard they understand.
>
> Who has believed what he has heard from us?
> And to whom has the arm of the LORD been revealed?

For he grew up before him like a young plant,
and like a root out of dry ground;
he had no form or majesty that we should look at him,
and no beauty that we should desire him.
He was despised and rejected by men,
a man of sorrows and acquainted with grief;
and as one from whom men hide their faces
he was despised, and we esteemed him not.

Surely he has borne our griefs
and carried our sorrows;
yet we esteemed him stricken,
smitten by God, and afflicted.
But he was pierced for our transgressions;
he was crushed for our iniquities;
upon him was the chastisement that brought us peace,
and with his wounds we are healed.
All we like sheep have gone astray;
we have turned—every one—to his own way;
and the Lord has laid on him
the iniquity of us all.

He was oppressed, and he was afflicted,
yet he opened not his mouth;
like a lamb that is led to the slaughter,
and like a sheep that before its shearers is silent,
so he opened not his mouth.
By oppression and judgment he was taken away;
and as for his generation, who considered
that he was cut off out of the land of the living,
stricken for the transgression of my people?
And they made his grave with the wicked

and with a rich man in his death,
although he had done no violence,
and there was no deceit in his mouth.

Yet it was the will of the LORD to crush him;
he has put him to grief;
when his soul makes an offering for guilt,
he shall see his offspring; he shall prolong his days;
the will of the LORD shall prosper in his hand.
Out of the anguish of his soul he shall see and be satisfied;
by his knowledge shall the righteous one, my servant,
make many to be accounted righteous,
and he shall bear their iniquities.
Therefore I will divide him a portion with the many,
and he shall divide the spoil with the strong,
because he poured out his soul to death
and was numbered with the transgressors;
yet he bore the sin of many,
and makes intercession for the transgressors.
(Isaiah 52:13–53:12)

"Surely he has *borne* our griefs and *carried* our sorrows."

"The LORD has *laid on him* the iniquity of us all. He was oppressed, and he was afflicted, yet he opened not his mouth; *like a lamb that is led to the slaughter,* and like a sheep that before its shearers is silent, so he opened not his mouth."

"He shall bear their iniquities."

Saint Peter, reflecting on this passage in light of Jesus's Passion, wrote, "He himself bore our sins in his body on the tree, that we might die to sin and live to righteousness. By his wounds you have been healed" (1 Peter 2:24).

The movie *The Passion of the Christ* has perhaps forever changed the way many of us experience those hours leading up to and including Jesus's death. The scourging scene wrecked me the first time I saw it. When the Gospel writers were describing what Jesus endured, they didn't need to elaborate for their readers. Their audiences were familiar with crucifixion and all that accompanied it. They regularly saw the bodies of men who had been scourged. Not us. We've never seen anything like that.

I remember well the first time I watched *The Passion of the Christ.* As I sat down in the theater, I knew everything that was about to happen, and still I was on the edge of my seat, as up until then these events had only been words to me. Foolishly, I thought I was prepared for the scene when the Roman soldiers took Jesus into the Praetorium and scourged Him. I wasn't. Not at all.

The scourging scene goes on and on and on. As Jesus's body was being literally ripped to shreds by the soldiers, I began to weep. Almost uncontrollably. As blow after blow tore apart Jesus's body, ripping open His back, the words of Isaiah and Peter came flooding into my mind: "With his wounds we are healed" (Isaiah 53:5). Between sobs I started to pray over and over again, "Oh, my God. Oh, my God. I am so sorry. I am so sorry. I am so sorry. I am so sorry. For all my sins, I am so sorry. This is what being 'the lamb of God' means. This was for me. Because of my sin. My bitterness, my resentment, my lust, my anger, my rage, my whatever. This was the price. This was what it cost. I am so sorry."

But there's a third thing that Jesus was doing on the cross. It's fairly common to hear that Jesus went to the cross because God loves us or to make atonement for us. It's not common, however, to hear that on the cross Jesus went to war to rescue us. The early Church often emphasized this dimension of what Jesus was doing. Yes, He was showing me the Father's love. Yes, He was making atonement for me. But He also was entering into battle to rescue me. He was fighting for me. And you.[18]

Remember again that the one on the cross is the One who made the universe, so things can't just happen to Him. Now, please don't misunderstand what I am about to say. In no way at all do I mean to convey that Jesus wasn't really suffering on the cross. He was! In ways infinitely worse than we can imagine. Jesus wasn't somehow playacting on the cross. Not at all. But though He was truly suffering, He was also actively engaging in battle.

I don't think this is how most of us think about Jesus. Certainly not in the Passion. Take a moment and find a crucifix or look up online a painting of Jesus on the cross. As you look, ask yourself, is Jesus the *victim* or is He the *aggressor*? Is Jesus on the cross being *hunted* (and caught), or is He *hunting*? At first glance the answers would seem obvious: He's the victim and He's the hunted. But He's not. Or better, He's not only these. He's *both* victim *and* aggressor. He's *both* hunted *and* hunting.

The Old Testament book of Wisdom includes a powerful passage that looks back on the Exodus, the liberation of the Jewish people from more than four hundred years of slavery under the pharaohs of Egypt. This event stands at the center of the Old Testament; it is the defining act whereby the Jewish people were miraculously rescued by God, brought into freedom, and set apart as His people. That event was real and yet was also a type, a foreshadowing, of the ultimate rescue mission God would later engage in. This wouldn't be a rescue from the tyranny and slavery of some earthly king but from the powers of Sin, Death, and Satan. Reflecting on that first exodus, Wisdom says,

> For while gentle silence enveloped all things,
>   and night in its swift course was now half gone,

your all-powerful word leaped from heaven, from the
royal throne,
into the midst of the land that was doomed,
a stern warrior. . . . (18:14–15)

This beautiful passage was more or less understood as poetry at the time that it was written in the first century B.C. Yes, it referred to a real historical event, the Jewish people being rescued from slavery in Egypt, but the image of a warrior leaping down from his royal throne in heaven into a land doomed with destruction, well, that was a poetic way to describe what had happened. In the person of Jesus, however, suddenly—astonishingly!—poetry became reality.

One very real day, probably in the month of March, in a town so insignificant that it's not even mentioned in the Old Testament, an angel appeared to a young teenage girl and invited her to do something, invited her to *be* something unthinkable and unimaginable. He invited her to be the mother of God's Son. And in that moment the words from the book of Wisdom were no longer poetry. They literally happened. "Your all-powerful word"—the One through whom and for whom everything was created—"leaped from heaven, from the royal throne, into the midst of the land that was doomed"—doomed to be enslaved, doomed to die by our own doing—"a stern warrior"! Suddenly, hidden away from the powerful and the wealthy, the God who made the universe begins to grow inside the womb of a woman He Himself created.

There's a twentieth-century church in Nazareth that is built on top of the ancient first-century ruins of the village where Mary lived. In the crypt of the church lies a much earlier church, built, tradition says, on the very house where the archangel Gabriel appeared to Mary so many years ago. In that crypt there is an altar engraved with a Latin inscription: "*Hic verbum caro factum est.*" The Word was made flesh *here.* "Your all-powerful word *leaped* from heaven . . ."

Back to the crucifix, though. Look again at Jesus on the cross. Does that look like a "stern warrior" to you?

Several years ago I encountered a two-word phrase I had never heard before, and it has forever changed how I understand the Passion of Jesus. It was the week before Holy Week, and I was preparing to celebrate daily Mass at the parish school where I served as pastor. As I sat in the chapel, out of nowhere I "heard" a phrase that until that moment I had never before heard in my life: "ambush predator." Now, you must understand, I grew up in the suburbs. I'm a city kid through and through. I don't hunt, I don't fish, and my idea of camping is a three-star hotel. Suffice to say, I had no idea what an ambush predator was.

As soon as I heard the words, though, odd as it might sound, I knew it was some sort of inspiration from God. God speaks to each of us in different ways, and one of the ways He speaks to me is through words, images, and ideas that enter into my mind. So in an attempt to gain further clarity on what I thought I was hearing in prayer, I did what many people in our day and age do as a first step to search for answers: I opened up my phone and googled "ambush predator." And then I started to laugh. What I sensed was an inspiration from God for understanding what Jesus was doing on the cross turned out to be more accurate than I could have imagined.

"Ambush predator," it turns out, is an expression used to describe various animals. Spiders, for example, are ambush predators. So are leopards, lions, snakes, alligators, and crocodiles. Ambush predators lie motionless and still, camouflaged by their environment, for one purpose: to attract prey. As I read the definition and looked at the various images on my phone, I realized this is a most fitting description of Jesus on the cross. On the cross Jesus was lying motionless and still, "camouflaged" with His environment, attracting prey. Again, don't misunderstand me. The misery He's enduring is very real. But it's not *happening* to Him. He's in control. As I noted earlier, on the cross Jesus is *both* victim *and* aggressor; He's *both* hunted *and* hunting. In the words of the book of Revelation, Jesus is both lamb and lion.

So what is Jesus's "camouflage"? Well, aside from His coming "in disguise," to use C. S. Lewis's description, once Jesus enters into the Garden of Gethsemane, that disguise becomes ever more . . . creative. There in the garden Jesus, preparing to enter into battle against the forces of hell all alone, begins to sweat blood. There, even though He has eluded capture time and time again, He allows Himself to be arrested. As part of the arrest, He *permits* Himself to be chained. Remember, we're talking about the creator of the universe! At the trial before the Jewish leaders, He *allows* a man He created to slap Him. People He created for friendship, for love, for communion, He *allows* to strike Him and to spit on Him. Then, leaving the Jewish courts, the judge of the universe *allows* Himself to be tried and condemned—by a man He had created and for whom He became a man to rescue. The camouflage gets more creative though.

Few experiences are felt as intensely as standing naked, utterly exposed, before a stranger. Yet here He is, the creator of the universe, violently stripped of His clothes, standing in front of His creation. He *allows* this. Then, the One whom angels adore and worship, *allows* others to mock and ridicule Him. Just imagine what the Roman soldiers are saying to Him as they do this. This was not an insignificant aspect of the degradation that preceded crucifixion; it was part of the ritualized sport. He then *allows* Himself to be chained to a pillar and scourged, torn apart, ripped to shreds by the Roman lictors. Those same soldiers plait a crown of thorns, and He *allows* them to push it into His kingly scalp. Finally, He *allows* the soldiers to nail Him to a cross.

Why?

In all of this, Jesus is revealing the Father's love, He's making atonement for our sins, and He's trying to lure in the prey.

Because on the cross, Jesus was hunting.

In *The Passion of the Christ,* this idea of Jesus hunting is hinted at in a strange scene that takes place right after Jesus takes His last breath. Just after Jesus dies, a drop falls from the sky (a tear from the Father?) and "explodes" as it hits the ground. Then we see an image of the devil, arms wildly outstretched, standing on dry, cracked ground, screeching at the top of his lungs. One would be tempted to think that it's a screech of glee, a cry of victory. But it's not. Instead, it's as if the devil is screaming, "Oh sh—nuts!" It's the scream of someone who realizes, against any and all expectation, that he has just been outmatched. "I had Him," we can almost hear the devil wailing, "and now I don't have Him. In fact, He actually has me!"

Jesus on the cross is the ultimate ambush predator, and He was hunting. All out of love for you. And for me.

Interesting as this might sound, you would be forgiven for thinking that perhaps I just have a hyperactive imagination. The image, though, of Jesus as an "ambush predator" isn't a new one. Not at all. Those precise words aren't used, but the idea behind them was commonly suggested in the early Church, especially at Easter.[19] In describing what Jesus was doing on the cross, bishops, priests, and saints employed various images that are akin to an ambush predator, even if, again, they don't use that expression.

Saint Augustine, for example, said that Jesus on the cross was like a mousetrap. His flesh acted like the cheese, whereas His divinity served like the bar, crashing down on the devil once he bit.

Saint Gregory of Nyssa suggested that Jesus on the cross was like a fishhook. His humanity was the bait, luring and attracting the devil to bite, but hidden within His divinity was a hook. Saint Isidore of Seville added to this image, saying that Jesus was the fishhook and His genealogy in the Gospels was something like the fishing line. And the one holding the rod, Isidore said, was the Father. He was trolling for Satan.

Several early Church preachers, though, are worth quoting at length. They show us that this understanding of Jesus going to war to rescue us was common within the early Church, even if it's something we rarely hear today. We have to use our imagination here to appreciate their preaching. Remember, the power that is Death has claimed every single person ever since the rebellion of Adam, ever since our first parents sold us into slavery. The kingdom of Death, the domain of Death, the lordship of Death has captured everybody. Thus Satan expects that he, through Death, will capture Jesus too. That's what he's been doing for century after century after century after century for millennia after millennia, ever since Adam.

This is why God comes in disguise. Satan is not wise, but he is not stupid either. He knows he's a creature and that he cannot defeat God. So God becomes a man and lives an ordinary life for many years, almost like a sleeper cell. Then, at the very moment when it looks as if He is defeated, Jesus springs a trap on Satan and his "firstborn"—Sin and Death. God, quite simply, cannot die. You can't kill God. So to liberate us from the tyrannical grip of the devil and Death, God takes a body so that He can "get inside" Death and Hell and despoil both from inside.

But enough of my attempt to explain this. Let's take a look at how two early Church figures preached on this. Saint Ephrem was a deacon who lived from A.D. 306–373. He grew up in Nisibis and later lived in Edessa, both located in what is now Turkey.

He was a renowned preacher and poet and was given the nickname, "The Harp of the Holy Spirit." Here is an excerpt from one of his Easter sermons:

> Death trampled our Lord underfoot, but he in his turn treated death as a highroad for his own feet. He submitted to it, enduring it willingly, because by this means he would be able to destroy death in spite of itself. Death had its own way when our Lord went out from Jerusalem carrying his cross; but when by a loud cry from that cross he summoned the dead from the underworld, death was powerless to prevent it.
>
> Death slew him by means of the body which he had assumed, but that same body proved to be the weapon with which he conquered death. Concealed beneath the cloak of his manhood, his godhead engaged death in combat; but in slaying our Lord, death itself was slain. It was able to kill natural human life, but was itself killed by the life that is above the nature of man.
>
> Death could not devour our Lord unless he possessed a body, neither could hell swallow him up unless he bore our flesh; and so he came in search of a chariot in which to ride to the underworld. This chariot was the body which he received from the Virgin; in it he invaded death's fortress, broke open its strong room and scattered all its treasure.
>
> At length he came upon Eve, the mother of all the living. She was that vineyard whose enclosure her own hands had enabled death to violate, so that she could taste its fruit; thus the mother of all the living became the source of death for every living creature.

But in her stead Mary grew up, a new vine in place of the old. Christ, the new life, dwelt within her. When death, with its customary impudence, came foraging for her mortal fruit, it encountered its own destruction in the hidden life that fruit contained. All unsuspecting, it swallowed him up, and in so doing released life itself and set free a multitude of men.

He who was also the carpenter's glorious son set up his cross above death's all-consuming jaws, and led the human race into the dwelling place of life. Since a tree had brought about the downfall of mankind, it was upon a tree that mankind crossed over to the realm of life. Bitter was the branch that had once been grafted upon that ancient tree, but sweet the young shoot that has now been grafted in, the shoot in which we are meant to recognize the Lord whom no creature can resist.

We give glory to you, Lord, who raised up your cross to span the jaws of death like a bridge by which souls might pass from the region of the dead to the land of the living. We give glory to you who put on the body of a single mortal man and made it the source of life for every other mortal man. You are incontestably alive. Your murderers sowed your living body in the earth as farmers sow grain, but it sprang up and yielded an abundant harvest of men raised from the dead.

Come then, my brothers and sisters, let us offer our Lord the great and all-embracing sacrifice of our love, pouring out our treasury of hymns and prayers before him who offered his cross in sacrifice to God for the enrichment of us all.[20]

As rich as Ephrem's homily is, however, there is another Easter sermon from roughly the same time period, that is, well, unlike anything I've ever come across. It was preached by Saint Epiphanius, the bishop of Salamis in Cyprus. Epiphanius was born somewhere around the year 310 and died in A.D. 403. The entire homily takes some forty-five minutes to preach, so I'll only share some excerpts here. It can be found, however, in its entirety in Appendix I.

> Yesterday, he was slapped: today, he strikes Hell's household with the thunderbolt of his Godhead. Yesterday, he was bound: today, he binds fast the tyrant with unbreakable bonds. Yesterday, he was condemned: today, he grants freedom to the damned. Yesterday, Pilate's minions mocked him: today, Hell's porters shudder to see him. . . .
>
> All the ranks of angels tremble, astonished and astounded, and they inquire among themselves, saying:
>
> What is this dreadful matter, fearful and frightful in manner? What is this grand and exceptional spectacle? The invisible God who is above us, the bodiless, is seen below as a man among men, naked and lifeless. Joseph and Nicodemus fearlessly give burial to him upon whom the Cherubim attend with reverent fear. When did he descend, who never left the heights? How did he go out, who is ever within? How did he come to earth, who fills all things? How did he depart unnoticed by all, who as God is ever with the Father on high? He who has never appeared to us at any time, has appeared to men as both man and man's friend. How is the Invisible seen? How is the Immaterial incarnate? How did the Passionless suffer the Passion? How was

the Judge brought to judgment? How did the Life taste death? How is the Uncontainable contained in a tomb? How does he dwell in a grave, who never left the Father's throne? How does he enter the door of the cave, who opened not the gates of heaven, yet opened the gates of Paradise; who broke not the doors of the Virgin's womb, yet shattered the gates of Hell; who opened not the doors before Thomas, yet opened the gates of the Kingdom to men; who kept unopened the doors and seals of the tomb? How is he numbered among the dead, who is free among the dead? How does the unwaning Light appear in darkness and the shadow of death? Whither does he go, whither does he descend, he who cannot be held by death? What is the reason, what the manner, what the purpose for his descent into Hell? Perhaps he goes down to bring up Adam, our condemned fellow-servant. Yes, surely he goes to seek the first-formed man like a lost sheep. Doubtless he wishes to visit even those who sit in darkness and the shadow of death. Doubtless he goes to loose from their bonds captive Adam and his fellow-prisoner Eve, he who is at once their son and God. So let us descend with him, let us assemble with him, let us hasten, let us skip, let us escort him, let us raise a shout, let us hurry, that we may see God's reconciliation with men, and the gracious Master's release of the condemned. . . .

Let us then make haste and journey in mind to Hades, that we may see how there at last, he masters with masterly might the most mighty master and tyrant, and with his brilliant lightning, as with a whole army, effortlessly subdues the ranks of that immortal infantry; Christ the Door having first burst open the exitless doors in the midst, and shattered the woodless gates of bronze by the wood of the Cross; by the nails having broken and sundered the age-old iron bars, by the bonds of his hands having dissolved the indissoluble bonds like wax, and by the spear in his divine side having pierced through the fleshless heart of the tyrant. There did he break the strength of the bow, when on the bow of the Cross, he stretched out the sinews of his divine arms like bowstrings. Therefore if thou followest Christ in silence, thou wilt presently see where he bound the tyrant, where he hung his head aloft, how he razed his dungeon and led out the prisoners, how he trampled the serpent, and where he displayed his head, how he freed Adam and raised up Eve, how he broke down the middle wall, where he condemned the cruel dragon, how he set up invincible trophies, where he put Death to death, how he spoiled corruption, and restored man to his primal dignity.

Accordingly, he who yesterday refused the aid of legions of angels in his economy, telling Peter, "I could even now set before me more than twelve legions of angels," today with God-befitting majesty, as both Warrior and Master, goes down by means of death to the depths of death and Hell to oppose the tyrant of death. . . .

Then Adam, the first-created and first-imprisoned of all men, held fast in chains with great security deeper down than all the rest, heard the Master's footsteps coming toward the prisoners, and recognized their sound as he walked about the prison, and turned to all the prisoners with him from former ages, and said:

"I hear the sound of someone's footsteps coming toward us; and if he has truly deigned to come unto this place, we are free of our chains: if we should truly see him here with us, we are delivered from Hell."

As Adam spoke these things and others like them to all his fellow-condemned, the Master entered in unto them, wielding the victorious weapon of the Cross. Upon seeing him, Adam the first-formed beat his breast in shock, and cried out to all those sleeping from times past, "My Lord be with you all!" And Christ answering said to Adam, "And with thy spirit." Then he took him by the hand and stood him up, saying:

"Awake thou that sleepest, and arise from the dead, and Christ shall give thee light. I am thy God, who for thy sake became thy son—for thy sake and thy posterity—who now speak and with authority command the prisoners, 'Go forth,' and them that are in darkness, 'Show yourselves,' and them that sleep, 'Arise.' Again I bid thee, Awake thou that sleepest: for I did not make thee, that thou shouldest be held captive in Hell. Arise from the dead: for I am the Life of mortals. Arise, my creation; arise, my form, made in mine own image.

"Arise, let us go hence; for we are one single, inseparable person—thou in me, and I in thee. For thy sake, I thy God became thy son; for thy sake, I the Master took upon me thy servile form; for thy sake, I that am far above the heavens came upon earth, and went under the earth; for thy sake, who art a man, I became as a man without help, free among the dead; for thy sake, who wast exiled from a garden, I was betrayed to the Jews in a garden, and in a garden was crucified.

"Behold my face which received spittings, that I might restore to thee thy primal in-breathing. Behold my cheeks which received blows, that I might set right thy marred form according the original image. Behold my back which received scourging, that I might loose the burden of thy sins laid upon thy back. Behold my hands which were nailed to the Tree for good, on behalf of thee who didst stretch forth thy hand to the Tree for evil. Behold my feet which were pierced and nailed to the Tree, on behalf of thee who didst wickedly run to the Tree. . . .

"I slept on the Cross and was pierced in the side by a spear, on behalf of thee who didst sleep in Paradise and bring forth Eve from thy side. My side healed the pain of thy side, my sleep shall draw thee out of sleep in the grave, my spear has stopped the sword which turned every way against thee.

"Arise then, let us go hence. I drove thee from the land of Paradise, yet I shall return thee no more to Paradise, but to a celestial throne. I barred thee from the archetypal Tree of Life, but lo, I myself, the Life, am now wholly united to thee. I placed Cherubim to keep thee out of Eden as a slave, but now I make Cherubim to bow down before thee as a god. Thou didst hide from God as one naked, but lo, now thou hast hidden within thyself the denuded God. Thou wast clothed in a shameful coat of skins, but I, being God, am clothed in the sanguine coat of thy flesh.

"Wherefore arise, all of you, let us go hence, from decay to incorruption, from death unto life. Arise, let us go hence, from darkness to everlasting light. Arise, let us go hence, from grief to joy. Arise, let us go hence,

> from bondage to liberty, from prison to the Jerusalem above, from bonds to God, from straitness to the bliss of Paradise, from earth to heaven. For to this end, I both died and rose again, that I might be Lord both of the dead and the living.
>
> Wherefore arise, let us go hence; for my heavenly Father awaits the lost sheep; the ninety and nine sheep, the angels, are waiting for the time when Adam their fellow-servant should arise, when he should ascend and return to God. A cherubic throne is set, and those who bear it aloft are ready and waiting, the bridechamber is furnished, the choice foods are made, the everlasting tabernacles and mansions are built, the treasuries of blessings are open, the kingdom of heaven has been prepared before the ages. The good things which eye hath not seen, nor ear heard, neither have entered into the heart of man, are laid up in store for mankind."[21]

We began this chapter asking for the grace of light to see Jesus ever more fully. Many people see Jesus as kind, gentle, compassionate, and merciful. Thanks be to God He is all of these! But He's so much more. Jesus is Lord, which is to say nobody else is. Jesus is absolutely and utterly unconquerable. He has no rival. As is commonly said when talking about sports figures, Jesus is the ultimate GOAT—the greatest of all time.

This war Jesus waged against Sin, Death, and Satan was all done out of love. For you and for me. Jesus on the cross, and in His resurrection from the dead, was not showing off. No, this is what love looks like. This is how much you mean to Him. That's why the gospel is extraordinary news. Not just news, not just data, and not just words.

Hundreds of years before Jesus was born, God foretold

through the prophet Isaiah all that He would do for us. Speaking about the seemingly hopeless situation of our race, God said:

> Can the prey be taken from the mighty,
> or the captives of a tyrant be rescued?

Who are the prey and the captives? We are. Who is the tyrant and the mighty? Satan and his minions. God goes on,

> For thus says the LORD:
> "Even the captives of the mighty shall be taken,
> and the prey of the tyrant be rescued."

How will this happen? God said,

> "I will contend with those who contend with you. . . .
> Then all flesh shall know
> that I am the LORD your Savior,
> and your Redeemer, the Mighty One of Jacob."
> (Isaiah 49:24–26)

Do you see that? God promised that He would fight for us! He would contend with those who contend with us. As a result, everyone will come to know that He is our Savior and Redeemer. I often think that the Church uses words that nobody really understands. *Redeemer* is one of those words. What's a redeemer? What have you ever redeemed aside from a coupon?

The Hebrew word for *redeemer* is *go'el. Go'el* was a family term; it referred to someone in the family who had various responsibilities toward other family members. For example, if a member of his family was kidnapped, it was the go'el's responsibility, his task, his privilege, to rescue the one who had been kidnapped. Or if one of his family was murdered, it was the go'el's task to avenge the murder.

God identifies Himself as *our* go'el. He identifies Himself as our kin, our family, our brother. Our race sold itself into slavery. Out of unimaginable love, God came as a man, "in disguise," to redeem us. Our race was murdered by the one Jesus called "a murderer from the beginning" (John 8:44). So the creator of the universe avenged us by defeating the one who has the power of Death (see Hebrews 2:14).

Recall the parable Jesus told, the image He used to help us understand the identity of the enemy? "When a strong man, fully armed, guards his own palace, his goods are safe." The strong man is Satan, his palace is the world, his goods are every single human person. Thankfully, that's not the end of the parable. Jesus goes on to say, "But when one stronger than he attacks him and overcomes him, he takes away his armor in which he trusted and divides his spoil" (Luke 11:21–22). When He spoke this parable, it was as though Jesus was taunting Satan, "I am going to break into your house!"

Imagine yourself back in the hands of the trafficker. You're locked up in a room, utterly hopeless. No one knows where you are. You've been there for so long you've lost track of time. One night, as you're trying to sleep (although sleep makes you dangerously vulnerable), you feel a touch on your shoulder. This is dangerous too, because you've come to learn that a touch means you're about to get hurt. You open your eyes, expecting the face of your attacker and are shocked to see another's face. This face is unlike any you've ever before seen. As He looks at you, He smiles, and you know He's not there to hurt you. But there's more than just a smile on His face. As you look at Him you have this awareness of strength. He gently bends down and begins to untie you, and He helps you stand up. His eyes never leave yours as He does all of this. Finally, He gently grabs your hand and begins to walk with you toward the door—the door that leads to freedom! But as you're walking toward the door, you experience two things simultaneously: exhilaration and terror. Exhilaration because you might actually get out of this hell, but terror because you know who's on the other side of the door.

The Man opens the door, and as you prepare to step across the threshold, you reflexively place your hands across your face and brace yourself, knowing who's out there. But the Man pulls your hands away from your face, and you see the one who has made your life so miserable. He's now tied up, harmless. He can't hurt you anymore! You know that this is all because of the Man who holds you in His hands. He turns, looks at you, and says, "You don't have to worry about him anymore. I've taken care of him. You're free."

What's in a name? *Everything* is in a name, most especially His name. The angel tells Joseph that Mary will bear a son. "You shall call his name Jesus," the angel instructs Joseph (Matthew 1:21).

Why?

What does *Jesus* mean?

It means "God saves."

He rescues.

He liberates.

He sets free.

From Sin and from sins.

From Death.

From Hell.

And from Satan.

Because that's how much you mean to God.

CHAPTER 5

SO WHAT?

IMAGINE GROWING UP IN A DYSFUNCTIONAL FAMILY. DAD'S AN ALcoholic. He and Mom fight all the time. Home is . . . loud. Nasty words are the norm, toward each other and toward you. Your home is simply not safe. Plates fly, quite literally. To protect yourself, you do everything you can to avoid being home. You play every sport, get involved in every extracurricular activity available—anything to stay away from home as much as you can. When you do finally have to go home, you sneak in as quietly as possible, praying everyone's asleep or perhaps passed out on the couch with the TV on.

As you grow older, you notice that across the street lives this amazingly happy family. Day after day, month after month, year after year you see and hear the kids your age outside playing. There's laughter, the likes of which you've never heard in your home. Most provocatively and attractively, you see and hear the dad regularly playing with the kids in the front yard and driveway. As he plays catch with them or shoots hoops, he's smiling, engaging with them in a way you can only marvel at. These kids look and sound like they feel safe with their dad. In fact, they are. You can't imagine this, as you've never felt safe with your dad.

One day you find yourself at home, alone. There's a knock at the front door and you go to answer it. As you open the door, you see the dad from across the street. He's wearing a huge smile as he looks at you. Then, with a warmth you've never heard in your dad's voice, he says, "Son, do you want to come and live with us?" Are you kidding me? You don't even pack. You run across the street and never look back. Moving from that first house to the second, from one dad to another, is one way to understand the many practical differences that Jesus's death and resurrection make in your life and mine.

In the last chapter, we began our exploration of the question, "What, if anything, has God done about the mess the world is in?" We saw that He's done nothing less than rescue us from the cosmic and terrifying powers of Death, Sin, and the enemy of our race. In this chapter, we want to drill more deeply into this question and focus our attention on the difference this makes. Or maybe we can put it this way: So what and now what?

As we have been doing repeatedly, let's start by asking for grace. In the last chapter, we asked for the grace of light to see Jesus just a little bit more clearly. Flowing directly from this greater clarity on the identity of Jesus, we want now to ask God to give us the grace of unshakable confidence in Him.

> *Father, Jesus said that when He was lifted up from the earth, He would draw all people to Himself.*[1] *As we continue to reflect, linger over, and gaze in our minds upon Jesus crucified and risen, I pray that You would draw us closer to You through Him. Help us to know Him more fully and fill us, who are living in a time with so much anxiety, so much fear, so much confusion, and so much unrest, with the gift of unshakable confidence in Him. Help us to understand that You are not nervous right now, so we don't have to be; that You are the creator of this universe, which is beyond anything we can comprehend, and that You hold us in Your hands. Show us as*

only You can that no one is stronger than You. Dispel any and all anxiety in us. Where there is fear, replace it with a confidence in You that no circumstance can shake. We ask all of this in Jesus's name. Amen.

Let's do a quick word association. I say "Jesus," and you think what? Most people, and especially most men, would answer something like this: "Jesus is kind. He's patient. He's gentle. He's merciful. He's compassionate. He's loving." Those are all true, but do they exhaust who He is? Do they fully help us appreciate what He's accomplished for me and you? To better understand who He is, then, let's examine just a few of the practical differences that Jesus's death and resurrection make in our lives.

First, Jesus has triumphed over the enemy. Jesus has defeated Satan. Saint Paul writes in his letter to the Colossians, "He disarmed the rulers and authorities and put them to open shame, by triumphing over them" (2:15). We could alternatively translate the first part of Paul's declaration like this: "He has despoiled and stripped naked the rulers and authorities." Who are "the rulers and authorities"? Death, Sin, and Satan.

Jesus, Paul goes on to say, has "put them to open shame." In other words Jesus has humiliated these powers, publicly disgraced them, and exposed them as losers. Finally, Paul writes, Jesus has *triumphed* over them. What does that mean?

In the Roman Empire *triumph* had a very particular meaning. A triumphal procession was a spectacular event held to commemorate a significant military victory. Everybody in Rome came out to watch and take part in it. Arches and enormous columns often were erected for such occasions. Some of these can still be seen in Rome today, like the Arch of Titus, built to commemorate the destruction of Jerusalem and the looting of the temple, or Trajan's Column, built to honor his victories in Dacia.

Triumph meant over-the-top, ostentatious parades designed to demonstrate the superiority of Rome over and against all others.

One of the best-known triumphs took place in the time of Julius Caesar. The Gallic Wars involved a series of battles that took place over eight years between Rome and the ruling chieftains of the kingdom of Gaul. Ultimately Julius Caesar led Rome to victory. The leader of the Gauls, Vercingetorix, was captured and hauled before Caesar, who was seated in an obvious position of superiority. As Vercingetorix stood there, his hands and legs chained, Roman soldiers roughly shoved him to the ground and pushed the Roman eagle—the emblem of Rome—to his lips. Forced to kiss the Roman eagle and acknowledge that he had lost, Vercingetorix was lifted to his feet. His clothes were then unceremoniously cut from his body. In an instant, this fierce and feared leader of Gaul was standing completely naked in front of the Roman legion. Soldiers then put him into a wagon that was more like a cage. Such was the beginning of a triumphal procession back to Rome.

The spoils of war—men, women and children—were paraded through the streets of the capital city. These once free but now hapless creatures would be enslaved to the Romans. Last among these spoils came Vercingetorix. Once proud, fierce, and frightening, he was now chained, humiliated, and naked. All of this was a dramatic way to indicate that the one who used to threaten and terrify Rome would never do so again. Finally, when the triumph reached its destination, this once mighty general was executed, the ultimate sign of both his defeat and of the greatness of Rome.

This is what's in Paul's mind as he writes about what Jesus has done to the enemy—the only enemy of the human race! He has *triumphed* over him. And the enemy *knows* it. He knows he has lost. He knows that he's been utterly defeated. He knows that Jesus is stronger than he is.

Why, though, doesn't it seem that Jesus has won? Why are things still such a mess? I've found the following analogy helpful in understanding this. Our situation is analogous to the time between D-Day and V-E Day. D-Day occurred June 6, 1944, when the Allies landed in Normandy. Once that happened, for all intents and purposes the outcome of the war in Europe was certain. Germany would be defeated. And everybody knew it. The Germans, the French, the English, the Americans—everybody. However, the fighting didn't stop that day. V-E Day, marking the surrender of Germany, was still eleven months away: May 8, 1945. That time included one of the fiercest battles of the entire war, the Battle of the Bulge. We are living now in something analogous to that time between D-Day and V-E Day. Jesus has already triumphed over the enemy, He has already defeated him. He hasn't, however, destroyed him. Yet. One day He will, though. And both sides know it.

Here's a second practical difference made by the death and resurrection of Jesus. We get new "spiritual passports." In that same letter to the Colossians, Paul writes, "He has delivered us from the domain of darkness and transferred us to the kingdom of his beloved Son, in whom we have redemption, the forgiveness of sins" (1:13–14). We could also translate this passage to read, "He has *rescued* us from the mastery, the control, the authority, or the power of darkness."

Think back to that child growing up in the dysfunctional family we started this chapter with. At a certain moment, the child moved. When does this happen for us? When does a person get rescued from the control and mastery of the kingdom of darkness?

When they get baptized.

Imagine that we all received something like "spiritual passports" when we were born. Despite how cute newborns are, if we could see these passports they would read, "This child belongs to the mastery, the domain of darkness." This isn't because they are nasty little children; it's because each person is born under the dominion of and enslaved to the cosmic powers of Sin and Death. They can't escape these on their own. But when a child, or an adult, enters into the waters of baptism, they get a new passport! If you could see it, the document would now read, "This person belongs to the kingdom of God." In baptism, by sharing in Jesus's death and resurrection, a person moves from one house to another, from the house of a cruel and abusive tyrant to the house of a good Father. If you are baptized, this has already happened! If you're not and you want a new address, freedom, and hope, well then, let's make this move a priority.

A third practical difference made by Jesus's death and resurrection is that He has rendered the power of Sin impotent. Now, I have to admit, I find this one a bit frustrating. Let me explain. We all still sin, obviously. We still do things, at least from time to time, that we know we shouldn't do and even hate doing. We're not yet what we want to be. We still say things we regret, make choices we know are wrong, entertain thoughts that don't belong. If Jesus has rendered the power of Sin impotent, why does this continue? Because we have memories, habits, and instincts. Personally, I'm more aware of my sinful tendencies now than I was in my youth. Yet it is true to say that the kingdom of Sin has no control over me. And it has no control over you if you belong to Jesus, if you've received a new spiritual passport, if you've moved from the home of a cruel tyrant into the home of a good Father.

In his letter to the Romans, Saint Paul says, "How can we who died to sin still live in it?" (6:2). What does he mean when he says we "died to sin"? When did I die to sin? Paul goes on to tell us, "Do you not know that all of us who have been baptized into Christ Jesus were baptized into his death?" (6:3). In other words, when we were baptized, when we shared sacramentally in Jesus's death and in His resurrection, we not only moved houses, not only received new spiritual passports, we also escaped from the power of Sin. It has no hold on me. Baptism, you see, is so much more than a public statement that you want to be a disciple of Jesus. Something really happens. You die. And you rise to new life. A new power enters into us—the power of the God who made the universe and who defeated Satan.

Paul continues,

> We were buried therefore with him by baptism into death, so that as Christ was raised from the dead by the glory of the Father, we too might walk in newness of life. . . . We know that our old self was crucified with him so that the sinful body might be destroyed, and we might no longer be enslaved to sin. (6:4, 6, RSVCE)

Paul is saying, in essence, that before baptism we were slaves to Sin. But not anymore! Sin, the *power* of Sin, has no domination, no mastery, over a baptized person. This is remarkably good news. It is not, however, an "all clear." It's not an announcement that the war is over. Rather, it's an announcement that now we actually have a chance to overcome because of the power of God alive within us. Before this, in actuality, we had no chance.

Saint Augustine's life provides a great and timeless illustration of the transformation we're talking about. Born in A.D. 354, Augustine is considered the first modern man. His *Confessions* is the first introspective autobiography. Augustine was gifted beyond measure intellectually and was relentless in his search for truth, beauty, and goodness. His mother, Monica, was a devout Christian. Though she had exposed Augustine to Christianity, he wasn't baptized as a child. Later, reflecting on the years before he was baptized and became a Christian, Augustine came to understand that most Christians go through two conversions: the conversion of the intellect and the conversion of the will. In the conversion of the intellect, a person is able to recognize that something is true or false but is usually unable to align their behavior with their thinking. In Augustine's case, there were years between these two conversions, and his primary challenge was chastity. Augustine had a mistress whom he loved very much and a sexual appetite that he greatly enjoyed indulging. Perhaps you have heard his prayer that effectively summarizes the tension between these two conversions that many of us go through. Recognizing that his behavior was not healthy, either for him or his mistress, yet not wanting to abandon it, Augustine prayed, "Lord, make me chaste. But not yet."

One day, however, Augustine had a profound encounter with Jesus. After many years of searching for the true, the good, and the beautiful; after many prayers uttered and tears shed by his mother, Augustine was baptized by Saint Ambrose in the cathedral in Milan, in a baptistry that even to this day you can visit. As he died and rose to new life with Jesus in this sacrament, Augustine tapped into new power, a power to which he had never had access before. Suddenly he experienced the power to become chaste. This wasn't because he tried harder. This wasn't the result of his own effort. No, this was because the power of Sin had lost its grip on him; he was no longer under its tyrannical dominion.

Here's another difference that Jesus's death and resurrection make: Jesus has not only rendered the power of Sin impotent, but He has also defeated the power of Death. Paul writes to his friend Timothy that Jesus has "abolished death" (2 Timothy 1:10).

What does this mean? Obviously, you and I still will die, as will everyone and everything we love. So what's Paul telling us? We could translate Paul's words like this, "Jesus has destroyed, wiped out, voided, and invalidated Death." In other words, He's caused Death to become toothless. Yes, it will still come to me and you, but Death has no claim on or power over us anymore. It won't be able to keep us in its grip.

This is extraordinarily good news. Jesus says to Death, "I have abolished you! Your power and claim are now voided as a result of My death and resurrection. You have no hold on those who belong to Me." And because of this, you and I can approach our own deaths and grieve the loss of loved ones in an entirely different way with confidence that it does not have the last word.

In the longest passage on the resurrection in the Bible, Saint Paul proclaims this great news with words worth meditating on:

> Behold! I tell you a mystery. We shall not all sleep, but we shall all be changed, in a moment, in the twinkling of an eye, at the last trumpet. For the trumpet will sound, and the dead will be raised imperishable, and we shall be changed. For this perishable body must put on the imperishable, and this mortal body must put on immortality. When the perishable puts on the imperishable, and the mortal puts on immortality, then shall come to pass the saying that is written:
>
> "Death is swallowed up in victory."
> "O death, where is your victory?
> O death, where is your sting?"
>
> The sting of death is sin, and the power of sin is the law. But thanks be to God, who gives us the victory through our Lord Jesus Christ! (1 Corinthians 15:51–57)

It's as if Paul is saying to Death, "You can't keep me. You won't win. You can't have me." Are you afraid of dying? If so, you're in good company—most people are. But we don't have to be.

The letter to the Hebrews says, "Since therefore the children share in flesh and blood, [Jesus] himself likewise partook of the same things, that through death he might destroy the one who has the power of death, that is, the devil, and deliver all those who *through fear of death were subject to lifelong slavery*" (Hebrews 2:14–15). What does that slavery look like? Commenting on this verse, Mary Healy astutely notes:

> We instinctively resist and recoil from everything that reminds us of our mortality—pain, deprivation, weakness, criticism, failure. This paralyzing fear influences many human choices on a subconscious level, leads to various forms of escapism and addiction, induces us to grasp the false security nets proffered by Satan, and keeps us from pursuing the will of God with freedom, peace, and confidence. It is the slavery from which Jesus came to set us free.[2]

Disciples of Jesus don't have to fear the power of Death. It can't and won't hold us. Nor do we have to be afraid of dying. This is why Paul can write something as audacious as, "For to me to live is Christ, and to die is gain" (Philippians 1:21). Gain! How? Why? Because Jesus has robbed Death of its power, and now it is simply the doorway into the fullness of life in which God has destined us to share. Pope Benedict XVI preached about this truth in an Easter homily some years ago:

> Christmas tells us that there is not only the tyrant, Death: there is God, who is Life, and this God can and

> will reach us; he has broken a way in to us. . . . But this answer is complete only if there is not just an entrance by which God can reach us but also an exit for us. . . . And this is the content of the message of Easter. Not only is there a door in, there is also a door out. Death is no longer a house with no exits, a place of no return.
>
> The ancient Church saw in this verse an interpretation of the article of faith "descended into hell," referring particularly to Holy Saturday. . . . The bolts of death's dungeon, of the world's dungeon, are wrenched off; the ramparts are thrown down; the gates are torn from their hinges. The one who has done this, Jesus, takes the long-imprisoned Adam and Eve—that is, humanity—by the hand and leads them to freedom. Life is not a waiting room leading to the void but the beginning of eternity. . . . [God] does not live in a distant castle, nor does he hide himself behind impenetrable anterooms.
>
> The door is open; it is called Jesus Christ.
>
> The celebration of Easter is intended to show us the radiant light that streams from this door.[3]

This approach not only changes how we face our own death but how we mourn the loss of loved ones. As a result of what Jesus has done for us by His death and resurrection, when we lose family members and friends, we are empowered to grieve in an entirely distinct way from those who are still held bound by the fear of Death.

Paul writes in 1 Thessalonians, "We do not want you to be uninformed, brothers, about those who are asleep [meaning, those who have died], that you may not grieve as others do who have no hope" (4:13). Note that Paul *isn't* saying we shouldn't grieve when we lose loved ones. Of course we should, and do! I cry often over the loss of family and friends. In fact, the appropriate, right, and genuinely human response to death is to cry. Jesus Himself cries at the tomb of His friend Lazarus, and in doing so He gives us permission to cry. What Paul says, though, is that we should not grieve like those who have no hope, like those who think that death is the end, pure and simple. For me this is most powerfully illustrated when we face the trauma of the loss of children.

As a priest I obviously have no children. I can't possibly fathom the pain and anguish of a parent losing any child, but perhaps especially a young child. I have stood beside and prayed with many grieving parents and have buried more children than I can count, from newborns to adolescents. Talk about feeling helpless. It often falls to me to say something in the midst of this excruciating anguish, but the simple truth is that there isn't anything to say. There are no words.

Amid all the tears, all the grief, all the anger and confusion, I have to remind myself to approach this with biblical lenses, from the perspective of "Where is this little one now?" If they're home, if they're with the Lord, if they're enjoying the kingdom of God, where there is no sickness, no pain, no loss, nothing that ever goes wrong, well, then, the *child* is not crying. The child doesn't feel as if he or she has missed out. No child in heaven is saying, "Man . . . I never got to drive. I didn't get to go to college. I never kissed a girl. I was robbed." When young people die, people often say things like, "They were so young. They had their whole lives in front of them." I understand that response if we're coming at it without biblical lenses. But such a way of speaking and thinking implies that heaven is less, not more. But this is not true. Please don't misunderstand me. I'm supposed to and do grieve like crazy over such painful losses. But the tragedy is not for the children; it's for us. I'm not sad for them; I'm sad for those of us who aren't able to hug them right now. But we will again one day.

And since Jesus has defeated the power of Death, between us and our loved ones who have died hangs a very thin veil. The communion we enjoyed on this earth we still enjoy, even if it's different for the time being. In the creed that many Christians recite, we profess that we believe in "the communion of saints." This is not some esoteric belief. Our belief in the communion of saints means a number of things, one of which is that Death is not strong enough to keep us from our loved ones. Because of what Jesus has done by His death and resurrection, they're not *dead,* at least not as the world uses that word. And since they're not dead, our friendship with them still lives, not just in our memories and photos but for real. "Love is stronger than Death" is not just a cute slogan. Love really is stronger than Death because God *is* love and He is stronger than Death. As a result, the friendships we once had with others here on earth, we still have, even when those friends are no longer visible to us. Because they're not dead, we can still talk to them, and if they're home with the Lord, they can still help us. Far more than we can imagine. This reality was powerfully brought home to me some years ago on a fall Saturday night.

I came home after a long day, quickly made myself a big bowl of pasta, and sat down to watch whatever football game was on TV. It happened to be a game between the University of Nebraska and Texas A&M. I don't have any particular affinity for either team, but I love college football, so I kicked up my feet, grabbed my fork, and dug into a bowl of Rigatoni alla Carbonara.

The game was being played at Kyle Field, the home stadium of Texas A&M. Kyle Field holds more than one hundred thousand fans (102,733 to be exact) and is known as "The Home of the 12th Man." For those who don't know anything about football, this name refers to the fact that the home crowd is considered to be the extra player on the field, as football is played with eleven players on each side. At this game the home team fans were all dressed in white to create a visually intimidating look for the opponent, in this case, the Cornhuskers from Nebraska. An important note: Texas A&M doesn't have cheerleaders; they have Yell Leaders. Yell Leaders have one job: to whip the crowd into a frenzy. Boy, oh boy, were they doing their job. Kyle Field was loud. I mean *really* loud. In fact, there was so much noise and so much energy in the stadium that the upper deck was bouncing. And the game hadn't even begun!

As I was watching all of this, I felt in my spirit God say to me, "John, that's heaven." Immediately, I remembered a passage from the letter to the Hebrews, "Therefore, since we are surrounded by so great a cloud of witnesses, let us also lay aside every weight, and sin which clings so closely, and let us run with endurance the race that is set before us, looking to Jesus, the founder and perfecter of our faith" (12:1–2). This passage comes after a lengthy description of what is sometimes called the "hall of faith"—a list of Old Testament heroes, men and women alike, who persevered and stayed faithful to God and loved their neighbor, even in the most trying of circumstances. As the author of Hebrews writes about these heroes, he is creating a word picture straight out of the world of sports. He's trying to help his audience, and us, understand that those who once competed in the game of life now surround us, much as fans surround players in a stadium. You and I are still on the field competing, running the race. They, however, have finished running. But here's the key: Nobody in Kyle Field that night was there to *watch* the game. Real fans don't go to a football game to watch the game. They go to do their best to change the outcome. That's why home field is "the 12th man." Every football team would rather play at home because one hundred thousand people cheering you on somehow helps you to achieve things that you could never do in your backyard in front of Mom and Dad.

So it is with those who have died and who surround us now. They're not simply watching. They're cheering us on. They're praying for us. They're asking God to give us all we need to be great, to play the game of life well, to stay faithful, to love God and our neighbor, even as they did. And one day, one real day, we will join them. Oh yes, we grieve, but we grieve with great hope!

Here's yet another practical difference that Jesus's death and resurrection make in our lives, and one that seems especially pertinent in our modern culture: By His death and resurrection, Jesus has canceled our sins. It's often noted that we live in a "cancel culture" right now. And quite honestly, good luck—you and I might be next. Who, after all, hasn't said or done something that would lead to our being canceled by one group or another? When I was first ordained, I was more than a little concerned about this because I was assigned to a parish where some of the guys that I used to live with, play basketball with, and party with went to the church. I wasn't exactly an altar boy in college. For those first few weeks, I kept wondering if one of those guys might stand up in the middle of my homily and say something like, "Hey, we knew him when he . . ." After some weeks of playing this scene out in my head, I finally decided that if someone did that, I would simply respond with, "He's right. I did that. And lots of other things too. But by the grace of God I've changed, and God has forgiven me."

Today's rampant cancel culture can lead many to live in fear like I did as a young priest. "What if people find out?" Well, here's the great news about what Jesus has done: God has already found out, and He's done something about what He found. He, too, has a cancel culture, you see. But He doesn't cancel people. He cancels sins. In his letter to the Colossians, Paul writes that in Jesus's death God was "canceling the record of debt that stood against us with its legal demands. This he set aside, nailing it to the cross" (2:14). Jesus's death and resurrection have obliterated, wiped away, and blotted out our sins, our most humiliating and shameful moments, choices, actions, and words. He did this with His precious blood, poured out on the cross in love for us. What amazing news! It's not as though I have a couple of shameful moments; I have pages and pages of them. And you might too. But all of these have been canceled by Jesus on the cross. God knows my sin, but He calls me by my name. He doesn't define me by my past, nor does He define you by yours. We aren't failures in His eyes, though we have failed now and then. And we're not His beloved addicts, although from time to time most of us (maybe all of us?) struggle with some kind of addiction. We are His beloved sons and daughters.

Closely related to this is yet another practical difference Jesus's death and resurrection make: By them we have been recreated. In 2 Corinthians Paul says, "If anyone is in Christ, he is a new creation" (5:17). The moment we were baptized, the moment we moved from the house of the tyrant to the good Father's home, we became new creations. The old passed away. How often do we say about somebody, "Well, you know, that's just my dad. He'll *always* be that way"? No, actually. That's not true. The beauty of the Christian life is that you can change. You can change today. You can change right now. Not by trying harder and rolling up your sleeves but by saying to the Lord, "I give up. I surrender. Help me. Change me. I'm tired of this." It can happen. It's been happening for two thousand years. It can happen to you. Nobody's *stuck*. "Behold," Jesus says, "I make all things new" (Revelation 21:5, RSVCE). Not some things. *All* things. Most especially,

He makes people new. God loves to do this. This is what God does best. He takes lives that are a mess and turns them into gold. He brings dead things back to life. Such is the extraordinary power of God.

Jesus's death and resurrection have also given us His own authority and power over the enemy. "Behold," Jesus says, "I have given you authority to tread on serpents" (Luke 10:19). Remember the serpent in Genesis 3? He is that subtle creature that God made who deceived our first parents out of envy of God's plan for us. Jesus has given us authority over him!

A word of caution: This does not mean that we should be reckless or foolhardy. We are always to have a sober awareness of our enemy, of his craftiness and power. The demons are angels and, accordingly, have intellects far greater than ours. Yet, because of what Jesus has done, we have authority over them. And we are supposed to exercise this authority.

This is perhaps especially encouraging for parents. Many parents lament, rightly so, about trying to raise a child in the midst of our current culture. A friend of mine says that raising a family today is like trying to build a house in the middle of a tornado. But moms and dads, you have authority over the enemy who is trying to seduce your children and deceive them into thinking God is their enemy and that they can be happier apart from Him. Exercise this authority! This is something you are especially able to do while they're still young and living at home. Imagine a son or daughter is struggling with fear, sadness, or depression. You can pray something as simple—and powerful—as this, "In the name of Jesus, I take authority over all spirits of fear, and all related spirits, and I cast you to the foot of the cross for Him to do with as He wishes." Then you can utter another simple prayer like, "In the name of Jesus, I declare that God is faithful, that He is a good Father, that He holds your life in His hands, and because

He does, you do not have to be afraid." You might exercise this authority by praying over a son's or daughter's room, either while they're asleep or when they're at school or camp or practice. Simply walk into their room and say something like, "In the name of Jesus, I claim this room for Jesus the Lord, the One who has triumphed over the powers of Sin and Death. You have no hold on my child. You can't have her. You can't have him. I take authority over you."

A well-known passage in Matthew can help us go a bit deeper with our understanding of the power and authority Jesus has given to His disciples. In Matthew 16:18, Jesus says to Peter, "I tell you, you are Peter, and on this rock I will build my church, and the gates of hell shall not prevail against it." Many people, when they hear or read this passage, think it means something like, "No matter how bad it gets, the Church will remain standing." That's not exactly what this passage means. Jesus says, "The gates of hell shall not prevail." Think to yourself for a moment. What are gates for? Have you ever been attacked by a gate? Gates are defensive structures. They're used for keeping people out or for keeping people in. When Jesus says, "The gates of hell shall not prevail against it," He means that hell has no chance against Him. Why? Because He has defeated it. And because He has defeated it, His disciples are to go on the advance—go behind enemy lines, if you will—and rescue those being held hostage by the trafficker. We are to do all we can to make this world more closely conform to how God created it to be—more genuinely human. Here's a key paradox, though: This advance happens most powerfully by imitating how Jesus won the victory—that is to say, by suffering. I will say more about this in the final chapter.

As I get older and older, I find myself more and more saying to God in prayer, "Who *are* You?" As I ponder God's desire to divinize us, to let us share in His own divine nature, I keep repeating this. No one but God would do something like this! Let's think about it: God creates everything out of nothing. He does so not out of need or boredom or lack but out of love. And the creature He most delights in is us, man and woman, made in His image and likeness. But soon, stunningly soon, we totally mess up His creation. We fall prey to the deception of the enemy, turn away from God, and sell ourselves into slavery. How would you respond to this if you were God? I'll tell you what I would do. I'd start over. I'd say to myself, "Ungrateful little things! I'll scrap that and make a new creature who will be grateful for all I've given and who will trust me." But God doesn't do that. He became a man to rescue us from the mess we made. As a result of all of this, God takes something that was perfect, for Eden was perfect, and makes it . . . better. Only God can and would do this!

And here's the thing: This is all about family. This is so personal to God. He didn't do all this just for the generic human race. God did all He did in Jesus for you and for me, by name.

I'm Italian, or at least my dad's side of the family is Italian. His family was from Formicola, a town so small that it doesn't show up on many maps. In the late nineteenth century, my dad's parents left there and settled in upstate New York. My grandfather was a tough old Italian immigrant who worked in a bicycle shop bending handlebars by hand. He was also gifted musically and used to conduct big bands in open-air parks back when that was the thing. I never met my grandmother, unfortunately, as she passed away before I was born, but I heard countless stories about her cooking, her faith, and her tireless love for her family.

My dad and his two brothers were drafted into the army shortly after the start of World War II. My dad served over in the Pacific theater, spending the war in Burma, China, and India. His brother Nick got the best deal, as he ended up playing the violin for the U.S. Army Orchestra in Kansas. My uncle Jim served in the medical corps. He had the toughest assignment, serving in North Africa and then later as part of the Allied troops invading Italy. Challenging as this was, he had the indescribable honor of liberating Formicola, the little town where his parents came from and where so many of his family were still living. To his mates in the army, the people on the streets were strangers, but not to Jim. They were cousins, aunts, uncles. Many of them knew him or knew about him through letters from his parents back to the family. He obviously wasn't able to spend a lot of time there, as the army was on its way north to Germany. For my uncle, the liberation of that town was deeply personal.

We began this chapter by asking God for the grace of unshakable confidence in Jesus. I asked what you think of when you hear the name *Jesus.* I suggested you might answer, "Kind, gentle, compassionate, merciful, forgiving," or something like that. To be sure, Jesus is all those things, blessed be He! But He's more.

Ultimately, Jesus is *Lord.* To say Jesus is Lord means nobody else is. He has no rival and no equal. He is absolutely unconquerable. When He made the decision to become man, though, when He went to war on the cross to defeat the powers of Sin, Death, and Satan, He didn't do that to stroke His own ego or as some sort of divine flex. He did it because God is all about family. Just as there were no strangers for my uncle Jim when the army entered Formicola and liberated his hometown, when Jesus went into and liberated hell, He didn't find any strangers. He didn't encounter some unknown, nameless mass of humanity. He encountered people He had created by name, people whom He loved into existence, about whom He knew everything.

One of the favorite icons of Eastern Orthodox Christians is known as the *Anastasis,* the Greek word for *resurrection.* In the icon, Jesus, surrounded by brilliant light, stands atop Satan, who has been defeated by the cross, which Jesus is holding in one of His hands. His other hand is grabbing the hand of Adam, our first parent. Right next to Adam is his wife, Eve. That long excerpt from Epiphanius that we saw in the last chapter describes this encounter. As the risen, triumphant, and unconquerable Lord sees our first parents, He says to them, in essence, "Come with Me and leave this place, for I did not create you to dwell in hell. I created you to abide with Me forever in heaven. So come, let us leave this place." He then did that with each and every person who was there. Like my uncle Jim's liberation of Formicola, Jesus's liberation of hell was so, so personal.

There's a moment in the Gospels when Jesus asks the apostles, "Who do people say that I am?" (Mark 8:27). They respond with various answers. After listening for a while, Jesus then asks them, "But who do *you* say that I am?" (8:29). I'd like to invite you right now to take that question and turn it around. As crucial as it is to answer Jesus's question for ourselves, it's also crucial to ask Jesus who He says we are. So take a moment, or as long as you need, and ask, "Jesus, who am I to You?"

Do you know who you are to Him? You're *family.* Saint John writes, "See what love the Father has given us, that we should be called children of God; and so we are" (1 John 3:1, RSVCE). The letter to the Hebrews says that Jesus is not ashamed to call us brothers and sisters (see Hebrews 2:11). This is your identity. God created you to be in His family.

The heart of the gospel isn't a bunch of rules or regulations or other things that so many people mistakenly think Christianity is all about. The heart of the gospel is the proclamation of what God has done for us, the God who made a universe that is ninety-plus billion light-years across. And the reason behind what He's done might just be this simple: You matter! You matter to God.

To Him, you're worth fighting for. You're worth dying for. You're worth the trouble of Him becoming a man and enduring the humiliation, the degradation, and the pain of the cross.

You are far, far, far more important than you ever dared to imagine.

This is the gospel.

Jesus is in fact Lord. He is utterly unconquerable. He has no rival and no equal. He has defeated the powers of Sin, Death, and Satan. But He doesn't just call you friend. He calls you brother or sister. And that's really good news. As we'll see in the last chapter, this truth is crucial to our mission as disciples, for God wants all His children to be reconciled to Him and to each other.

CHAPTER 6

CONVINCE ME

THE WRITERS OF THE GOSPELS RECORDED SEVERAL STORIES THAT can make us scratch our heads. For those relatively unfamiliar with them, their portrayal of the apostles is anything but positive. In fact, if the writers were attempting to convince people of the apostles' brilliance, faith, and heroism, they did a terrible job. Of course, that's not why the Gospels were written. They were written so that those who hear the stories of all that Jesus accomplished might surrender and turn their allegiance to Him (see John 20:31).

One particular head-scratcher appears on the final page of Matthew's gospel. The story is also very consoling, at least to me. Jesus's crucifixion has already taken place. He's died and been buried, and then bodily resurrected. Over a period of forty days, He has frequently appeared to His disciples. He's shown them the wounds from the nails in His hands and from the lance in His side; they've placed their fingers into those wounds. He's eaten with them. He's answered the questions they must have asked about what He was doing after He was taken down from the cross and placed in the tomb. He's taught them things that only now they could understand. The joy, the sheer euphoria, of the disciples must be beyond what any of us can imagine. They were daily in the company of someone who had not only come back from the dead but had also conquered Death itself. What's more, this was their *friend*, a friend who was in fact stronger than Death.

Then comes the head-scratching and consoling part:

> Now the eleven disciples went to Galilee, to the mountain to which Jesus had directed them. And when they saw him they worshiped him, but some doubted. (Matthew 28:16–17)

"Some doubted." Really? After all they had seen and heard over the previous forty days, they still doubted, still wavered, still hesitated?

Yes. And I for one am greatly consoled by this. Their doubt, wavering, and hesitation make me feel better about my own.

This is more than a comforting passage, however. Something is being revealed to us—something very important to our journey through the story that is salvation history. We said earlier that the gospel is not ordinary news but extraordinary, explosive, and life-changing news. The stated, up-front goal of the proclamation of the gospel is that a person will be overwhelmed by the events that are proclaimed, and moved to surrender, to entrust his or her life in faith to the God who has rescued us from Sin, Death, and our true and only enemy, Satan. But in order for that to happen, in order for us to surrender, we need more than mere words—powerful as they can be and are. As the scene on the mountain with Jesus and the apostles tells us, we also need more than sight.

We now arrive at the fourth and final big question in this book: "If God has done anything about the mess the world is in, how should I respond?" Perhaps we could reframe that to ask, "What's the logical, reasonable, intelligible response to someone who rescues you from a tyrant's occupation, especially if that someone is the One who made the universe and the tyrant is Satan?"

As with the earlier questions, we want to ask God for a specific grace as we consider this question. The grace? We want to be overwhelmed.

Grace in its simplest form means "gift." But it's more than that. Grace is also power. It's something that God gives that changes you and me. So then let's take a moment—especially those of us who relate to those doubting disciples on the mountain—and ask for this gift:

> *Lord, we ask You to do right now what only You can do: Take all that we've heard, all that we've contemplated, all that we've considered, all that we've reflected upon, all that we've discussed; the things inside us that we haven't even found a way to talk about, that we're musing over—and help us to know that these aren't just words, that this isn't just data. Help us, as only You can, to know it's true. Whatever is resistant within us, come and remove the obstacles. Help us to hear Your voice. Help us to understand not just with our intellect but with everything we have and are. Help us to understand, Father, what You have done for us in Jesus and how we should respond. All of this we ask in Jesus's name. Amen.*

I would suggest that there are two general responses to what God has done to rescue us. First, there's an *inward*, more personal response. Second, there's an *outward*, more mission-oriented response. In chapter 7, we will concentrate on the inward, personal response. Chapter 8 will address the outward, mission-oriented response. Before we can break open those responses, however, we need to talk about who it is who makes the response possible.

Why? Well, because reading all that we've laid out so far is not enough. Reason and logic, while important, are not enough. The disciples on the mountain disbelieving while *looking at* the risen Jesus are proof of that. The overwhelming reasons to not just believe but *think* that Jesus bodily rose from the dead and was seen not only by His disciples but also by people who did not follow or believe in Him (most especially a man named Saul) are there for anyone to consider.[1] I would gently but firmly suggest that it takes greater faith *not* to believe this is true. But again, reason and data and words are just not enough. We need something else. We need someone else. That someone else is the Holy Spirit.

Some of us struggle with understanding God as Father, perhaps because our own fathers weren't the best examples. I was blessed to have an amazing father, one who truly modeled for me the love, patience, and faithfulness of our heavenly Father. I know that my experience is increasingly rare, but even though I had a great model of God as Father, I still struggle. Jesus, for many of us, can be somewhat easier to relate to. After all, He is a man like us in all things but sin, and I can picture myself sitting beside a lake or at a workbench and speaking with Him. The Holy Spirit? In art He's often portrayed as a dove. How do you have a relationship with a bird? Okay, He's *not* a bird, but in my experience He's the hardest person of the Trinity for many of us to get our heads around.

Space does not allow for anything even approaching a comprehensive treatment of the Holy Spirit here. Mindful that I do not have the scope to write about all that is important and worth saying, what I would like to offer is a very, very short primer focused on the action of the Holy Spirit in regard to our inward and outward responses to what the Father has done for us in Jesus. I'm going to consider how the Spirit helps us and empowers us to surrender in faith, and how He mobilizes us for mission. Let me at least, though, share a few foundational observations.[2]

Who exactly are we talking about? Well, we're talking about the third person in the Most Blessed Trinity. God has revealed Himself as a Trinity of persons: Father, Son, and Holy Spirit. While these three persons all share the same nature, and thus are all divine, They are distinct persons. What exactly does that mean? "Nature" answers the question, "*What* is that?" "Person" answers the question, "*Who* is that?" The Holy Spirit, then, is the third person of the Trinity.

This third person is not some late arrival to the story of salvation history but has been present from the beginning, in the first chapter and verses of Genesis. "In the beginning, God created the heavens and the earth. The earth was without form and void, and darkness was over the face of the deep. *And the Spirit of God was hovering over the face of the waters*" (1:1–2).

All throughout the Old Testament the Spirit is present, moving and acting.[3] His action and presence are evident in a most powerful way when the archangel Gabriel announces to Mary of Nazareth that she is most highly favored and has been chosen by God to be the mother of the Son of the Most High. "How shall this be?" she asks the archangel. "The Holy Spirit will come upon you," the archangel answers, "and the power of the Most High will overshadow you; therefore the child to be born will be called holy, the Son of God" (Luke 1:34–35, RSVCE).

Immediately after Jesus's baptism by his cousin John the Baptist in the Jordan River, the Holy Spirit leads Him into the wilderness. There, before He begins His public ministry, Jesus faces the enemy of the human race, the one who deceived our first parents (see Luke 4:1–13). Later, as Jesus draws nearer to His Passion, He begins to speak to the apostles much more deliberately about the Spirit, telling them that He will send another "Helper" to them (see John 14:16–31). After Jesus's death and bodily resurrection He says to the disciples: "Behold, I am sending the promise of my Father upon you. But stay in the city until you are clothed with power from on high" (Luke 24:49).

In other words, something momentous is about to happen to the followers of Jesus. That something is Pentecost. Until that day, the disciples had been less than courageous—*even though they had seen the risen Jesus with their own eyes.* On the day of Pentecost, however, these same men burst onto the streets of Jerusalem to tell all the crowds gathered in the city for the Jewish feast about the great things God has done in Jesus, the things promised by prophets of old. And all of this happens as a result of the Spirit, who appeared to them in their meeting place as a mighty wind and tongues of fire (see Acts 2:1–4).

This third person of the Trinity, then, is equated in a special way with power, and that power enters into a person when he or she is baptized. The apostle Peter, on that same day of Pentecost, proclaimed the gospel to an audience that was more or less familiar with the early parts of the biblical narrative but who never expected it to be fulfilled in a crucified and risen Messiah. The crowds, however, are so moved by Peter's preaching that they ask what they should do in response. Peter tells them, "Repent and be baptized . . . and you will receive the gift of the Holy Spirit" (Acts 2:38). For the men and women who respond, the Spirit inhabits them in an entirely new way. The same happens for anyone today when he or she is baptized.

This is why the apostle Paul writes, "Do you not know that your body is a temple of the Holy Spirit within you, whom you have from God? You are not your own, for you were bought with a price" (1 Corinthians 6:19–20). Remember the various things Jesus accomplished on the cross? One of those things was that He made atonement for us. He became sin for you and me (see 2 Corinthians 5:21). He offered up His life for you and me by name. This is the "price" Paul is writing about. When we were created, we were given the gift of our lives. When Jesus suffered and died for us, we were given those lives back, rescued from the hands of the trafficker. For anyone who has been baptized, our bodies are now temples of God, temples of the Spirit.

"The Spirit of God *dwells in you,*" Paul says in Romans 8:9. What does that mean? A wise priest-mentor of mine used to say, "The Holy Spirit is in us the way heat is in hot water." That's a mighty image. *How* is heat in hot water? It's everywhere! So, too, is the Spirit in us. He inhabits our every dimension—our minds, our imaginations, our memories, our wills, our intellects. Everything. He has moved in, if you will.

Scott Hahn and Curtis Mitch write, "The Spirit is the presence and power of God in the life of the believer, the animating principle of Christian morality and spirituality. In short, the indwelling of the Spirit makes it possible to live victoriously as a disciple of Jesus Christ."[4] This is a remarkably hopeful reality; because of baptism I now have access to power to live differently, the same power that changed Augustine's life so profoundly.

How many of us regularly fall into the trap of thinking, *It's all on me*? My experience, both personally and in walking with thousands of people as a priest, is that many of us go through life gritting our teeth, clenching our fists, and trying harder to be good, to be better, to be the persons we want to be. I know I did that for years. The good news is that you can stop trying harder. Let me give you an image. I love to golf, and a favorite quote of mine from a golf coach is, "Try less hard." Why? Tension in sports constricts muscles and reduces your ability to play well. I've always found this a great image for life as a whole. "Try less hard." That doesn't mean that we don't have to do anything at all. We do! But what we primarily have to do, paradoxical as this sounds, is surrender.

This is what we need to do with God, and at least for me, it's incredibly hard. We need to let Him in, let Him move in our thoughts, our desires, our wills, our speech. This doesn't mean we are supposed to be passive, like puppets on a string. Hardly. It means, rather, that we are to fully and freely cooperate with God's grace, to be actively receptive—like Mary when she surrendered to God in Nazareth. Mary serves as a wonderful example of what some call "vulnerable listening," or "vulnerable attentiveness." This is "a listening that is combined with trust," trust in a God who loves, acts, and rescues.[5]

Just as the Holy Spirit fell in power upon those doubting disciples and convinced them beyond what their reason—crucial as it was and is—could do, so the Holy Spirit comes and convinces you and me that everything we've been talking about thus far is true. Jesus truly came to rescue us out of love for us. As the Spirit does this, He moves us to surrender, for we can only surrender to someone we trust. As He moves us to surrender, He also gives us hearts that are eager to go and rescue others who are now as we once were, living the nightmare of life apart from God.

In the next two chapters, we will look at how the Holy Spirit moves us to surrender and how He gives us hearts that are mobilized for mission, eager to rescue others. Right now, though, we want to concentrate on what must come first: We need Him to convince us, as only He can, that all we have been talking about is true, that out of His boundless love, Jesus came to rescue us.

Let me briefly unpack for you how the Holy Spirit works in us. From my experience, in most of us the Holy Spirit doesn't work linearly so much as in a spiral formation. What do I mean by that? When I was younger, I thought that growth in the spiritual life progressed along a straight line. We begin at point A, master that, and move on to point B. Having gotten that down, we then move on to C, and so on. I thought of the spiritual life the way I thought of education: You have to take certain prerequisites, and then, once having passed those, you move on to the next class.

The Holy Spirit doesn't usually work like that. Instead, He moves in many of us in a pattern that resembles a descending, circular staircase. He starts "up top" and steadily walks down, deeper and deeper and deeper and deeper. In other words, He takes point A and He just keeps going deeper and deeper and deeper and deeper. I don't know about you, but I'm not sure I've even gotten to point B. For most of us, point A, where the Holy Spirit begins at the top of the staircase, is identity.

In my experience, many of us—no matter the outward impression we make—are insecure. Because of this, we try to find our identity in all sorts of things. For a lot of us this started when we were young. Longing to be accepted, esteemed, seen, and loved, some of us found our identity in sports or grades or musical talent or physical appearance.

Just the other day I happened to read an author commenting on how common it is for a group of fifty-five-year-old men to gather together and start walking down memory lane, revisiting events from high school. This walk is exhilarating for some but agonizing for others, since these discussions inevitably remind some that they were "cut" during tryouts for whatever sport is being fondly recalled by the other men. And though it all happened decades earlier, the emotions come rushing back! No matter how successful these men have been in their lives since that moment, they keenly feel the devastation of their name missing from the piece of paper taped to the coach's door.

Jesus says in the gospel of John: "I will ask the Father, and he will give you another Helper, to be with you forever, even the Spirit of truth. . . . You know him, for he dwells with you and will be in you" (John 14:16–17).

In the original Greek, the word *Helper* appears as *Paraclete.* That word can be translated in a number of different ways, and is replete with legal connotations. It is frequently employed when describing matters that occur within a courtroom. It refers to a person who is tasked with pleading another person's case. Sometimes *paraclete* is translated as "comforter" or "advocate" or "helper." Those are all fine translations, and they're commonly found in various versions of the Bible. However, for me, the most powerful translation of *paraclete* is "someone who answers the cry."

So what's "the cry" being answered? Keeping in mind that the struggle for most of us is identity, I would suggest there are two cries. The first is, "Am I loved?" Maybe even, "Am I lovable?" Because of some things that happened to me as a child, I have a constant temptation to fear that I'm not loved. Along with that is a constant dread that I'm not good, that I'm "wrong"—not that I've done wrong, but that *I am* wrong, that I'm damaged. Perhaps you struggle with something similar or know someone who does.

The second cry that arises from within us is, "*Can* I love?" This is really more like, "Can I change?" Why is this a cry? Because it's hard to love. Oh, it's easy to love the people you like, but it's hard to love everybody. Come to think of it, it's hard to love the people you *like* all the time too. Don't we constantly struggle to better love our spouse, children, parents, and friends? Perhaps a way to rephrase this cry might be, "Can I get better at this? Can I become the man or woman I want to be?" As I get older, it's my most honest, humble acknowledgment. I'm just not who I want to be yet. I long to be more. I long to know ever more deeply that I'm loved not for any accomplishment, not as a reward, but just for who I am. And I desperately want to love others more consistently.

I had a particularly illuminating experience in prayer some years ago. I had been a priest for a good twenty years or so when this happened. Some challenging things were taking place within my family. The Lord was using those challenges to expose a wound in my life, not so He could rub my nose in it but so that He could bring it to my attention and then begin to heal it. In prayer I could sense the Spirit revealing to me that I had spent much of my life as a priest more or less trying to win the Father's love and acceptance, mostly because deep down I dreaded being unlovable. He showed me a young boy constructing something and then bringing it to his father, as if to say, "Here, look what I've made. Am I good enough now? Am I loved now? Do I make the cut? Am I accepted? Am I in?" And the Spirit revealed to me that the Father loved me before I did any of that. In fact, it was God who enabled me to do anything good to begin with. I could sense the Father saying to me, "This is all well and good, but in a certain sense it's irrelevant." Not because it doesn't matter, but because I don't have to do anything to win His love. I don't have to earn it. "I love you, John," He said. "Not because of anything you've done or haven't done, and despite all of those not very good things in your life you have done!" With this realization, it was as if the foundation of my life collapsed. I honestly didn't know what to do with this.

I don't think I'm alone in this experience. Most of the people I have been privileged to walk with as a priest routinely acknowledge to me that they have only known in their lives "reward love"—love given as a result of some sort of achievement or behavior. By and large, we are used to being loved for what we've done. But to be loved *for who we are* is a completely different experience.

This is one of the things that the Holy Spirit does in us. The answer to those cries and questions above is a resounding "Yes!" You *are* loved! You *are* good! You *can* love! And you *can* change! Not by trying harder but by letting the Spirit take over and invade your life, by giving Him permission.

As the Spirit does this, He reveals both who God is and who we are. He reveals that God is my Father and your Father. Not just *a* Father or *the* Father. He's *my* Father. By virtue of our baptism we can call Him what Jesus calls Him.

Saint Paul, again in his letter to the Romans says, "You did not receive the spirit of slavery to fall back into fear." What fear? That I'm alone. I'm on my own. I've got to achieve enough to matter. I've got to measure up. I've got to accomplish something. And so much more. Paul says, No! "You have received the Spirit of adoption as sons, by whom we cry, 'Abba! Father!' " (8:15).

Some years ago I was counseling a family who had adopted several children and wanted to adopt another young boy who was living in another country in rather deplorable conditions. He had spent most of his young life in orphanage after orphanage, experiencing various, often-brutal forms of abuse. The family who wanted to adopt him was very well off, materially speaking. More important, however, they were a family brimming with love. Over the course of several months, it was as if I were watching a split screen, with the young boy on one side and the family here in the States on the other. The boy had no idea how his life was about to change, and I don't think he could have even imagined such a profound transformation. As I prayed for this young child one day, I thought to myself, *Son, you are about to win the lottery. You are about to go from there to here. Your life is going to be turned upside down in a most remarkable way!*

This experience helped me better understand what happens to us all when we get baptized. God does something in this sacrament. He brings us into His family. And the Holy Spirit, who begins to dwell in us as a result, cries out within us, "Abba!" This word is an incredibly intimate term, one that Jesus uses when He prays to His Father. *Abba* is not only a term of endearment but also a term of confidence, certainty, and reliability.

A friend shared a helpful story about this remarkable word that the Spirit cries out from within us. He had lived in Jerusalem for a number of years, both studying and teaching. He said it wasn't unusual to be walking around in a grocery store and hear a little child, alone in an aisle and feeling lost, lift up his hands and cry out, "Abba!" The cry expressed the child's confidence that, as soon as the father heard his voice and that word, he would emerge from wherever he was, pick up his son or daughter, and everything would be okay. This is "Abba."

This cry, inspired by the Holy Spirit from within us, reminds us that God is a Father who sees us, knows us, loves us, and takes care of us. Because this is true, I don't have to be anxious or fall back into fear. Yet how many of us live riddled with fear! "What if . . . ? What if . . . ? What if . . . ? What if . . . ?" If you're a disciple of Jesus, you don't have to worry about what-ifs. This doesn't mean that nothing hard, challenging, or painful will happen to us. Jesus has not promised us an easy life. But He has promised us that God is faithful and reliable, and that He will give us what we need in each moment. We don't have to worry about those things, however. God will provide. He'll take care of you and He'll take care of me. In fact, even before we ask for something in prayer, our Father knows what we need (see Matthew 6:8). Though I do not know what the future holds, I do know who holds the future.

Shortly before the events of His Passion, Jesus tells His apostles, "All that I have heard from my Father I have made known to you" (John 15:15). How is that *possible*? Jesus is the eternal Son of God who has been in an eternal conversation, an eternal communion with His Father. How can He say, "All that I have heard from my Father I have made known to you"? Maybe, maybe—I'll leave certainty to better theologians—"everything" is summed up in one word: *Son.* In revealing to us our deepest identity—son or daughter—Jesus changes everything for us.

Who am I? Who are you? Beloved daughter or beloved son. Not just daughter or son. But beloved daughter or beloved son in whom, God says, "I am well pleased." This is not the result of some accomplishment or achievement on our part. God's love is entirely gratuitous. This doesn't mean that the way we live our lives doesn't matter. It does, to be sure. But His love comes first. He loves; therefore I am, therefore you are. There is nothing you or I could do to make God love us more than He does at this very moment. Saint Paul reminds us that God proved His love for us in that while we were still sinners, still His enemies, Christ died for us (see Romans 5:8, 10). When we had turned our backs on Him. When we were held captive by the powers of Sin and Death. But now "the Spirit himself bears witness with our spirit that we are children of God" (Romans 8:16). He testifies deep within you, in a way that mere words on a page cannot, that *you* are a child of God.

What is the gospel? The gospel is power. It's not just words. It's not just news. It's not even just extraordinary, explosive news. It's *power.* The gospel itself is power. All that we've been talking about is power. The events that we've been describing are power. The power that is able to overwhelm us, as we saw earlier in the book as a result of hearing the story proclaimed.

It is because of the power of the gospel that I believe so strongly that we need to take time every year as preachers to just preach the gospel—the heart of the story. We need to give people an opportunity to be overwhelmed and entrust their lives to Jesus in faith. In education, teachers usually begin the school year with some time of review. But how often do we do that in the Church? Instead, I fear that many of us who preach presume something that in fact hasn't happened in all the people present: an overwhelming encounter with God.

We can make space for this encounter by setting aside a month or so to preach the four big questions we have been breaking open in this book: *Why is there something rather than nothing? Why is everything so messed up? What, if anything, has God done about it? And if He has done anything, how should I respond?* And with these big questions the four words as well: *created, captured, rescued,* and *response.* If we don't know these things, then faith is easily reduced to keeping a bunch of rules. But if I know who God is, why everything exists, why everything is so messed up, what He's done about it—and that He did it for me—well, now that changes everything.

Let's return, though, to where we began this chapter. How does this actually happen? How do I get overwhelmed by the gospel? A few years back a woman was interviewing me, knowing that I am adamant about setting aside time to preach the core content of the gospel. She asked me, "How do you convince people of all of this?"

I looked at her and said, "How do I do what?"

"How do you *convince* people of this?" she repeated.

"I don't."

She was clearly puzzled by my response. After a few moments she continued, "Then how does this *work*?"

I told her, "I'm just a mailman. I deliver the mail as best I can and trust that God will do the rest."

To be clear, not everyone is overwhelmed and entrusts themselves to God every time someone preaches the gospel. God moves in different ways in different people. Sometimes it takes a long time. Sometimes it's almost immediate. You learn as a preacher that sometimes you're throwing seeds and sometimes you're watering what another has sown. Sometimes you see amazing fruit, but that's often because somebody else has been sowing long before. How this happens is mysterious to be sure, but the point is that it's not on the preacher to convince anybody. That's the beauty of this. A story from the Gospels illustrates this point.

On Easter Sunday, Jesus appears to Mary Magdalene and says to her, "Tell my brothers to go to Galilee, and there they will see me" (Matthew 28:10). When I was studying in the seminary, preparing to go out and preach the gospel, this passage gave me so much comfort. It lifted so much of the pressure I had put on myself to try to convince people. As I repeatedly prayed with this, it was as if I could hear the Lord tell me what He was telling Mary: "Don't worry about convincing them of anything. I'll take care of that. Just tell them where they can meet Me." The beautiful truth is that no herald of the gospel has to worry about convincing anyone. Do we need to know what we're talking about? Of course. Do we want to present the gospel as reasonably and attractively as possible? By all means. But feeling as though I have to convince another person? That's God's work.

And He wants to do that now.

You might prefer to stop reading right now and finish this chapter at a chapel where you can read and pray in front of the Blessed Sacrament. Or maybe you just want to find a quiet place in your home. Please, though, do whatever you need to do to get into a space that allows you to be prayerful, to listen to the Lord.

It's time now to allow the Lord to go to work. It's time now to invite the Spirit, the Paraclete, the One who answers the cry, to come and speak to us as only He can. Even as I write these words, I'm doing what I am asking you to do. It's not like I've got this all figured out or don't need the Spirit to move in my life too. A priest I know who has been ordained for almost thirty years was asked a few years ago, "When did you decide to become a priest?" He answered, "This morning." I love that answer! I have to choose every day. All of us do. A common danger for those of us who are already Christians is that we get used to this. We get used to the extraordinary news of what God has done for us. We get used to the magnificent—what a tragedy.

God wants you and me to know, as only He can enable it to happen, that all that we've been talking about so far is not just words. It's true. So, again, please put yourself in a place where you can be with the Lord.

As you enter this time of prayer, and in the pages that follow, I'm going to offer some suggestions for how you might consider talking to God. By all means, feel free to adapt them as you desire. When you're in that place, pray something like this:

> *Holy Spirit, take me to the cross. Use my imagination, my senses, and whatever else You need to use, to help me to be there. Help me to see Jesus on the cross.*

As you continue to pray, confidently ask the Holy Spirit to help you to see yourself there. See yourself looking at Jesus on the cross, the One through whom the universe was made, out of love without any effort. Jesus on the cross is the One who "landed in disguise" for you. He is the One who took on human flesh for you. He is the One who became a man for you. He is the One who went to war for you. He is the One who did it all in the most extraordinarily creative and clever way by entering into hell and liberating it from inside.

Ask the Holy Spirit to help you to see Jesus hanging on the

cross. Ask the Spirit to help you to see His eyes, still open. Ask the Spirit to help you to see Him looking at you as you're there looking at Him.

As you ask for this grace, pray something like this:

> *Spirit of God, move in me right now in such a way that I can see Jesus on the cross looking at me personally. Spirit of God, help me to know that Jesus is on the cross for me. As only You can, convince me of this truth. Convince me that Jesus is on the cross for me.*

As you pray this, ask the Spirit to help you to hear Jesus speak to you. Hear the Lord talking to you from the cross. Hear Him calling you by name. Ask the Holy Spirit to help you hear Jesus tell you: "I'm here on the cross for you. I'm doing this for you. I'm showing you how much the Father loves you. I'm showing you what you're worth to Him. I'm giving you a chance to start all over again, no longer defined by your past. Out of love for you, I'm going to war against the powers of Sin, Death, and Satan in order to rescue you. I see you! You matter to Me! You're worth the trouble of My doing this for you!"

> *Holy Spirit, as only You can, convince me that God is my Father. Show me that He is good, faithful, kind, compassionate, patient. Show me that He is love.*

Many of us have had very bad examples of fatherhood. We can't grasp God as a good father. Perhaps we tend to run from the image of God as a father. Maybe this image frightens us. But God is not like those hurtful fathers. He's sheer goodness, love, and faithfulness. If your own father wasn't a great example, consider asking the Spirit to help you enter into that scene we imagined earlier, where we're living in a dysfunctional family but across the street is an amazingly loving father. Ask Him to help you to see and hear the good Father coming to the door of your house, knocking, wanting to know if you're tired of living in the tyrant's house and want to join His family. A family of infinite love. A family of abundant life.

> *Please come, Holy Spirit, and heal all my wounds, the bad memories, the hurtful things that were done and said to me. Replace those words even now in my mind with new and powerful and healing words from the Father. Help me to know that I'm seen. Help me to know that I'm delighted in. Help me to know that I'm loved. Help me to know that I'm worth the trouble He went to for me. Help me to know that I'm worth dying for.*

The Spirit can do this. The Spirit can overlay the voices in our memories from years and years ago, the ones that caused the wounds to our identity. He can replace those words with new words right now. This is how He re-creates us. Perhaps you've never received affection from our Father. Perhaps you've never heard Him say, "I love you." If so, ask the Spirit right now:

> *Help me to hear the Father say, "I love you."*

Trust that God is moving. He wants to bring healing. In fact, He wants to do this more than we want Him to. The cross is the proof.

As you're able, let's keep asking the Holy Spirit to act as only He can.

Holy Spirit, convince me that I am God's beloved daughter, or God's beloved son. Holy Spirit, help me to see the Father looking at me, telling me, "I delight in you."

The Spirit wants to help you to see the Father looking at and delighting in you. "You're mine," He says. "The apple of My eye." You might be seventy-two years old as you read this, and yet you still don't know, don't believe this. God wants to convince you and me of this core truth.

Holy Spirit, overwhelm me now.

Try to pray this over and over.

Holy Spirit, overwhelm me now. Overwhelm me with all that I've just read.

Whatever image might have impacted you most in the previous pages, ask the Spirit to bring it back to mind. As that happens, say something like this to the Spirit of God:

I've had enough of reading. I've had enough of trying hard. I've had enough of trying to convince myself of these things. Do now what You do as only You can do. Please. Overwhelm me.

Finally, allow me to close with a prayer:

Father, I thank You for whatever You're doing in those who are reading this right now. Help them to remember the look, the words, or whatever it was that was impacting them. I pray that as they read the pages that follow,

You will continue by the power of Your Spirit to convince them of the truth of Your love. Help us all to know that Jesus truly became man, truly went to the cross, truly went to war for us—for each of us by name. Help us to know that we're loved. That we're Your sons, Your daughters. Help us to know that we don't have to worry about measuring up. That it's all a gift. That our true identity is in You. That we don't have to be afraid. That we can call You, the creator of all that is, Father.

CHAPTER 7

I GIVE UP

"REPENT AND BELIEVE IN ME!"

Those words probably sound familiar to you. They were spoken by a man who appeared in Judea in the first century. But it wasn't John the Baptist, nor was it Jesus of Nazareth. Okay, those two did say similar words, but they weren't the only ones who said them. A man named Joseph ben Matthias said them too. Who? I propose that understanding who Joseph ben Matthias was, and what he meant by those words, can help us better understand what Jesus meant when He said them. We'll come back to this shortly.

We are still working our way through the fourth big question: "How should I respond to all that God has done for me in Jesus?" The word tied to this big question is *response.* Having looked at the One who makes this response possible, the Holy Spirit, we are now able to turn our attention to what our response should be. As with much of what we've talked about already, I won't be able to do this adequately; there's simply too much I could say. So let me concentrate on a few things in particular.

As I mentioned in the last chapter, there is both an internal, personal response and an external, more mission-oriented response. We'll concentrate on the external response in chapter 8, but in this one, let's concentrate on the more internal one.

As Jesus was dying on the cross, immediately before He gave up His spirit, the gospel of John tells us, He cried out, "I thirst" (see 19:28–30). Before we look at what exactly Jesus was thirsting for, it's worth noting that He "gave up his spirit" is an unusual way to describe someone's death. When my mom was dying, she didn't "give up her spirit." She died. She wasn't in control. It was different with Jesus. Saint John is reminding us that, no matter how it appears, Jesus was in control throughout His passion. He was both victim and aggressor, both hunted and hunter. He was drawing "the strong man" close. "The ruler of this world" had no power over Jesus; His life was not being taken from Him. He laid it down. For you. For me. Out of love. Why? Because *you matter*. You're worth the trouble. To God you're worth dying for.

For what precisely was Jesus thirsting on the cross? Certainly, on a natural level He was thirsting for water. Pinned up like an insect on the wood of the cross, every drop of fluid pouring out of His body, Jesus was experiencing massive dehydration.

But Jesus was thirsting for something more than water.[1]

In the gospel of Luke, Jesus asked, "When the Son of Man comes, will he find faith on earth?" (18:8). In view of this, I think what Jesus is thirsting for is faith. But what exactly *is* faith?

Perhaps George Michael, the 1980s pop star, can help us out. Michael, after all, wrote a song called "Faith," so there are bound to be some golden nuggets there, right? He croons on and on in the chorus,

> 'Cause I gotta have faith.
> I gotta have faith.
> Because I gotta have faith, faith, faith.

Alas, so much for profound insights. Songs like this only serve to reinforce the all-too-common idea that faith is primarily, if not exclusively, tied to emotions and feelings, with little or no grounding in fact or reality.

I remember watching a particular football game years ago. One of the teams playing was 0–8. As the halftime whistle blew, the sideline reporter raced across the field to interview the coach of the winless team, which, true to form, had exhibited yet another dismal display in the first half. The reporter thrust the microphone into the coach's face and asked what he thought about his team's performance in the first thirty minutes. "I know you can't see it out there," he said, "but I feel there's been a lot of improvement and I believe we're going to turn this around and win." The sideline reporter then handed the airways back to the anchors in the studio. Commenting on the coach's remarks, one of them said, "Well, I guess that's what *faith* is—confidence in the absence of evidence."

No! That is *not* what faith is. At least that's not what biblical faith is. Before we address what it *is,* however, let's address a few other common misconceptions about faith.

First, faith is not a *feeling.* To be perfectly honest, I rarely feel anything in my relationship with God. Maybe that helps some of you who likewise struggle in this way. Sometimes, to be clear, there are feelings, but most of the time there's nothing. In that regard, faith is a lot like love. Isn't it true that we often discover how sincere our love for another is when we don't feel anything? Faith is similar to that sometimes.

Second, faith is not *blind.* Faith isn't belief in the absence of evidence. All too often we see the media, in countless ways, speak of Christians or portray Christians much like those football announcers thought of the coach: foolish, blind, naive, gullible, and worse. Perhaps some Christians are these things, but to have faith, as we will see, is not foolish, blind, and naive. Some of the greatest thinkers of all time—Thomas Aquinas, Augustine, Edith Stein, Gregor Mendel, Sir Isaac Newton, Blaise Pascal, to name just a few—were men and women of faith.

Third, faith isn't *mere* intellectual assent. Intellectual assent, as we'll see, is an aspect of faith, but it doesn't exhaust what it means to say, "I believe." The letter of James says, "You believe that God is one; you do well. Even the demons believe—and shudder" (2:19). Yikes! Faith can't be reduced, then, to simply acknowledging that God is real. Because of misconceptions like these, some have argued that we should abandon using the word *faith* in church altogether, since it reinforces an inaccurate understanding of our proper response to the gospel.[2]

What, then, *is* faith? What does it mean to say, "I believe"?

The Greek word for *faith* is *pistis,* and it doesn't mean anything close to what we saw above. *Pistis* has many meanings, including "confidence, fidelity, trustworthiness, assurance, guarantee, and loyalty." Each of these conveys the sense that faith is a *response* to something that is credible or to someone who is credible. Let's focus our attention for a moment on that last word, *loyalty.* As we do so, let's return to Joseph ben Matthias.

Joseph was a Jew, a Pharisee, and a general in Galilee during the fateful conflict between the Jews and the Romans in the first century. He ended up defecting to the Roman side in the conflict and is now known to us as the historian Flavius Josephus. His writings offer many valuable insights and perspectives on that era of history.

When Joseph said, "Repent and believe in me," he wasn't saying, "Stop sinning, believe in me, and you'll go to heaven." Hardly. He wasn't the leader of a cult; he was a general fighting a war. His words meant something more like, "Stop thinking the way you are and *become loyal* to me." This, then, is one of the significant dimensions of faith: loyalty. And it's one of the things for which Jesus is thirsting.

In other words, Jesus is looking for a response that trusts Him in response to all that He has already done for us. And what has He done for us? He has defeated Sin, Death, and Satan. And He did this by laying down His life for us on the cross, in the greatest act of love ever unfurled before human eyes. In other words, nobody is more credible, more trustworthy, more deserving of our loyalty than He is, for nobody has done anything that can remotely compare with what He has done for us.

Matthew Bates, in a wonderful book called *Salvation by Allegiance Alone,* argues that faith has three significant aspects: intellectual assent, public confession, and genuine obedience. I said above that faith isn't *mere* intellectual assent, but, to be clear, there *is* an intellectual component. To have faith, or to say, "I believe," means to intellectually agree to all that the creeds of the Church propose. This means not just believing but *thinking* that the following are true. Jesus

- preexisted with the Father;
- took on human flesh, fulfilling God's promises to David;
- died for our sins in accordance with the Scriptures;
- was buried;
- was raised on the third day in accordance with the Scriptures;
- appeared to many (including those who were not His disciples—like Saul of Tarsus);
- is seated at the right hand of the Father as Lord; and
- will come again as judge.[3]

Before we dive a bit more deeply into this, let's pause briefly and state an obvious truth: Everyone lives by faith. We have to, for there is simply no way any of us could verify for ourselves all the things we hold to be true. A crucial question for us to consider is whether or not the people we put our trust in are credible. This is especially true when dealing with history and even more so with ancient history. With this in mind, I would argue that nobody is more credible than the apostles of Jesus with regard to the things listed above. Why? Because of how they died.

The closest companions and friends of Jesus died horrific deaths. Now, lots of people in history have died horrific deaths, but the apostles died solely because of their testimony about Jesus and especially their testimony that they had encountered—on many occasions—Jesus bodily risen from the dead after He was crucified. All they had to do to escape being tortured to death was to say that they had made it up, that the claims of His resurrection were part of a hoax that got out of hand, or something along those lines.

But none of them did, whether they were thrown off the top of the temple in Jerusalem, crucified, beheaded, burned alive, or any of the other horrific methods of torture the apostles experienced. Now consider this: Nobody dies for what they know to be a lie. Lots of people may die as a result of believing in a lie, but *nobody* dies for what they *know* is a lie. Life is far too precious. The testimony offered from those first friends of Jesus about His resurrection, as well as the other things listed above, is, historically speaking, far more credible and trustworthy than anything else I know of from history.[4]

The second aspect of faith, according to Bates, is the public confession of Jesus as Lord. Here is where faith becomes political. We would do well to remember the immensely subversive and political nature of the New Testament and what it means to be a Christian. "Jesus is Lord" were dangerous words to speak at the time of the apostles. The Roman Empire had a lord; his name was

Caesar. When Saint Paul started proclaiming that Jesus is Lord, he was saying that Caesar was a pretender, a fraud. Oh sure, he was the ruler of the empire, but the world was not in his hands and he was not the "savior"—a common title for Caesar—of anything. Jesus, Paul said, was—and is—Lord and Savior.

"Jesus is Lord" can be dangerous words to speak today too. To have faith in Jesus is to be willing to publicly declare that we pledge our allegiance to Him above anything and anyone else—political party, favorite football team, even our family. As good citizens who love our country, we certainly need to vote; and as sports fans it's more than okay to root for our favorite teams. As sons and daughters, brothers and sisters, and moms and dads, we should love our families. But our allegiance belongs to Jesus above all else. Why? Simply because of what He has done for us: He has rescued us from Sin, Death, and Satan. As rich, meaningful, and special as the many relationships we have in our family and among our friends, nobody has done for us what Jesus has.

Finally, the third aspect of what it means to have faith, according to Bates, is genuine obedience. Not perfect obedience, thank heavens, or most of us would be doomed. Jesus says, "Not everyone who says to me, 'Lord, Lord,' will enter the kingdom of heaven, but the one who does the will of my Father who is in heaven" (Matthew 7:21). In other words, what we do with our bodies, our lives, our words, and our actions matters greatly.

Now, we all fail many times in our journey through life. We are all weak and frail, and though Jesus has defeated the power of Sin, we still have memories, habits, and instincts that frequently cause us to stumble and fall. All the saints (except Mary) struggled with sin, and some of them mightily. I fail daily to be the man I long to be.

Weakness, however, is different from obstinacy. It's one thing to stumble; it's another thing to outright reject something Jesus teaches. As we trust in His love made manifest in His laying down His life for us, let us never outright reject what Jesus teaches us, for He is trustworthy like no other.

The oh-so-encouraging news is that God deals patiently with us in our weakness. A priest friend of mine is fond of repeating that it is an ironclad law that, no matter how many times we fall, so long as we never give up, so long as we ask God to forgive us, so long as we try again to be the men and women He has created us to be, we always win.

Bates's threefold description of faith reminds me of a conversation I once heard between a man and some teenagers. Trying to help them better grasp what faith is, he painted a word picture. "To have faith," he said, "is to lean so far over on God that if He wasn't there you'd fall down." *This* is faith. In other words, to have faith, to believe in God, is to surrender ourselves to Him, to entrust ourselves to Him—in our thoughts, our words, and our actions.

Over the past few years, I have found a certain bodily posture and Scripture passage immensely helpful in daily reminding me to intentionally choose to surrender to God. The gesture is lying prostrate on the floor. This is the posture assumed by a man when he is ordained as a deacon or a priest. This is not at all a gesture of humiliation or debasement but rather one of total surrender. As human beings we express ourselves through our bodies, so this is a tangible way of freely entrusting myself to the Lord each morning. As I lie there, I simply pray, "Here I am again, Lord. I surrender everything to You again today. I choose, this morning, to follow You. Help me to stay loyal to You in all my actions and words and thoughts." Though this gesture is found in the ordination ritual for a priest and deacon, it's by no means exclusive to that ceremony. A number of my friends who are not priests or deacons also find this gesture to be a helpful and powerful way to start their day in prayer. You might try it too.

The Scripture passage that has been increasingly helpful for me as I start my day is Psalm 24:7: "Lift up your heads, O gates!" As I pray with these words, I see in my mind's eye something like a medieval walled city. Outside the city stands a visitor asking to be let in through the gate of entry. The walled city is me; the visitor, of course, is Jesus. Because He will not force His way in, He calls to me as He stands outside the door of my heart, the wounds visible in His hands, feet, and side. He wants to know if again today I will let Him "occupy" my life—not to take away my freedom but rather so that I might be truly free. As I pray with this passage, I ask the Holy Spirit to give me the grace again to yield, to surrender, to let Jesus, the true King, enter. I pray for the grace to "lift up the gates" of my mind, my imagination, my will, my memory, my body—everything—and to let Jesus enter in anew and reign as Lord.

As you're reading this, you may think it all sounds like a bit . . . much. It is!

I think the reason that this can be difficult for so many people is that they've never met God. They've never been overwhelmed. After all, how can I surrender to someone I don't know? Blind dates don't usually end in marriage proposals! In my experience most people don't know God personally; they don't have a deep friendship with Him. They know *about* Him, at best. They've heard about Him. But He's something of a "rumor." They don't *know* Him. I think this is true both in the Church and in the world at large.

So let's go a bit deeper.

We started this chapter with the words "Repent and believe!" We took a quick look at what it means to believe and to have faith. In the Gospels, faith is always paired with repentance. Let's take a quick moment, then, to better understand what repentance means, for it too is often misunderstood.

Perhaps somewhat surprisingly, "Repent!" is one of the first words out of Jesus's mouth in Mark's gospel (1:15). This hardly sounds like an encouraging first word from the eternal Son of God as He steps onto the stage of human history. That's probably because many of us hear it as though Jesus is scolding us, saying something like, "You idiots! You're doing everything wrong." But that's not what Jesus is saying.

The Greek word for *repent* is *metanoia,* which means "a change of mind." Saint Joan of Arc is credited with observing, "All battles are first won or lost in the mind." How true that is! My mind—that is, my thinking—gives birth to what comes out of my mouth and what I do with my body.

A crucial first step in the Christian life, then, is to change the way I think or, better, to ask the Lord to help me change the way I think. Saint Paul in his letter to the Romans says, "Do not be conformed to this world, but be transformed by the renewal of your mind" (12:2). Another translation of that passage reads, "Don't let the world around you *squeeze* you into its own mould, but let God re-mould your minds from within."[5]

Don't most of us experience the world daily trying to squeeze us into its own mold? The news, social media posts, movies, podcasts—all of these and more—routinely place into our minds patterns of thought that are anything but godly. A Christian author once commented, "Most of us have not so much Christian minds as worldly minds with Christian patches."[6] I know this is true for me many days. So we need to ask the Holy Spirit to give our minds light, to help us to think clearly and to see things as they really are.

This changing of our thoughts, this renewal of our minds, is especially significant with regard to surrendering to God. As we consider this, it's worth noting that there is an easier part in this surrender and a much more challenging part.

The easier part is making a decision to cling to the God who rescued us. Once we come to know who Jesus is and what He's done; once we come to know how He invaded Death's fortress in His chariot, broke open the stronghold, and set the captives free; and once we know that all of this was done personally for us by name, well, then, it becomes easier to surrender to Him.

I am profoundly aware that Jesus liberated me from "enemy occupation." I know He pulled me out of the hands of "the human trafficker." In response I want to cling to Him for dear life, mindful that no one else has done for me what He has done for me. So why is this still so hard?

Well, in order to cling to Jesus, I have to stop clinging to other things. I don't know about you, but if I'm honest with myself, most days I'm trying to cling to some things while at the same time trying to cling to Jesus. Maybe you are too. This doesn't work out very well. What are these other things to which I'm clinging?

In one of his letters to the small Christian community in Thessalonica, Saint Paul writes to honor that little band of early believers because, after the gospel was preached to them, they "turned to God from idols to serve the living and true God" (1 Thessalonians 1:9). In other words Paul commends them for having stopped clinging to idols and having begun surrendering to God.

Wait a minute. *Idols*? Really? In the twenty-first century we're talking about *idols*?

Yes. Though I doubt any of us has a golden calf or a statue of Zeus in our front yard, we all struggle with idols. Here's how one person defines an idol:

> An idol . . . is *anything* more important to you than God, *anything* that absorbs your heart and imagination

> more than God, *anything* you seek to give you what only God can give.
>
> A counterfeit god is *anything* that is so central and essential to your life that, should you lose it, your life would feel hardly worth living.[7] (italics mine)

Ouch. I don't know about you, but when I came across those words, I realized I have more than a few idols. I can easily and almost habitually cling to a lot of things. And I find it can be very hard to let go. What are some of the more common idols we struggle with? Health, children, sports, reputation, pleasure, wealth, time, career, sex, independence, titles, politics, and more.

Idols like these not only keep us from surrendering to God, they also keep us from genuine happiness. Arthur C. Brooks, a popular author, speaker, and Harvard professor, routinely helps his graduate students in their search for true happiness. One of the ways he does this is by helping them identify which of the following is most important to them: power, pleasure, riches, or fame. These are the four primary idols with which we all struggle. Most of us, he argues, can probably eliminate one or two right away, but it's usually impossible to say honestly that we don't struggle with at least one of them. Whichever one is hardest to eliminate might be the idol we most need to concentrate on, so that we can surrender to the One who alone can make us truly happy.[8]

At this point, let me encourage you to stop reading for a moment and take a few minutes to reflect on what your idols might be. Perhaps you'll want to grab a journal and write down some of the idols in your life. Take as much time as you need. With confidence in the One who rescued us, who loves us, and who wants us to be truly free, let us ask the Holy Spirit to gently shine a light into our minds and show us those things that we're clinging to and need to let go of in order to more fully surrender to the God who is Love.

* * *

BEFORE MOVING ON to the final chapter, let me address one other personal and intimate response we should consider to all that God has done for us in His Son: thanksgiving. After all, it would certainly be more than appropriate to thank God for saving us from hell!

Does God have a preferred way to be thanked? I would argue that He does, but how He prefers to be thanked might be surprising for some of us.

Christians often are tempted to spend their time reading the New Testament to the exclusion of the Old Testament, since the New Testament deals with Jesus and the spread of the gospel message and the Old Testament can be downright confusing for many of us, as we saw when talking about the first chapters in Genesis. That said, if we just skip the Old Testament, we severely hinder our understanding of the story, the role of Israel in the story, and how Jesus and His saving deeds are foreshadowed in the Old Testament. Saint Jerome, a great Scripture scholar from the early Church, wrote, "Ignorance of Scripture is ignorance of Christ." Perhaps you've come across that line before. What's noteworthy is that Jerome wrote those words in a commentary on Isaiah—and Isaiah is in the Old Testament! In other words, "ignorance of the Old Testament is ignorance of Christ." The Bible is, after all, one story with one ultimate Author, and the Old Testament foreshadows and prepares for all that God will fulfill in the New.

At the risk of being far too simplistic, I would suggest that the Old Testament has a center. That center is an event. In a certain sense, everything is either building up to this event, describing it, or looking back at it and anticipating how it might somehow be fulfilled in a new way. The central event is God's dramatic rescue of the people of Israel, the descendants of Abraham, from slavery to Pharaoh and the Egyptians.

The Israelites had been enslaved in Egypt for four centuries. Throughout the course of these many, many years, they had not only no freedom but no hope, for to be a slave was to be a kind of living tool, furniture with a soul, if you will. A master could do absolutely anything he or she wanted to his or her slaves.

Then, after hundreds of years, seemingly out of nowhere, God dramatically acted! He chose and called Moses to lead His people out of slavery, out of Egypt—the "house of bondage." With mighty signs and wonders, He rescued His people from Pharaoh's tyranny, oppression, and dominion.

This central event of the Old Testament is known as the Exodus. Interestingly, this event had—and has—a meal connected with it. The meal is known as Passover. The instructions for how to celebrate this meal were given by God through a man, Moses. The instructions were, and are, very precise. Here's the key, though: Up to this very day, when our Jewish brothers and sisters celebrate this meal, they believe the event somehow becomes present.

A passage in Psalms suggests that the Lord has established a memorial for himself (see 111:4). In the Greek Old Testament, the one heard by most of the Jewish people before and at the time of Jesus, that verse reads, "The Lord has established an *anamnesis* for Himself." *Anamnesis* is much richer than a mere memorial, at least the way we tend to use that word. *Anamnesis* means more than just recalling something in our mind. It means something is becoming present—now. Again, when our Jewish brothers and sisters celebrate Passover, they believe the event that happened more than two thousand years ago somehow becomes present. They are being delivered from slavery. In the Mishnah, a compilation of rabbinic texts from just before and after the time of Jesus, it says

> In every generation, a man must so regard himself as if he came forth himself out of Egypt, for it is written . . . "It is because of what the Lord did for me when I came forth out of Egypt" (Exodus 13:8). Therefore, we are bound to give thanks . . . and to bless him who wrought all these wonders for our fathers and for us. He brought us out from bondage to freedom, from sorrow to gladness, and from mourning to a Festival-day, and from darkness to great light, and from servitude to redemption; so let us say before him the Hallelujah.[9]

Commenting on this text, Catholic scholar Brant Pitre writes,

> With these words, we see quite clearly that for ancient Jews, the Passover feast was not just a remembrance of what God had done for their ancestors. In some mysterious way, they saw each Passover, "in every generation," as a way of sharing in the original act of redemption. Although living centuries after the first exodus, the father would speak of the event as if it were something he himself had experienced.
>
> In other words, ancient Jewish celebrants did not just remember the exodus; they actively *participated* in it.[10]

This is, obviously, a most extraordinary thing. And the psalm tells us *God* has established this. This was *His* doing. He wanted this *anamnesis,* this memorial, to be celebrated so that the people would never forget where they had been and what God had done for them. They were once slaves. But God *did* something. He brought them out of slavery into freedom. It is necessary to remember again and again that our God is one who rescues and liberates, a God who loves. Otherwise, He would have left them in slavery.

What happens when we turn to the New Testament, the fulfillment of all this foreshadowing—is there a center there too? Yes. At the center of the New Testament is also an event, something either being anticipated, described, or looked back to and reflected on over and over again. The event, of course, is Jesus's death and resurrection, what's often called "the Paschal mystery." This event takes place over several days, starting on Holy Thursday, and includes Good Friday, Holy Saturday, and Easter Sunday. This event is also a most—*the most*—dramatic rescue from slavery. Not slavery from Pharaoh and Egypt but slavery from the tyranny and oppression of Sin, Death, and the trafficker, Satan.

Lo and behold, this event also has a meal connected with it. In this meal, however, the instructions don't come from God *through* a man. Instead, God gives the instructions *as* a man. And just as it is for our Jewish brothers and sisters with Passover, when this meal is celebrated, the event also becomes present. This is truly sublime. This is the Mass.

In the Mass, the events of Jesus's Passion, death and resurrection are made present again. This is not to say, as many misunderstand what Catholics believe, that Jesus dies again somehow—not at all. He has died once and for all and is now seated at the Father's right hand in glory.[11] However, the events of the Paschal mystery are sacramentally made present. And those who are gathered become contemporaries of these wondrous events. All of this is very clear once we understand how the Jewish people understood what goes in Passover. When we properly understand this, you and I will be able to better see how we are invited to respond when the Mass is celebrated.

Saving Private Ryan is one of my all-time favorite movies. While inspired by real-life events, the movie tells the fictional story of a World War II soldier, James Ryan, and a series of events that take place to rescue him shortly after the invasion of D-Day.

The film begins with an older Ryan visiting the Normandy American Cemetery in France. His wife, children, and grandchildren accompany him. Though he's much older than they are, he's far in the lead, clearly heading somewhere with great intentionality. It becomes clear that he hasn't been to this site in a long time. In fact, he hasn't been there since June 6, 1944. His family seems to have only a vague idea as to why exactly this place is so important to him. Ryan is obviously searching for a particular grave. After making his way through rows and rows of headstones, he finds it. Like so many of the others, this grave is marked with a cross. As he stands there, the camera slowly zooms into his eyes and then just as slowly pulls out, and the viewer suddenly finds himself in 1944.

Saving Private Ryan is actually one long flashback, with the exception of roughly ten minutes at the beginning and ten minutes at the end. In between, we have access to the events that took place in those fateful days and discover why it is that Ryan is so eager to visit this particular grave—it marks the resting place of the man who died saving his life, Captain John H. Miller.

In the final minutes of the film, we find ourselves back at the cemetery. Ryan still stands tearfully looking at the cross atop Miller's tomb. Ryan's wife can see that he is deeply moved, but it's also clear that she doesn't know why. Then follows one of the most poignant dialogues I've ever seen and heard on film, but I'll let you discover that on your own, in case you've never seen the movie.

For the purposes of what we're talking about, Ryan and his family members serve as a powerful image for the vastly different ways people walk into a church. Some people enter a church and their eyes are immediately focused on the crucifix. These people are like the older Ryan, tearfully looking, some days at least, at the One they know saved their lives at the cost of His own. Other people, however, are like Ryan's children or grandchildren, more or less wondering what they're doing there. Just as John H. Miller was simply a name on a headstone for them, so Jesus is only a name for many people.

Until we hear the gospel and it overwhelms us.

When that happens, the crucifix and the Mass change wondrously. We enter knowing, "I'm here for *Him*! *That's* the One who saved my life!" And when we're there, when we're present at Mass, you and I are not just hearing about what happened two thousand years ago, we're becoming present—sacramentally, wondrously, mysteriously present.

And here is the scandalous claim of the biblical story: The God who made all of this—the universe, the earth, the mountains, you and me in His image and likeness—*this God* went to war on the cross for us, to rescue us, to rescue you.

Some time ago I was leading a retreat, preaching many of the things that we've been looking at in this book. Near the end of the day during a break, an older man came up to me and asked if I had a moment for a question. "Sure," I told him.

He looked at me and said, "Father, I think I understand most of what you've said. But there is one thing I don't understand at all."

"What's that?" I asked.

"Why?" he responded. "I don't understand why God would do this—especially for me."

Here's the answer, for that man, for you, for me, and for every person on the face of the earth. One of my favorite ways to understand what it means to say "I love you" is the expression "You're worth the trouble." When a mother wakes up in the middle of the night to care for her crying child, why does she do it? Because that little one is worth the trouble. When my dad sacrificed his time and personal preferences to sit beside my mom day after day, year after year in her hospital bed, why did he do it? Because she was worth the trouble. God, the creator of the universe, hanging on a cross, says to you and to me: "You are worth the trouble."

I once came across the story of a young man who was similarly befuddled by the extraordinary depths to which God went to rescue us. He also asked why, and the priest he spoke with replied, "Because Love does things like that." His answer tells me that I don't really know what love is. I wouldn't have done that for my creature. Now, I hear parents routinely say that they would die for their children. I have no doubt that many in fact would. But that's something very different. That's not the equivalent of what God did. God is not a creature. God is the creator. The creator of all that is. And this creator became a creature to rescue us. In a most painful and humiliating manner. God laid down His life for His beloved creatures. Because you matter. And Love does such things. And God is Love (see 1 John 4:8). He's not *loving.* God *is* love.

Now we draw near to an even more scandalous reality. What does love want? It wants many things, to be sure, like the true good of the beloved. But I think love especially wants one thing. Love wants union. This is why a man and a woman, when they love each other and get married, are not content to just say, "I love you." Oh, that's important, and we should all say it more than we probably do. But love wants more. It wants to show itself. So we buy the beloved gifts, flowers, rings, and all sorts of other things. But love is consummated when the lover and the beloved, the husband and wife, give themselves to each other and become one. Why? Because love wants union. If God is love, and He is, then what does God want? God wants union. With us.

Here is the shocking answer to the question, Does God have a preferred way to be thanked? Yes. He wants you and me to let Him give us something. He wants nothing less than for us to let Him give us Himself. This is what happens when someone comes forward and receives the Eucharist at Mass. God gives Himself and in so doing we become one with Him.

This is one of the reasons Sunday is so important to the biblical story. From the beginning, from the moment Jesus ascended, Christians have gathered Sunday after Sunday. Many early believers described Sunday as the day they could not live without. Why? Because it is liberation day. It is the day Jesus triumphed over the grave and gave the human race hope.

When believers gather on Sunday, the Scriptures are proclaimed and the story is told, but it's not just the retelling of things that happened long ago. When the Scriptures are proclaimed at Mass, the events are happening anew.[12] And when we move into that meal, which is so much more than a meal, that Jesus Himself gave instructions for, the event is happening. We become contemporaries of the cross. We become contemporaries of the resurrection. We become partakers of the foretaste of heaven and the banquet of heaven. The first Christians said they couldn't live without Sunday because they couldn't live without Him. You see, it's not enough to hear God loves me. I need to know it. I want to taste it.

Years ago I was visited by a wonderful and enthusiastic young evangelical woman. She was looking for some financial support as she was about to embark on a mission. During the conversation, she sheepishly asked me, "Father, can I ask you a really personal question?"

"Sure," I said.

"Do you have a personal relationship with Jesus?"

I smiled and answered, "Well, I eat His body and drink His blood every day. I'm honestly not sure how much more personal it can get!"

As important as personal faith is, though, it's equally important not to reduce being a disciple of Jesus to this intimate and personal encounter. God's desire is for all His children to be gathered together again, reconciled both to Him and to one another. He created us to be His family. So, mindful that the enemy is the enemy—and nobody else is—that God is a good Father, that Jesus is Lord, and that this world is crying for God, even if it doesn't know it, I would like to argue that His call to follow Him is nothing less than a call to join the resistance and to go out into this world that He loves. What might that look like? Let's turn the page to find out.

CHAPTER 8

GO, TURN THE WORLD UPSIDE DOWN

IN ALL THAT WE'VE LOOKED AT SO FAR, I'VE REPEATEDLY SAID THAT Jesus's death and resurrection are for us, personally. However, His death and resurrection also have profound social and political repercussions. As various authors have noted, the gospel is not about our "getting out of here" and going to heaven so much as it is about God rescuing His creation and reigning as King and rightful Lord, and about us being restored to that mission given to us way back at the beginning to govern His good creation in His image and likeness.[1] In other words, the consequences of the gospel are personal but not private.

I've heard a bishop friend of mine repeat on several occasions that the Church has three options right now. The first option is to look around at all that's happening and just give in, capitulate to "the spirit of the age."

Some of us might be familiar with the expression "the new evangelization." This concept was first introduced by Pope John Paul II and has been repeated by all the popes since. It's new, John Paul II said, in "ardor, methods and expression."[2] Those of us who are tempted by this first option would do well to remember that what we might call "the old evangelization" actually worked. What do I mean by that? Well, perhaps you know that Christianity was considered an "illegal superstition" in the Roman Empire for more or less 250 years. A Christian, legally speaking, did not have the right to exist from the time of Emperor Nero up until the time of Emperor Constantine. This isn't to say that Christians were constantly subject to persecution during that time. Periods of persecution came and went, depending on a variety of factors, including the tolerance of the emperor and the region of the empire in which they were living. It is to say, however, that Roman law prohibited the practice of Christianity. In fact Christians were actually considered "atheists" by the Romans because they did not acknowledge the gods of the empire. As such, they were seen as seditious and a threat to the security and well-being of the empire, whose fate depended on the good pleasure of the gods. If those gods weren't acknowledged and worshiped, so it was thought, the empire was in jeopardy. However, some two and a half centuries later, Christianity became the official religion of the Roman Empire. How did that happen?

It's commonly said that history is written by the winners. That is often the case, but not for the history of the early Christian Church. From the year A.D. 64, when Nero began rounding up and executing Christians in the Circus of Caligula and Nero on Vatican Hill, until the early part of the fourth century, Christians were in ever present danger. They were thrown to wild beasts in the arenas, crucified, set afire, sent as slaves to the mines, prohibited from publicly gathering at their cemeteries, and more. And yet . . .

The witness of their lives was so radically different in almost every way that the empire was gradually won over. Their approach to marriage, education, women, and caring for the sick and poor was so vastly different, so hopeful, so filled with a new way of understanding human dignity that the faith grew, despite the persecutions and the laws. We will return soon to the witness of these early Christians, and especially their witness to an entirely new kind of community that the empire found both attractive and threatening.

A second option for the Church today is to look around at all that's happening and decide to build a kind of Christian "ghetto." This option is perhaps best summed up by the expression "The hell with the world. Let's hunker down!" This seems to be a more tempting option for serious disciples than the first. I know more than a few people, all well-intentioned, I'm sure, who live in a kind of Catholic or Christian bubble, isolated from the world at large, content with spending their time, at least their free time, with like-minded believers. Tempting as this might be, this is not the attitude that we are called to have. Jesus teaches us that we are "the salt of the earth," the "light of the world,"[3] and "leaven."[4] All these images show a faith lived not for its own sake but for the sake of others. Salt flavors and preserves, light enables those who can't see to see, and leaven works by touching the dough. Christians are not called to escape, but rather to engage in and interact with the world. As N. T. Wright puts it, Jesus didn't rescue us *from* the world but *for* the world.[5]

To engage, then, is the third and only real option for the Church. But how? I find myself often thinking about this question, and I repeatedly come back to two things that are essential. The first is unshakable confidence in the lordship of Jesus. As we saw, to say Jesus is Lord is much more than the mere ending of a prayer; it's a reality. It means nobody else is. He has defeated, though not yet destroyed, the powers of Sin, Death, and Satan, and He is not nervous, anxious, or worried right now. He holds the world and each of us in His hands. "The counsel of the Lord stands forever, the plans of his heart to all generations," the psalmist sings (33:11). Personally, maintaining confidence in God's lordship isn't much of a struggle for me. The problem is, it's not enough. We need something else, and I struggle mightily with that something else: conformity to Jesus's heart. The Lord showed me this in prayer recently in a most humbling fashion.

I was praying one Sunday morning during the season of Advent just before Christmas. The Scriptures I was reading all centered on that real day when Jesus will return to judge the world and make all things new. As I lingered with this in prayer, I found myself thinking about all sorts of people and how they might react on that day of judgment. Sheepishly, I'll admit I don't even know many of these people. Some of them are celebrities, figures frequently in the news, politicians, and others whom I just don't like very much. As I continued in prayer, I imagined, with no small degree of delight, the look on their faces when they saw with their own eyes the truth about Jesus. I was looking forward to seeing them "get it" on that day in return for various things they had done. Suddenly, I sensed the Lord jolting me out of my delight. "John," I heard in my spirit, "I don't want anyone to 'get it.' I died for the ungodly—and that includes you!" To engage, then, we need both confidence in Jesus's lordship and a greater share in His heart—that is, a love for each and every person we encounter and a desire to see them come to understand what He has done for them by name. These two things are the how, if you will. But what exactly are we to be doing right now?

A few years ago, I received an email from a woman who has since become a dear friend. She began by telling me she was a marine and went on to say that she and a group of fellow marines had been listening to our ACTS XXIX podcast *You Were Born for This.* "You guys sound like marines!" she said. I immediately felt five inches taller. She said that the episode she was listening to prompted her to share some things with us that might be helpful for the work we do. She wanted to know if we could talk, and I immediately told her we'd love to.

Many things in that conversation stood out for me, but one in particular has stayed with me ever since. Marines, it turns out, much like the Church, are fond of acronyms. One of the acronyms they commonly use is IOT. It stands for "in order to." Officers in the corps have a responsibility to make sure that all of those under their command have absolute clarity on every mission. For example, we're landing in Okinawa *in order to* do what? We're advancing on that hill *in order to* what? We're going into that village *in order to* what? Without clarity on the IOT, communication can break down, morale can quickly fall apart, and if and when things get dicey, people can die.

In chapters 4 and 5, we broke down the mission of Jesus. In marine-speak, God became a man *in order to* what? Many things, of course, but I argued especially for three: 1) to reveal to us the Father's love; 2) to make atonement for our sins; and 3) to go to war to rescue us from the powers of Sin, Death, and Satan. In this final chapter, let's focus on our mission as Jesus's disciples. Jesus sends us out *in order to* . . . what? This mission is increasingly urgent in this anxious, fearful, and divided world, a world so prone to demonize "the other."

As I mentioned in chapter 6, we are called to both an inward, personal response and an outward, mission-oriented response to all that God has done for us. These are something like two sides of the same coin. Here's a thought that might help explain this. Only God is able to create. The enemy, the devil, can't create. He can only mar, deface, twist, and distort God's good creation—both "out there" in the world and "in here" in my heart and mind. Imagine, then, for a moment, that your life, especially your interior life, is like the map of a country. On this map are various things: thoughts, imagination, memory, will, and more. If I'm honest, when I look at the map of my life, Jesus's flag flies high in certain parts more or less all the time. In other words, He really is the Lord of those areas. Unfortunately, in more areas than I'd like to admit, the enemy's flag flies high, at least from time to time. The *internal* mission, then, is to cooperate with the Holy Spirit and let Him take back territory in my life that properly belongs to God. This internal mission is a steady growth in holiness, rooting out sin, abandoning various idols, growing in virtue, and gradually letting God lay claim to every dimension of my life.

What about the other side of the coin, though? What's the *external* mission? What does Jesus send us out *in order to* do? The answer to this question, I believe, comes from understanding what Jesus was doing on that first Easter.

When Jesus rose from the dead, He wasn't simply showing off. No, on Easter Sunday Jesus began the re-creation of this universe—a universe that He loves and that came into existence through Him. And when He returns it will not be to take us away, although I think that's what many people imagine. No, on that day Jesus will be revealed to all as the true and only King of heaven and earth, and every knee will bow to Him and confess that He is Lord. On that day He will judge everyone according to what we have done. On that day the dwelling of God will be with men and women. On that day the heavenly Jerusalem will come down (we won't go up!). On that day there will be no sickness, no sadness, no sorrow, no death, no goodbyes, no crying. On that day Jesus will make all things new.[6]

If Jesus was beginning on Easter the re-creation of this world that God loves, then our mission, rightly understood, is to continue that mission until He returns. Perhaps you're familiar with the song "The City of God." It's not an especially good song, and the theology is a bit wonky. The refrain includes these words, "Let us build the city of God." Here's the problem: Nobody can build the city of God. Nobody except God, that is. We can, however, build *for* the city of God. And this is a way to understand the mission. Let's see how we can do this.

Jesus says to His disciples, "You are the light of the world. . . . [No one] light[s] a lamp and put[s] it under a basket, but on a stand, and it gives light to all in the house" (Matthew 5:14–15). Why don't you put a lit lamp under a basket? It's stupid, that's why. It makes no sense. Not only would you set the basket on fire, but it would defeat the whole purpose of lighting the lamp. You light lamps so that people in the dark can see.

The Greek word translated as *lamp* in this passage is *lyknos.* A lyknos was a portable lamp, about the size of a small television remote control. Who is "the lamp" Jesus is talking about? You are. I am. Who picks up the lamp? Jesus. What's "the stand"? Wherever you and I happen to be at any particular moment: the grocery store, football field, classroom, waiting room, medical lab, government office, or any other place we can think of. What's "the house"? The world that God loves and that we live in. I am fortunate to have one of these first-century lamps. It sits next to my bed, so that upon waking I am instantly reminded that I have a mission to do today. When I see that lyknos, it encourages me to ask God to use me, broken, selfish, and sinful as I can be and am. I beg Him to somehow "shine" His life and love through me on to others.

I noted earlier that C. S. Lewis described Christianity as "the story of how the rightful king has landed" in disguise. But he went on to write something even more explicit with regard to our mission. The king, Lewis says, "is calling us all to take part in a great campaign of sabotage."[7] That's the mission.

Now, lest you get nervous about language like that, and perhaps rightfully so given the age in which we're living, let's make clear right away that the "weapons" we are called to fight with are love, truth, goodness, beauty, mercy, integrity, forgiveness, character, kindness, compassion, and other positive qualities. Once again, let's remember who the enemy is: the devil and his minions. It bears repeating over and over again: No human being is my enemy. That's not to say that people don't do wicked things. Of course they do. But they're not the enemy. They're just rebels, rebels to win, just as I was once a rebel and was won over by the love of God.

Let's get even more explicit on the IOT. Without trying to be exhaustive, for that would be impossible, let me offer eight specific missions for us as disciples of Jesus. He sends us out into the world in order to be the following:

- agents of hopeful lamentation
- agents of redemptive suffering
- agents of sabotage and resistance
- agents of re-creation
- agents of restoration
- agents of reconciliation
- agents of healing
- ambassadors

As we'll see, some of us are called to do *some* of those things at *different* times in our lives. All of us, though, are called more or less daily to do the first two.

Agents of Hopeful Lamentation

IF YOU'VE BEEN baptized, that was no mere ritual that took place; something really happened to you, as we saw when we looked at the practical differences Jesus's death and resurrection make in our lives. Baptism really washes away, or cancels, sin; it really transfers us from the dominion of darkness—the cruel tyrant—into the kingdom of God's beloved Son, to the home of a good Father; it really makes us new creatures; it really causes us to become temples of the Holy Spirit; it really incorporates us into the body of Christ; it really makes us adopted sons and daughters of God; and it does more besides.[8]

Baptism also makes the person who receives it a priest. More precisely, a baptized person shares in Jesus's own priesthood. This is commonly referred to as "the priesthood of all believers," as distinct from the ordained or ministerial priesthood. Saint Peter reminds the early Christian community that they are "a chosen race, a royal *priesthood*" (1 Peter 2:9). Peter is talking to all the people, men and women, who have been reborn in baptism. The seer in Revelation writes, "To him who loves us and has freed us from our sins by his blood and made us a kingdom, *priests* to his God and Father" (1:5–6). Likewise, the seer is referring to everyone born anew of water and the Holy Spirit.[9]

In my experience, while many people may have heard this, they don't know what this means. What's the big deal about being a priest? What do priests have?

Priests especially have *access*—access to God.

This might not sound like a big deal at first, but nobody had access to God in the Old Testament once the temple in Jerusalem was constructed. (Okay, one guy did, once a year, with a rope around his waist—in case he died!) A man or woman couldn't just stroll into the Holy of Holies and sit down for a chat with God. On Good Friday, though, as Jesus breathed His last on the cross, the gospel writers tell us that the veil that closed off the Holy of Holies in the temple was torn—from top to bottom. In other words, *God* tore the veil. Jesus's death and resurrection opened up for us entrance into God's courts. Now we can do something that would have been impossible and unimaginable for our Jewish brothers and sisters at the time of the temple. We can go into God's presence anytime we want. If you or I tried to walk into the White House to meet the president, we would certainly be turned away and perhaps arrested! If we tried to walk into our doctor's office without an appointment, more than likely we would be told that we need to call and schedule a visit. If we walked in and tried to see the CEO of virtually any organization, we would probably be told it's simply not possible. By virtue of our baptism, however, which makes us all priests, we have access to God and can talk to Him anytime! This is genuinely astounding. What, though, are we supposed to do once we're there?

There's a momentous scene in the history of Israel that I find helpful in understanding this mission of being an agent of hopeful lamentation. Esther was a Jewish girl, married to King Ahasuerus, a pagan ruler. At a time when her people were in mortal danger, Queen Esther longed to approach Ahasuerus to plead on their behalf. King Ahasuerus's right-hand man, Haman, out of envy and malice, was plotting to kill all the Jews in the realm. The king was unaware both of this plot and of the fact that Esther was Jewish, as her ethnicity had been hidden from him. Perilous as the situation was, nobody could approach the king unless he granted an audience, and you couldn't just call up his executive assistant to request an appointment. One day, though, the king noticed Esther standing outside the hall and motioned for her to come in. She had been granted access, and that access resulted in her and all the Jewish people being rescued from Haman's wicked plot.

This image of Esther is with me every morning as I walk into the chapel to pray. It's as if I see myself standing outside this massive hall, majestic and beautiful beyond description. I see angels attending and worshipping the King of kings and Lord of lords. I see our Lady and the saints in joyful fellowship. I especially see the Lord Himself seated on His glorious throne. And just as King Ahasuerus saw Esther outside the courts and extended his scepter, granting her access, so the Lord looks at me and, smiling, does the same. He reminds me that because of all He has done we can approach Him. And just as Esther brought the plight of her people before the king, so we are allowed to bring the many plights in our families, our communities, our schools, our country, and our world before the true King. No, we're not just "allowed." This coming into God's courts is one of the privileged missions that belongs to us as disciples. We are called to bring our own lamentations, and the lamentations of the whole world, before the King—not as if we're making Him aware of something He doesn't already know, but because in solidarity with the human race we feel the pain of others. As disciples of Jesus we are all called to stand, sit, kneel, or lie prostrate in agonized prayer for the world, our spouse, our children, coworkers, friends, classmates, leaders—everyone and anyone.

N. T. Wright reminds us that even as creation is groaning as it awaits the return of the King, so we also groan while awaiting the fullness of redemption (see Romans 8:22–23). This groaning is intimately tied to our mission of being priests. Wright observes, "We are called—in the Messiah's spirit—to share the pain of the world. . . . Our vocation," he continues, "places us, right now, where the world is in pain, *so that . . . we can be in prayer right there.*"[10]

Wright further explains this particular mission:

> To live and announce that message [Jesus is Lord] in and to the world, with the world in its current state, means engaging with the world's reality, its turmoil, its

> trouble, its tears. And we can't simply say "Well, that's all right, because Jesus is the answer." Nor can we say, "Well, of course the world's a mess, because it doesn't know Jesus; but we're alright, heading for salvation somewhere else; we don't really belong here, we're just passing through." . . . No: part of our primary calling as followers of Jesus is to lament: to stand in the place of pain in humility, sorrow and hope. . . . It's what we are called to do as we stand in prayer at the heart of a world in pain.[11]

This, then, is the first mission that belongs to all of us: to be agents of hopeful lamentation. We are *hopeful* because Jesus is Lord, and He has defeated Sin, Death, and Satan; He is trustworthy and good, He knows what He is doing, and He will make all things new one real day. But we *lament* because the world right now is groaning in pain—so much pain—and so we also are to be in pain as we read the news and live with and in the heartaches of our own families and our own brokenness. The Benedictine abbot Jeremy Driscoll, summarizing this mission, says, "It is the priest's work to bring another before God in prayer."[12]

Agents of Redemptive Suffering

PRIESTS, HOWEVER, ALSO offer sacrifices, and this is a second mission we are all sent by Jesus in order to do. Saint Paul, in his letter to the Romans, exhorts Christians this way: "Present your bodies as a living sacrifice, holy and acceptable to God, which is your spiritual worship" (12:1). Paul draws on imagery here that is somewhat humorous, though also painful. Sacrifices in Paul's day often involved animals being placed atop an altar, where they were slain and then sometimes burned as an offering to the Roman gods and goddesses in an attempt to either win the favor of the gods or appease their wrath. In his exhortation, Paul is telling us that we are called to place *ourselves* on the altar, not to win God's favor or appease Him but in grateful response to all He has already done for us, and also so that we can become holy, set apart for Him (the literal meaning of *sacrifice*). A key difference, however, is that you and I are to be *living* sacrifices. The challenge with a living sacrifice is that the body keeps crawling off the altar! Each day, then, we have to choose to crawl back on, to decide to give ourselves back to the One who created and rescued us.

This call to offer ourselves as a sacrifice involves more than at first meets the eye. One of the more challenging verses in the Bible is Colossians 1:24, where Saint Paul writes, "In my flesh I am filling up what is lacking in Christ's afflictions for the sake of his body, that is, the church." What in the world could be "lacking" in the sufferings of Christ? Does Paul mean to convey that what Jesus did in going to war to rescue us was close but not quite enough to accomplish all that He came to do? Hardly. The only thing "lacking" in Jesus's afflictions is our participation in them.

Let's note that there are two distinct kinds of suffering. On the one hand, we might voluntarily take on certain sufferings, like fasting or some other act of penance. On the other hand, there are involuntary sufferings that come to us, such as chronic pain, cancer, and depression. As disciples of Jesus we are sent to be agents of redemptive suffering, to unite our sufferings, big and small, to the cross of Jesus for the sake of the world. This is immensely important since, with regard to involuntary suffering, it's not a question of whether it will come to us but only how and when.

The culture at large usually sees suffering as a waste, of virtually no value whatsoever. Men and women in nursing homes and hospitals, or confined to their own homes, or wherever pain may find them, can be strongly tempted to think that what they are going through is in vain. Disciples of Jesus know a different story. Or they should. If you and I had been there on that day we now call "Good Friday" and seen Jesus on the cross between the two thieves, we would certainly have thought to ourselves, *What an utter waste.* We would have believed that nothing good would come from His suffering.

We would have been wrong.

Disciples of Jesus understand that He rescued us by His suffering on the cross, wherein He revealed to us the Father's love, made atonement for our sins, and went to war to defeat the powers of Sin, Death, and Satan. Disciples of Jesus likewise understand that Jesus didn't promise us that if we believed in Him, He would protect us from any and all suffering. Instead, the New Testament is filled with passages that affirm we will suffer with and for Jesus before we enter fully into His kingdom.[13]

As it was with Jesus on the cross, so it is with us when we suffer. It is not a waste or in vain—at least it need not be. When we suffer we can *use* it. God can do great things through it. In a previous era those who were suffering were often encouraged to "offer it up." That might strike us as being a bit passive. Some have found it more helpful, remembering Paul's words in Colossians 1:24, to actively unite what they're going through—chemotherapy, a migraine, chronic back pain, depression, or any other way that suffering comes to us—to the cross of Jesus, trusting that one day they will understand how God is using this. The important thing is to understand that nothing we are enduring right now, no matter how painful, need be in vain!

My mom spent most of her final years in intense chronic pain. Pain is often measured on a scale of 1 to 10. Many days her pain was something like 15. When she was younger, shortly before I was born, my mother had an accident that led to numerous surgeries, many of which only made the pain worse. This went on for years. Then, when I was in junior high school, she experienced a miraculous healing, something right out of the pages of the Gospels or the Acts of the Apostles. I mention this because my mom experienced and knew God's power firsthand. She knew that miracles are not confined to the past. However, later in life, when ferocious pain returned, she came to understand that the same Lord who had once healed her was now inviting her to do the very thing Paul had done so many centuries before: fill up in her own flesh what was lacking in the sufferings of Christ for the sake of others.

My mom, then, without romanticizing the pain, learned to pray in a new way. She learned to crawl atop the altar out of love for the sake of others. When I asked her about this once, she told me that she said to the Lord, "Jesus, you know that I do not want this pain and that I so want You to release me from it. But I trust that this is not in vain, is not useless, is not meaningless—anymore than Your cross was. So I unite this to Your cross." Then, somehow, she got the idea to start writing down names of people who were in need. At first it was just a few—my dad, her children, her grandchildren and great grandchildren. Over time, however, the list grew. She started to write down prayer intentions on legal pads beside the hospital bed where she lay most of the day or on the kitchen counter around which she would slowly walk in an attempt to ease the pain. She might note the names of a couple who were having marital difficulties. A young man who was suicidal and battling depression. A girl who was pregnant and considering an abortion. Leaders of nations. People seeking discernment for huge decisions. It was overwhelming to see how many names—and how many legal pads!—there were.

Gradually, people began to hear about this. They would ask me or my siblings to please ask my mom to write their name, or the name of a loved one, on her legal pads. When my mom finally died and her pain was over, I had an image of Jesus walking with her, taking her on a sort of tour. As they walked, He showed her various homes, and they were able to look inside and see the people. That couple who had been struggling in their marriage and had managed to stay the course. The young man who had persevered through the depression. The young mother and the child she had chosen to keep. On and on they walked together, and after each house, Jesus simply smiled at my mother and said to her, "It was by My grace that they were able to do those things. But your participation in My cross helped them. Well done, good and faithful servant!"

These first two missions, then—agents of hopeful lamentation and agents of redemptive suffering—belong more or less to all of us, all of the time. There are other missions, however, that belong to some of us some of the time. Let's turn our attention to those now.

Agents of Sabotage and Resistance

JESUS SENDS SOME of us out into the world in order to be agents of sabotage and resistance. *Sabotage* is defined as "the deliberate attempt to damage, destroy, or hinder a cause or activity" as by civilians or enemy agents in a time of war.[14] I hope we all realize, sobering as it is, that we are in fact in a time of war. We have been ever since that tragic day when our first parents sold our race into slavery. (We just need to keep reminding ourselves over and over again who the real enemy is.)

Sabotage, though, isn't a biblical word; it's a French word, and the Bible wasn't originally written in French. *Resistance,* though, is a synonym of sabotage and it is a biblical word. *Resistance* means taking action in opposition to something or someone. You might remember this passage from 1 Peter: "Be sober-minded; be watchful. Your adversary the devil prowls around like a roaring lion, seeking someone to devour. Resist him, firm in your faith" (5:8–9).

When I was younger, I used to think this meant, "When temptation comes, don't cave!" And there's truth in that interpretation, to be sure. When the enemy tries to move us away from the Lord, away from acting with integrity and love, we are to resist him, we are to stand strong.

However, there's another meaning of *resistance,* one where we're more on offense than defense. At certain times we are to oppose the devil. To fight against him. To take action in opposition to him. I, for one, desire to do as much as I can in proclaiming the gospel to do damage to the enemy's kingdom. To help people see his lies. To help those who are now as I once was: enslaved, ensnared, fearful, anxious, living without hope. Let me offer an example of someone who did this.

On December 1, 1955, a woman was coming home from work. She took the bus every day both to and from work. She was sitting in the eleventh row on the bus because in the city where she lived the first ten rows were permanently reserved for white people. She wasn't white, so she sat in the eleventh row. The first ten rows filled up quickly and the bus driver asked everyone to move back. He *told* everyone to move back, actually. Three people immediately moved back; this woman didn't move. Irate, the bus driver ordered her to move. She wouldn't move. Fed up, the bus driver called the police and the woman was arrested. She was officially charged with resisting the orders of a bus driver! The woman was jailed overnight, and four days later a 381-day bus boycott began in Montgomery, Alabama. The woman's name? Rosa Parks. Explaining afterward why she wouldn't move, Rosa answered, "People always say that I didn't give up my seat because I was tired, but that isn't true. I was not tired physically. . . . No, the only tired I was, was tired of giving in."[15]

Many people are familiar now with Rosa Parks and rightly identify her with the struggle for civil rights. Countless cities across the United States have streets named for her. Sadly, though, few people seem to know that what animated her was her faith. She was, her biographer Jeanne Theoharis wrote, a "staunch and devout Christian."[16] In her memoir *Quiet Strength: The Faith, the Hope, and the Heart of a Woman Who Changed a Nation,* Parks herself would put it this way: "I learned to put my trust in God and seek Him as my strength."[17]

Parks later said about her experience on that Montgomery bus: "I felt the Lord would give me the strength to endure whatever I had to face. God did away with all my fear. It was time for someone to stand up—or, in my case, sit down. I refused to move."[18]

Rosa Parks understood that the idea that some people were greater or lesser than others simply because of the pigmentation of their skin was a demonic lie from the pit of hell. That idea should be resisted and opposed with every fiber of our being. Her faith enabled her to see what other people couldn't: There is no greater than or lesser than in the human race. There aren't "some" important people. All people are important. All people have dignity. All people have worth. All people are cherished by God. All people are willed into existence by God. All people are redeemed by the precious blood of Jesus. All people are destined to be divinized.

All people.

So Rosa Parks resisted, and that resistance led to the overturning of an unjust law. There's much, much more work to be done, to be sure, but she started something. I see Parks as an amazing agent of sabotage. A forty-two-year-old woman coming home from work who decided not to move.

Let me offer another example of an agent of sabotage. *Unsere*

Besten ("Our Best") was a German television series that chronicled the lives of the greatest Germans of all time. The lineup was based on the rankings of television viewers. A twenty-one-year-old college student, together with her brother, ranked fourth as a key historical figure. The same young woman was voted "the most important woman of the twentieth century" in 2003 by the German women's magazine *Brigitte.* The woman's name? Sophie Scholl.

Sophie Scholl grew up in a Lutheran family in the 1920s and '30s.[19] Like all young people in Germany at that time, she was compelled to be a member of the Hitler Youth. It didn't take long, however, for Sophie to learn what the Nazis were doing. She was especially repulsed by the Nazi ideology *Lebensunwertes Leben* (meaning "life unworthy of life"). She came to see this was a demonic ideology and had to be resisted. Such resistance required great courage, however, and ended up costing her life.

Sophie's letters and diary are evidence of a young woman with a deep faith in Jesus. On February 12, 1942, she wrote:

> I have decided to pray in church every day. . . . When I look at people around me and also at myself, I feel awed by humanity because God came down to earth for its sake. Yet, this is what strikes me as most incomprehensible. . . . Yes, one should always bear in mind, when dealing with other people, that God became man on their account. To think that one feels too good to condescend to many of them! What arrogance![20]

In another diary entry, she wrote:

> I call aloud to you, I call "you," even though all I know about you is that my salvation resides in you alone. Do

> not turn away from me if I fail to hear you knock; open my deaf, deaf heart.[21]

In one last entry, she wrote:

> I pray for a compassionate heart, for how else could I love? I who am so shallow in everything must pray for everything. A child can be compassionate, but I too often forget the sufferings that ought to overwhelm me, the sufferings of mankind. I place my powerless love in your hands, that it may become powerful.[22]

Sophie's faith was profoundly influenced by great figures like Augustine, Thomas Aquinas, and John Henry Newman. She grasped the dignity of every human being, as evidenced in her compassion for humanity in her diary entries. Sophie quickly became active in a resistance movement formed by her brother Hans and several other students at the University of Munich. The movement started at the university as students became aware of the demonic ideology of the Nazi regime and the devastation it was causing at home in Germany and abroad. The students called themselves "the White Rose." These young students were the first resistance movement coming from inside Germany since Hitler had come to power, and they gave hope and encouragement to those who opposed the goals of his regime.

The students spoke out against the German leaders, especially Hitler, and sought to arouse like-minded individuals in Germany to stand with others who were anti-Nazi and willing to say so. This was a dangerous, life-threatening endeavor.

At one point Sophie asked her boyfriend, Fritz Hartnagel, a soldier in the Wehrmacht, if he would help her obtain a duplicating machine. When he asked why, she told him that she planned to copy subversive material.

"Do you realize," he asked her, "that this could cost you your head?"

"Yes," she told him. "I understand that."[23]

What was it that the members of the White Rose resistance movement actually did? They printed fliers. Six fliers, to be exact.[24] After copying them, they would board trains and head to various cities throughout Germany. Once they got off the train, they mailed the letters to other cities, thus giving the impression that the movement was much larger than it actually was. After a fierce search by the Nazis, Sophie and her brother were finally caught on February 18, 1943. An employee at the University of Munich, Jakob Schmid, had seen them tossing a shower of leaflets from the top balcony of one of the university buildings.

Sophie, her brother, and the other members of the White Rose were agents of sabotage. They told people what was really happening. They told the truth. They did what they could to help people see beyond the propaganda espoused by the government and to know about the death camps and other atrocities. "Somebody, after all, had to make a start," Sophie told Roland Freisler, Hitler's notorious "hanging judge," at her trial. "What we wrote and said is also believed by many others. They just don't dare express themselves as we did."[25]

For those who want to learn more, there's a most inspiring movie titled *Sophie Scholl: The Final Days.* Filmed in German with English subtitles, it covers mostly her interrogation by the SS and is based on the transcripts the Nazis kept. Their fixation on documenting things in this case turned out to be most useful in providing a glimpse into this heroic young girl's mind and heart. Sophie Scholl was beheaded at the tender age of twenty-one on February 22, 1943.

Agents of Re-creation

REMEMBER THAT SAINT Paul writes, "Therefore, if anyone is in Christ, he is a new creation" (2 Corinthians 5:17). His words help us understand yet another mission some of us are sent out into the world to do, one that is increasingly important in view of the New Great Depression we discussed earlier. We could look to any number of people as examples here, but the one that is personally most striking for me is Dorothy Day.

In her youth, Day was an atheist, a communist, an anarchist, an alcoholic, sexually promiscuous, had an abortion, and twice tried to kill herself.

Then, shortly after Christmas in 1927, Dorothy Day became a Catholic.

Day went on to become one of the people most disturbing to my conscience. People who knew her said, "To meet Dorothy Day was to wonder afterward, 'What just hit me?'"

Day dedicated her life to the poor, the homeless, the underemployed, the unemployed, and others who were relegated to the margins and fringes of society. If she and I had ever had the chance to sit down and talk, I imagine we would have gone rounds on a whole host of topics. And she would have won every single one of them. I imagine she would have said to me, "But, Father, Jesus said _____ in the Sermon on the Mount. Why don't you believe that? Why don't you live like that?" And I would have had no answer.

Day didn't pick and choose with regards to different aspects of the faith. She wasn't what is sometimes called "a cafeteria Christian." She wholeheartedly embraced everything the Church taught, whether about sexuality or the means for achieving peace.

She went to Mass and prayed the Rosary daily. In fact, she spent *three hours* every day in prayer. She was radically in love with Jesus. But her faith and love for God weren't confined to a chapel. She went out. And when she went out, she let herself be used by Jesus to re-create others even as He had re-created her. One American bishop said of her, "Day was a reminder of how the world will be. Not everyone is called to be a pacifist, but Dorothy was a reminder that one day there will be no war."[26]

Dorothy Day was a brilliant lamp in Jesus's hands, reminding each and every person she encountered that they mattered, they were loved, they were of inestimable value to God, they were worth the trouble. Her mere presence, not to mention her words and her smile, communicated these things. Jesus sends us out to be these kinds of people.

Day, together with her good friend Peter Maurin, started what were known as "houses of hospitality." These places arose across the country at the initiative of people in the pews, not bishops or priests, with the purpose of caring for men and women who were in need of food, clothing, love, and dignity as a result of the Depression and other factors often related to it. These houses of hospitality also served to bring people into an encounter with the power of the gospel. These houses were an extraordinary example of the integration of Dorothy Day's faith into every aspect of life. "As it is now," she wrote in 1938, "under the dubious hospitality of the city and state, it is as though God were unknown. There is no reminder to morning and evening prayer. Men have lost the sense of their own dignity, that dignity which they possess because Christ shared their humanity."[27]

Her hope was for some two thousand such houses to crop up across the United States. In the same 1938 article, Day shared with her readers some of the fruits from the first houses that had opened. "As soon as the feeding began—*as soon as the mood of hospitality began to make itself felt*—lines formed at the door, and continued day after day"[28] (italics mine).

We need such "houses of hospitality" today! For those who are materially poor, yes, but perhaps as much for those who are living the nightmare that is life apart from God. "To those who sit around and say, 'Why don't the priests do this or that?'" Day quipped, "we should reply, 'Why don't *we* all?'"[29] When more than 75 percent of people don't go to church, this might be the opportune time for the people in the pews to see that their homes, even more than their churches, are the primary place where evangelization can and should take place. Indeed, we at the ACTS XXIX ministry would argue that we should see our *homes* as the place where the world meets the Church. After all, those who have encountered Jesus and have come to know all He has done for us know countless people who don't go to church. They live in their neighborhoods, work with them, work out with them, serve on various committees at schools, and so much more. And it is far easier for most people, for many reasons, who don't yet know God and His love to cross the threshold of the home of a neighbor and friend than it is to cross the threshold of a church.

Agents of Restoration

SOME OF US are sent out on mission by Jesus to act as agents of restoration. Whereas agents of re-creation help to make people new, agents of restoration help to make systems, structures, professions, and fields of industry new.

In the gospel of John, Mary Magdalene is the first one to arrive at Jesus's tomb on Easter Sunday. Shocked to find it empty, she runs to tell the disciples, who are hiding in the upper room. Peter and the disciple whom Jesus loved hear this news and run to the tomb. After peering in and finding it just as Mary had said, they depart. Mary, however, stays.

> Mary stood weeping outside the tomb, and as she wept she stooped to look into the tomb. And she saw two angels in white, sitting where the body of Jesus had lain, one at the head and one at the feet. They said to her, "Woman, why are you weeping?" She said to them, "They have taken away my Lord, and I do not know where they have laid him." Having said this, she turned around and saw Jesus standing, but she did not know that it was Jesus. Jesus said to her, "Woman, why are you weeping? Whom are you seeking?" Supposing him to be the gardener, she said to him, "Sir, if you have carried him away, tell me where you have laid him, and I will take him away." Jesus said to her, "Mary." She turned and said to him in Aramaic, "Rabboni!" (which means Teacher). Jesus said to her, "Do not cling to me, for I have not yet ascended to the Father; but go to my brothers and say to them, 'I am ascending to my Father and your Father, to my God and your God.'" Mary Magdalene went and announced to the disciples, "I have seen the Lord"—and that he had said these things to her. (John 20:11–18)

There's much we could say about this passage, but I only want to call our attention to one thing. In the post-resurrection appearances of Jesus, people didn't immediately recognize Him.[30] Amid her tears and confusion, Mary looked at Jesus standing there but didn't know it was Him. She thought He was the gardener, John tells us.

And she was right.

He was the gardener. He is the gardener. God created Adam and placed him where? He put him in a garden. In this garden, God gave Adam the task of exercising dominion on the earth.

Genesis tells us that God used to walk in the garden and converse with His creation.[31] On that first Easter Sunday, the day when the re-creation of this world God loves began, God and the "New Adam" (Jesus is both!) are once again walking in the garden. He's exercising dominion on the earth. He's restoring everything. Again, *re-creation* happens personally to individuals. *Restoration* is something more systemic. Something is being brought back to the original plan for which God created it.

If you're old enough to remember President Richard Nixon and the Watergate crisis, you probably remember Charles "Chuck" Colson. Colson was a brilliant—and shady—political strategist, renowned for his "dirty tricks" and largely responsible for the landslide victory Nixon won in 1972. He once notoriously said that he would "walk over" his own grandmother if necessary to ensure the reelection of Nixon. Colson was later convicted and sentenced to prison for his involvement in illegal actions surrounding Daniel Ellsberg, a former Pentagon official who had leaked what came to be called the "Pentagon Papers."

Born in Boston on October 16, 1931, Colson was the only child of his hardworking parents. Due to their hard work, he was able to attend a prestigious preparatory school with children from "the upper crust." Though offered a full ride to Harvard University, he turned it down—to the shock of the admissions officer. Instead, Colson enrolled at Brown University, where he became a member and leader of the Young Republicans and a champion debater. Upon graduating from Brown, he immediately joined the United States Marine Corps. Colson later received a law degree from George Washington University.

In 1956, Leverett Saltonstall, the senior senator for Massachusetts, hired Colson as an administrative assistant. This role brought Colson into contact with Richard Nixon, who "dazzled" Colson with his ideals and thinking.[32] Over time, Colson went on to become a self-described "hatchet man" for Nixon and was a key figure in Nixon's 1972 presidential campaign. Among other "dirty tricks" he spearheaded, Colson leaked (untrue) rumors about Federal Reserve Chairman Arthur Burns and helped unearth a picture of Senator Edward M. Kennedy dancing with an actress in Paris.[33] He also gathered an "enemies list" of various individuals—politicians, journalists, and activists—who were considered dangerous to the Nixon White House.

The high (or low) point of his "tricks" was when Colson agreed to a command from Nixon to blacken the reputation of former Pentagon official Ellsberg, who was suspected of the Pentagon Papers leak. These papers were instrumental in changing the public perception of the war in Vietnam.

"Get Colson in," Nixon told his chief of staff. "He's the best. It's the Colson type of man that you need."[34]

This affair eventually led to Colson's conviction for obstruction of justice. He resigned from the White House in March 1973, and in June 1974, Colson pleaded guilty to a single charge of "disseminating derogatory information to the press." He was sentenced to one to three years in prison.

As all of this was happening, Colson unexpectedly had a life-changing encounter with the person of Jesus in late summer 1973. Thanks to both the witness of a dear friend, Thomas L. Phillips, and the book *Mere Christianity,* belief in God and in what He had done in the person of Jesus became both attractive and reasonable to the former atheist. Jonathan Aitken, his biographer, wrote that Colson "transferred his huge drive, intellect and maniacal energy from the service of Richard Nixon to the service of Jesus Christ."[35] He took his newfound faith into prison, and that same faith—those biblical lenses—enabled him to see that something there wasn't working as it should. Seeds were being planted for his becoming an agent of restoration.

In prison, Colson was surrounded by often resentful inmates who constantly thought of escape. From his experience in confinement, he observed that there had to be a better way to care for inmates:

> I saw the absolute futility of the prison system. There's no way you can take a bunch of criminals, stick 'em in a dormitory where they sit around at night comparing the crimes they committed and how they're going to do it next time, and expect to rehabilitate them. It's demeaning, it's demoralizing, it doesn't give people aspirations to do the right thing. It almost encourages the wrong thing. So I got out of prison and I realized: This isn't working.
>
> That's what got me to start the prison ministry.[36]

In his autobiography, *Born Again,* Colson confided, "I found myself increasingly drawn to the thought that God had put me in prison for a purpose and that I should do something for those I had left behind."[37] In 1976, Colson founded Prison Fellowship, the nation's largest Christian nonprofit serving prisoners, former prisoners, and their families, and a leading advocate for criminal justice reform. Here is their mission statement:

> Prison Fellowship works to restore America's criminal justice system and those it affects. We help men and women replace the cycle of brokenness that landed them in prison. We advocate for justice reform and activate grassroots networks to do the same. We equip wardens to bring restorative change to their facilities. We care for prisoners' families and help strengthen the bond between children and their parents who are be-

> hind bars. We call the Church to lead the way in caring for those impacted by the criminal justice system. And we do it all from a biblical worldview.[38]

Prison Fellowship currently operates throughout the United States and in more than one hundred countries.[39]

Colson had an encounter with Jesus. He had an experience with a system that wasn't working. We need the prison system, of course, because unfortunately people still do harmful things and people need to be protected. Colson saw firsthand, though, that the system could greatly benefit from reform. He wanted that reform to be shaped by the biblical narrative, the biblical story.

Chuck Colson is a model for everyone who is "out there" working in the world. You might be a teacher, physician, politician, engineer, actor, coach, or nurse. The mission isn't simply to do the work ethically. Remember, all the enemy can do is bend, deface, and distort God's good creation. This includes systems, structures, and professions. The mission, therefore, is to do all we can to "bend things back" wherever we work in order to be more in conformity with how God created it to be.

Agents of Reconciliation

IN THE MIDST of an increasingly divided culture, many of us would do well to remember the piercing words of Aleksandr Solzhenitsyn: "If only there were evil people somewhere insidiously committing evil deeds, and it were necessary only to separate them from the rest of us and destroy them. But the line dividing good and evil cuts through the heart of every human being."[40]

Given where things are today, perhaps few missions are as vital as being agents of reconciliation. In the United States, we are almost literally at each other's throats. We are increasingly quick to demonize "the other," and our capacity for rational discourse on even the simplest of topics is rapidly dissipating. In this day and age, as in every time, politics is very important, but it can't fix the problem. Law, too, is very important, but it also can't fix the problem. The key to problem-solving is to identify the problem. So what's the problem? As Solzhenitsyn so accurately put it, the problem is the human heart. Every human heart. Starting with mine.

In a letter to the Christians in Ephesus, Saint Paul writes,

> In Christ Jesus you who once were far off have been brought near by the blood of Christ. For he himself is our peace, who has made us both one and has broken down in his flesh the dividing wall of hostility . . . that he might create in himself one new man in place of the two, so making peace, and might reconcile us both to God in one body through the cross, thereby killing the hostility. (Ephesians 2:13–16)

Now, I don't know what you hear or see in that passage, but Paul was probably talking about a real wall that stood in the temple in Jerusalem. The temple consisted of a series of demarcations, if you will, made up of various courts into which only certain categories of people could enter. There was a Court of the Gentiles, a Court of the Women, a Court of the Israelites, a Court of Priests, and at the very heart of the temple the Holy of Holies.

Archaeologists have discovered a fragment from a wall that probably separated the Court of the Gentiles from the Court of the Women. It reads, "No foreigner may enter within the balustrade around the sanctuary and the enclosure. Whoever is caught, on himself shall he put blame for the death which will ensue."[41] We often sit in church and hear various excerpts from the New

Testament about Jews and Gentiles without having any idea of what the relationship between these ethnic groups was like. These people, at least many of them, absolutely hated each other.

Until they met Jesus.

Then everything changed. They didn't simply begin to tolerate each other, as today we're so often told to do. They began to love each other. They began to lay down their lives for each other. They reconciled to each other and began to call each other brother and sister. This dramatic reconciliation between people who used to hate each other was one of the things that turned the world upside down and won over the Roman Empire to Christianity. We desperately need this again today.

Let me share the single most inspiring story of reconciliation I have ever heard in my life. In fact it might be the most amazing story I've ever heard. I've been to the Auschwitz concentration camp three times. For some reason known only to God, I read *Night* by Elie Wiesel when I was nine years old. Ever since, I've felt an especially strong affinity for what the Jewish people endured in what is often simply called "the Shoah."[42] I don't ever want to step foot in Auschwitz again. It's hell on earth. I think it's haunted. I was there for the first time in 1990. It was brutally cold, and the wind was howling. Blowing through the padlocked doors of some of the remaining stables in which the prisoners were housed, the wind sounded like ghosts from years past screaming to get out.

The commandant of Auschwitz was a man named Rudolf Höss. Born in 1900, Höss grew up in a rigid Catholic family. He once considered becoming a priest, in fact. That all changed when, as a teenager, he thought, mistakenly, that the priest had broken the seal of confession and revealed to his parents something Höss had done at school. "My faith in the sacred priesthood had been destroyed," he recalled, "and doubts began to arise in my mind for the first time."[43] Höss made the decision to never trust a priest again and shortly thereafter left the Catholic Church.

Höss served in World War I first in the Red Cross, and over time was renowned for his bravery and leadership skills. He became the youngest sergeant in the army and returned home loaded with medals.

Having heard Adolf Hitler speak in 1922, Höss was captivated and joined the Nazi party. Shortly thereafter, he was imprisoned for his involvement in a murder and was released in 1928. He married in 1929 and appeared to be headed for the tranquil life of a farmer with his wife and children. However, in 1934, Heinrich Himmler invited him to reenlist. He did, both out of great affection for his country and because of the fond memories he had of his fellow soldiers in World War I. His aptitude for leadership again shone forth, and Höss was sent to Dachau in 1934 to begin his tenure in concentration camp administration. He moved to Sachsenhausen in 1938 and served there until May 1940, when Rudolf Höss became the commandant of Auschwitz. In 1941, after a meeting with Himmler and other Nazi leaders, Auschwitz was turned into an extermination camp. When Höss was captured after the war, he acknowledged—not confessed or expressed remorse, but simply acknowledged—"I was commandant of Auschwitz until 1 December 1943 and I estimate that at least 2,500,000 victims were executed and exterminated there in gas chambers and crematories. At least a further half million people died from hunger and sickness, which adds up to a total amount of about 3,000,000 deaths. This figure represents about 70 or 80% of all persons who were sent to Auschwitz as prisoners."[44]

The Nazis ruthlessly arrested, imprisoned, and often executed those whom they considered political enemies. This included academics and clergy. The Jesuits were both of these. In 1940 the Jesuit community serving in what is now known as Kraków was among those sent to Auschwitz. The gestapo arrested all the priests and brothers at the provincial house, with the exception of the superior, Father Władysław Lohn. For whatever reason, Lohn wasn't home that day. When he returned and saw that the brothers were missing, he inquired among the neighbors and was told they had been arrested and taken to Auschwitz.

Lohn then did something I still can't fathom: He broke into Auschwitz.

The guards captured him and brought him to Commandant Höss. Lohn demanded his brothers be released. I imagine Höss thought the priest was out of his mind. The commandant did not let the Jesuits go free, but for some reason Höss was overcome by the daring and faith of this brave priest and decided to let him go unharmed. And so it was that Father Władysław Lohn was kicked out of the most notorious Nazi death camp by the commandant himself.

Both Höss and Lohn survived the war.

On March 11, 1946, the British army captured Höss, who had been hiding under the name Franz Lang since the Nazi surrender. The British beat him, as one can only imagine, as soon as they found out who they had in their hands. Like other Nazi war criminals, Höss was taken to Nuremberg for trial. His testimony was given in April 1946, and he was then handed over to the Supreme National Tribunal of Poland in May 1946. The Polish found him guilty on April 2, 1947, and sentenced him to be executed. At Auschwitz.

First, though, Höss was imprisoned in a town called Wadowice, about twenty miles from Auschwitz. Wadowice was the town where a man named Karol Józef Wojtyła was born on May

18, 1920. Wojtyła would later become Pope John Paul II on October 16, 1978. In Wadowice, Höss awaited transfer to the camp where he had overseen the murder of nearly three million people.

Knowing he was to be executed, Höss wasn't afraid of dying so much as he was afraid of being tortured, since he was back in Poland where he had committed such heinous atrocities. He understandably expected the guards to do anything and everything to make him suffer for his crimes. But the torture never happened. Instead, he encountered something most unexpected. As a result, something extraordinary started to happen within his heart.

Höss wrote a statement in which he declared, "In Polish prisons I first experienced what human compassion means. In spite of all that had happened I was shown a human compassion that I never expected and which shamed me profoundly."[45] This "human compassion," over the course of two short weeks, had an overwhelming effect on Höss.

> In the seclusion of my detainment I arrived at the bitter knowledge of how enormous my crime against humanity has been. As commander of the Auschwitz extermination camp I executed part of the horrible human extermination plans of the "Third Reich." Thereby I caused the greatest harm against humanity and human solidarity. . . . I am atoning for my responsibility with my life. May God forgive me my actions one day.[46]

Through the guards, it seems, God was working in this man who was responsible for such unimaginable evil. They were serving as agents of reconciliation in Jesus's hands. Another agent, though, was about to enter Höss's life. Re-enter, actually.

On April 4, 1947, Höss heard the bells of a nearby church

ringing and asked to speak to a priest. The Nazi commandant wanted to go to confession. April 4 that year was Good Friday—the day Jesus cried out from the cross, "Father, forgive them, for they know not what they do" (Luke 23:34). For several days the prison staff tried to find a priest who could speak enough German to hear Höss's confession, but all such clergymen were dead. More than likely at the hands of Höss.

Informed that no confessor could be found who could understand him well enough to hear his confession, Höss suddenly remembered the man he had kicked out of Auschwitz, a man he knew from his encounter spoke fluent German: Father Władysław Lohn. "Find that man," he told the guards.

The guards found Father Lohn in Lagiewniki, Poland. He just happened to be serving as the chaplain at the Shrine of the Divine Mercy, the shrine venerating where Jesus had instructed a young Polish religious woman, Sister Faustina Kowalska, to have an image made of Him with the inscription "Jesus, I trust in You." Jesus told Faustina that her mission was to be His "secretary of mercy." He wanted to make known to all the world, and especially to those most in need and in greatest despair over the evil they had done, that there was nothing He couldn't or wouldn't forgive if someone was truly repentant. You would be hard pressed to find a person more in need of mercy than Rudolph Höss.

And so it was that on April 10, 1947—Thursday of Easter week—the week that celebrates Jesus's triumph over the powers of Sin, Death, and Satan—Father Władysław Lohn entered the cell of the man once known as "the animal" in Auschwitz. I imagine Lohn entered that place with much the same mindset as Ananias who, many centuries before had entered another place and stood face-to-face with another man who had blood on his hands: Saul of Tarsus. And I imagine Lohn—fully aware that Höss had done unfathomably wicked deeds beyond human comprehension, and yet also aware that the real enemy of the human race is someone else—greeted him with the word *brother,* much like Ananias had Saul.

The priest who had been kicked out of Auschwitz because of his daring became an agent of reconciliation for the commandant who had killed nearly three million people—including the priest's Jesuit brothers.

The following day, April 11, Lohn returned to Höss's cell and brought him the Holy Eucharist. The guards testified that Höss received communion like a small boy, on his knees, weeping all the while. Lohn himself, much later in his life, said, "In all my years I have never seen anyone receive Holy Communion with such devotion. I have no doubt that Rudolf Höss is in heaven."[47]

The day after this, Höss wrote to his wife,

> Based on my present knowledge I can see today clearly, severely and bitterly for me, that the entire ideology about the world in which I believed so firmly and unswervingly was based on completely wrong premises. . . .
>
> And so my actions in the service of this ideology were completely wrong. . . . My turning away from my belief in God was based on completely wrong premises. It was a hard struggle. But I have again found my faith in my God.[48]

Rudolph Höss was hanged at Auschwitz on April 16, 1947, on a gallows especially built for him by German POWs.

When I first heard this story, one that has largely escaped public notice, it was as if I had an image of Jesus, the unconquerable One, the One who came to make all things new, to rescue His creation, prying Höss's life out of Satan's hands. As He did so, it was as if I could hear Him taunt the only real enemy of the human race with these words: "You. Can't. Even. Have. Him."

Jesus had told Sister Faustina in one of her visions, "Let the weak, sinful soul have no fear to approach Me, for even if it had more sins than there are grains of sand in the world, all will be drowned in the immeasurable depths of My mercy."[49]

The world, our world, right now, desperately needs agents of reconciliation. Disciples of Jesus know, or *should* know, like no one else knows, that one of the things God does best is to take people who used to hate and despise each other and turn them into friends. Not just people who tolerate each other. *Friends.*

Agents of Healing

JESUS ALSO SENDS us out as His disciples in order to be agents of healing.

As He was sending the seventy-two disciples out on mission, Jesus told them,

> Whatever house you enter, first say, "Peace be to this house!" And if a son of peace is there, your peace will rest upon him. But if not, it will return to you. And remain in the same house, eating and drinking what they provide, for the laborer deserves his wages. Do not go from house to house. Whenever you enter a town and they receive you, eat what is set before you. Heal the sick in it and say to them, "The kingdom of God has come near to you." (Luke 10:5–9)

"Heal the sick in it." In the original Greek that's in the imperative tense. To heal is a *command.*

As we have noted often, we live in a time that is being called the New Great Depression. We are surrounded by men and women, young and old, desperately in need of healing. Often they are the people closest to us. Under our own roofs. Such was the case in my life.

My mom and dad are the two greatest people I've ever known. No other person even gets close. They were married for sixty-six years. My siblings and I often say to each other that we won the lottery when it comes to parents. I honestly can't fathom what kind of man I would be without their love and their example of married life. They taught me more or less everything I know. Their relationship wasn't always so strong, though. Like every couple, they faced many severe storms in their marriage. One storm several years in was so severe that they almost quit. Thanks be to God, they didn't.

My dad was the first of my parents to die. At his funeral, shortly before we walked into the church, I heard my mom say the most amazing words I've ever heard one human being say to another. Before I tell you what she said, let me set the stage.

My folks came from vastly different backgrounds and often shared with us humorous stories of their first encounters with each other's families. My dad, as I mentioned earlier, was from upstate New York. He was born and raised in a little town in the Mohawk Valley, the son of two Italian immigrants. My grandparents were lower to middle class. And very Catholic. My mom grew up in Grosse Pointe, Michigan, one of the most prestigious areas in metro Detroit. Her parents were quite wealthy. And Methodist.

My mom was one of four children, the only daughter of Lyle and Golda Fife. Her dad, my grandfather, was the most intimidating man I've ever met. A self-made man with little formal education, Lyle was immensely successful. He started his own business, Fife Electric, when he was still a young man. He was a phenomenal athlete, even once in a while joining the Detroit

Tigers for spring training in Florida. Given his love for business and sports, he decided to partner with several others to buy the Detroit Lions. Here was a man who had it all, or seemed to. (If you ever get a chance to visit our ACTS XXIX offices, you can see the 1957 World Championship blanket the NFL gave to the Lions after their last championship victory. It's on proud display!)

Lyle was my mom's hero. She, in turn, was the apple of Lyle's eye, being his only daughter. A visit from her brothers when she was at the University of Michigan, however, brought everything crashing down.

Like many people away from home for the first time, my mom was excited to have family come and visit her. Her brothers, however, proceeded to tell her news that shattered her tender heart. Their dad was having an affair and had walked out on their mom.

It seems their father had for some time been quietly moving things out of the house. When he left in the morning for work, he would put an extra shirt in his briefcase or maybe a pair of pants. On colder days, he would wear an extra sweater under his topcoat. This went on for weeks. Then one day my grandmother walked into the bedroom, opened the closet, and saw that all of Lyle's clothes were gone. She had never suspected a thing.

When my mother heard this, she went ballistic. In an instant, the man who had been her hero became public enemy number one. She hated her father intensely. A bitterness began to take root in my mom, one that perhaps feels familiar if you have experienced this kind of betrayal.

My dad met my mom around this same time. My dad had attended Albany State College out of high school, then was drafted and served three years in World War II, as I mentioned before. Thanks to the GI bill, he was able to attend the University of Michigan when the war was over.

My parents quickly fell in love and were married on August 5, 1950, at Saints Peter and Paul Church in Detroit. My grandfather wasn't at the wedding. My mom didn't invite him. In fact, every wedding gift he sent to them, she sent back. Unopened. Every card he sent to them, she sent back. Unopened. She didn't talk to her father for years. And the hatred and bitterness took a stronger and stronger hold inside her heart. By the grace of God, my mom and grandfather had an extraordinary reconciliation later in his life, but that's actually another story for another time.

As my dad got to know my mom, he came to realize that there was profound hurt in her life. Behind her carefully constructed facade, he could sense an immense identity wound deep inside her. From the outside, my mom was beautiful and intelligent, an athletic woman who appeared to have everything going for her. Inside, however, her heart had been torn apart, leaving her feeling rejected, unloved, and unwanted. My dad knew this. My dad also knew that God had brought him into her life to be a means by which these wounds could be healed.

Marriage is a sacrament. One of the simplest definitions of a sacrament is that it is a visible sign of an invisible reality instituted by Jesus that gives grace.[50] For example, the visible sign in baptism is water. The invisible reality is sin being washed away and the person dying, being buried, and rising to new life in and with Jesus. The visible sign in the Eucharist is what looks and tastes like bread and wine. The invisible reality is the body, blood, soul, and divinity of Jesus.

What's the visible sign in marriage? Well, if you're married, *you are.* Not you as a couple, or rather, not first you as a couple.[51] You, the husband, or you, the wife. What's the invisible reality? The love of Jesus. Whoa! Do you understand this? If you're married, you are entrusted with the mission of making Jesus present to your spouse. By your words—both what you say and what you don't say; by your actions—both what you do and don't do; by your mercy; your compassion; your kindness; your gentleness; your fidelity; and so much more, you are supposed to make Jesus present.

To do such a thing obviously requires much more than just goodwill and hard work. Anyone who's married knows that rolling up your sleeves and trying harder just doesn't work at a certain point. That's why when a couple is married in the Church, they are given grace. This is given during what is somewhat inaccurately called "the nuptial blessing."[52] What's grace? Well, grace is a number of things, to be sure: sheer gift, God's unmerited favor, a share in His own life, and more. But I tend to think of grace, at least the grace given in marriage (or ordination), as "spiritual steroids."

Steroids are illegal in athletics because they give the athlete an unfair advantage in competition. Here's the thing, though: God wants you and me to win! He wants us to win at the "game" of becoming the men and women that He created us to be and that we deep down desire to be. So He gives us help. On the day that a couple gets married, He gives them supernatural strength to be and to do the very things He has brought them together to be and to do. From that day forward, the couple is not on their own. They have access to power—God's power.

To be what? To do what?

To make Him present and tangible in their relationship with each other.

Perhaps you're familiar with the prayer Anima Christi, composed by Saint Ignatius of Loyola, who we have come across before. It goes:

Soul of Christ, sanctify me.
Body of Christ, save me.

Blood of Christ, inebriate me.
Water from the side of Christ, wash me.
Passion of Christ, strengthen me.
O Good Jesus, hear me.
Within your wounds hide me.
Permit me not to be separated from you.
From the wicked foe, defend me.
At the hour of my death, call me
and bid me come to you
That with your saints I may praise you
Forever and ever. Amen.

"Within your wounds hide me."

This doesn't mean, "Tuck me safely away from all harm so I can't get hurt." It means, "Wherever there is pain in Your body, Lord, place me. Wherever someone is in need, let me be like a healing ointment to bring relief, Lord." Over the course of sixty-six years, my dad was intentional and deliberate in trying to be just that for my mom. Like all people, he had his shortcomings and failings, but on August 5, 1950, knowing her shattered heart, he set about the mission entrusted to him that day by God. He wanted to make it clear to my mom that after God she was absolutely and without question the most important person in his life. I could share countless stories of how my dad cooperated with this power (and my mom did, too, to be clear), but I'll just tell you how it all ended, with those words I heard my mom say at my dad's funeral.[53]

On February 19, 2016, I had the honor and privilege of celebrating my father's funeral. A retired cardinal was there, as were several bishops, a result of my dad spending years serving and assisting the Church in countless ways after he retired from his professional career. Twenty or so priests had vested and were lined up, ready to join me in praying for my dad and for our family. I was in the back of the church with my three sisters and brother, each of us constantly wiping the tears that seemed to stream endlessly from our eyes. The good folks from the neighborhood funeral home were preparing to close the casket. Just before they did, however, my mother rolled her wheelchair over to the casket, gently placed her hand on her husband's embalmed and hardened hands, and said: "Honey, because of you, I know who God is."

And with that, the funeral directors closed the casket, and my mom, elegant even in a wheelchair, slowly pushed herself away.

The young girl's heart—a heart that had felt shattered, rejected, disposed of, and unlovable—came to know by her husband's life, words, and actions that in fact she was chosen, cherished, priceless, and worth dying for.

"Heal the sick!"

If you're married, this is the mission. Make God present, tangible, to your husband or wife. Heal his or her heart. For behind the facades we all so carefully construct lie bruised, grieved, and broken hearts.

Ambassadors

FINALLY, WE ARE sent out as agents in order to be ambassadors. Saint Paul writes:

> All this is from God, who through Christ reconciled us to himself and gave us the ministry of reconciliation; that is, in Christ God was reconciling the world to himself, not counting their trespasses against them, and entrusting to us the message of reconciliation. Therefore, we are ambassadors for Christ, God making his appeal through us. (2 Corinthians 5:18–20)

To hear the word *ambassador* is to think immediately of an embassy. What's an embassy? An embassy is the headquarters of people tasked with representing their government in a foreign country. This is one of the best descriptions I know of the Church. We are the headquarters of the kingdom of God serving in "occupied territory," to use Lewis's language. An embassy is led by an ambassador, who serves as the representative of the leader of his or her country. In a certain and very real sense, each and every one of us is an ambassador. We're all representatives of our country's leader. That leader, of course, is God, our good Father, who sent His Son to rescue us from Sin, Death, and Satan. An embassy, remarkably, isn't subject to the laws of the host country. What are the laws of the "host country"? In our case, Sin and Death. We're not bound by these anymore, thanks to Jesus's death and resurrection. We are not just free from Sin and Death, though. We're also not bound by all the ways the laws of Sin and Death manifest themselves: hatred, anger, division, gossip, slander, lust, greed, pride, unforgiveness, and so much more. Finally, an embassy offers asylum and protection from arrest and extradition.

Again, I find this to be a powerful image of the Church, and all that the Church is supposed to be. Tragically, however, all too often we are not fulfilling this role. Somebody should be able to walk into a church and immediately see that the people inside are different. They should see people who have virtually nothing in common. They should see a gathering that is astoundingly diverse: every color and ethnicity; rich, poor, and in between; young and not so young; some arriving in BMWs and some on their bikes; people who root for different teams and belong to different political parties. At the center of all the diversity, though, is Jesus. Their allegiance, their loyalty, belongs to Him. This is because they've come to know who He is and what He's rescued them from, and so they've said to Him, "You can have it all." And because of Him they're serious about loving one another. They are intentional about laying down their lives for one another. A unity exists here that the world can't imagine or replicate, for only God can unite such vastly different people into one. This kind of love and unity is amazingly attractive, and if and when people see it, they want to be a part of it.

Personally, the most powerful example of an "ambassador for Christ" I've ever come across is Saint John Paul II. I was fortunate to live in Rome from 1992 to 1996. I lived in the shadow of this pope, who has to be one of the greatest men who ever lived.

Karol Józef Wojtyła was born on May 18, 1920, the youngest of three children. Karol's mother, Emilia, died when he was eight years old. His sister, Olga, died before he was born. Karol had a brother, Edmund, with whom he was very close, even though Edmund was thirteen years his senior. By the time Karol was in university, however, Edmund had also died, as had his father, also named Karol. "At twenty," he shared later in life, "I had already lost all the people I loved."[54] In addition to these deep pains, he grew up in Poland, a country that one of his biographers described as having lost World War II *twice*—first to the Nazis and then to the Soviet Union.

His life is almost impossible to summarize, though many moving biographies and videos about him are well worth reading and watching to get a sense of this most amazing man. By the time I arrived in Rome, I was more than familiar with his reputation as a gifted athlete, poet, playwright, actor, and mystic. Oh, and he not only had survived an attempt on his life but also had then visited the man who tried to murder him—and forgave him!

The cardinal of Detroit, Adam Maida, who had sent me to study in Rome, was not only a cardinal but also Polish. In short, that meant he was in Rome a lot. As a result, I was fortunate to meet John Paul II more times than I can honestly remember. Somewhat embarrassingly, we were invited to so many private Masses with him that many times I said no, aware that another opportunity would probably come in a month or so.

Meeting Pope John Paul II was an utterly overwhelming experience. Immediately, in a way I can't quite put into words, you knew you were standing in the presence of greatness. I remember the first time I met him like it was this morning. He said something to me that I will never forget and that I've rarely shared. My goal the first time I met him was simply not to say or do something stupid. I recall Cardinal Maida walking side by side with the pope, introducing him to each one of us personally. When they finally got to me, it was as if he looked into my soul and said, "John, let's be honest: You don't have anywhere near the gifts that I have. But you can still be great. So be great." To be clear, he didn't actually say those words. But he might as well have! I left that encounter so inspired to make something of my life, so desirous not to let down this man—or, of course, God.

You may remember that almost immediately after he was elected pope, he began to repeat the words, "Do not be afraid!" Here was a man who grew up in Poland, who was an orphan by the age of twenty, who had lost his brother, who endured World War II, who had been run over by a truck and left for dead by the Germans, who then "lost" World War II again (to the Soviets), and these are the words he kept repeating? This is extraordinary. Of all the people in the world who had reasons to be afraid, it was this man. Yet he was telling not only the Church but the entire world not to be afraid.

With utmost confidence in the power of the gospel, he proclaimed to all the world at his first Mass as pope:

> Do not be afraid. Open wide the doors for Christ. To his saving power open the boundaries of States, economic and political systems, the vast fields of culture, civilization and development. Do not be afraid. Christ knows "what is in man." He alone knows it.
>
> So often today man does not know what is within him, in the depths of his mind and heart. So often he is uncertain about the meaning of his life on earth. He is assailed by doubt, a doubt which turns into despair. We ask you therefore, we beg you with humility and trust, let Christ speak to man. He alone has words of life, yes, of eternal life.[55]

One can notice here, in his own words, what we've been talking about in this chapter, namely the call to let the gospel into various dimensions of life—politics, culture, development—so as to transform them.

Saint Paul writes, "We are ambassadors for Christ, God making his *appeal* through us" (2 Corinthians 5:20). What is the appeal?

There are a number of ways we could answer that, but here's how I read it: "You can defect! You don't have to live in the home of a cruel tyrant (the devil) anymore. You don't have to live under the laws of Sin and Death. You don't have to live in a dysfunctional family. You can leave that home and move into this other home. You have a good, good Father. You're His beloved son or daughter. He offers you abundant life and true freedom. You can be a part of this other family—the family of God, the Church."

In other words, as I mentioned above, people are supposed to walk into our churches, look around at those assembled there, and say to themselves something like this: "Well, I'll be. This is real. These people get it. These people are different. They don't talk about unity; they're united. They don't talk about love; they love." Nowhere have I found a better articulation of this mission than in one of the prayers found in the *Roman Missal,* the book clergy use when they celebrate Mass. It reads:

> O God, in the covenant of your Christ
> you never cease to gather to yourself from all nations
> a people growing together in unity through the Spirit;
> grant, we pray, that your Church,
> faithful to the mission entrusted to her,
> may continually go forward with the human family
> and always be the leaven and the soul of human society,
> to renew it in Christ and transform it into the family of God.
> Through our Lord Jesus Christ, your Son,
> who lives and reigns with you in the unity of the Holy Spirit,
> God, for ever and ever.[56]

We Were Born for This!

MY WHOLE LIFE I have felt a deep and often painful longing to be great. That's what my father encouraged me to be. John Paul II reinforced this and built on the example and witness of my dad. I'm convinced that every single person deep down wants to be great; no one wants to be mediocre. What does real greatness look like? The world around us often encourages us to think greatness looks like wealth, possessions, athletic prowess, academic and professional achievement, this, that, and the other thing. There's nothing wrong with any of those. In fact, they're good, or can be. But they're not the measure of true greatness.

True greatness is measured by love. True greatness is measured by responding to all that God has done for us in His Son, Jesus.

Jesus's parable of the good Samaritan is perhaps familiar to you. Perhaps it's overly familiar, though. It's probably based on a true story. It was common for people to get beaten up while traveling from Jerusalem to Jericho. A lot of robbers hid along that road. So Jesus tells the story of a man who travels from Jerusalem to Jericho and on the way is assaulted. He's beaten, stripped, left for dead in a ditch. Which means what? It means there's no way to identify him. He has no clothes. Clothes are a distinguishing characteristic. And he can't talk, which means you can't tell where he's from. And he's been left for dead.

Who is the man in the ditch? I am. You are. The human race is. And along finally comes someone from outside the victim's community and sees him. The next words are often translated in English to say that the man "had compassion" (Luke 10:33). This is a really weak translation. The original reads something more like, "his heart was wrenched open" when he saw the man in the ditch. As his heart is wrenched open, he takes action to care for the injured man, to bring him back to life.

Who is the good Samaritan? Jesus. Jesus is the one who, in that conversation in heaven we imagined earlier, saw the situation of Adam—and of you and me—and said, "I'll go. I'll bring them back. I'll bring them home." God's heart was wrenched open in mercy for you and for me, and He was moved to do something about our situation, to rescue us from cosmic powers we could never escape on our own.

Here's the thing: Each day you and I meet people who are figuratively lying in a ditch. They've been beaten. Left for dead. They're walking around without any clue about what they're made for, why they're here, where they're going. They may even have tons of stuff. But they're still walking dead. They're like I was many years ago. Or maybe like you were. And God sends us to them. Like a person picking up a lamp, Jesus wants to pick you and me up and place us in a space where He can shine brilliantly through us, despite all our imperfections, to give people hope.

In our ministry at ACTS XXIX, we see in Saint Joan of Arc a particularly inspiring example for our day and age. Winston Churchill wrote of her, "Joan was a being so uplifted from the ordinary run of mankind that she finds no equal in a thousand years. . . . She embodied the natural goodness and valour of the human race in unexampled perfection. Unconquerable courage, infinite compassion, the virtue of the simple, the wisdom of the just, shone forth in her."[57] Even a man like Mark Twain, hardly a paragon of faith, was utterly captivated by Joan.

As Joan was setting out on the mission the Lord God had uniquely commissioned her for, she was approached by someone and asked, "Aren't you afraid of doing this?" She answered, "No. I'm not afraid. God is with me. I was born for this!"

So were you.

So was I.

You and I don't just "happen" to be alive right now. It's not a historical accident that you're here. God could have chosen to create you to be alive in any moment in history—third-century Guatemala or seventeenth-century France. But He didn't. He created you and me to be alive now, and He's given you and me gifts, natural and supernatural, so we can bring renewal, healing, transformation, and hope to a world that is increasingly desperate. God wants to use you and me to continue the mission and the work of His Son, which He began on Easter Sunday, until that glorious day when He returns and finally makes all things new.

At the conclusion of a wonderful little book called *The Christian Cosmic Narrative,* we read:

So, the battle for humanity will go on until the One who rules all destinies decides that the time of fulfillment has arrived. Christ continues in every age to build his Kingdom, to assault the powers of evil, to attack the fortress of darkness, and to set its captives free. Satan angrily attempts in every age to fend off that attack, trying to maintain his deceitful but now fragile sway over human souls, and to cling, however vainly, to his illegitimate power.

Into that battle, into the complexities and mysteries of a graced creation, into a zone of light and shadow, of high hope and quiet despair, of beauty and corruption, sprung from a race of rebels, some allied to and enslaved by the Devil's tyranny and others struggling together against it by God's power, one fine day, each of us was born. Conceived from all eternity in the mind of God, created by him with a high purpose and a hoped-for destiny, we were brought into existence under the watchful and loving eye of the Lord of the Universe himself.

In the high-stakes drama all around us, we have each been given a part to play, one that bears our name and no one else's. We each have the mercy of God to receive, a self to put to death, a Kingdom to gain, a battle to fight and spiritual enemies to slay, comrades to aid, rebels to win over, and a life of love to build, as we fulfill our task of inhabiting and reflecting the bright life and love of God refracted uniquely through each of his children.

If the Father's hopes for us are fulfilled, we will embrace the part we have been given.

We will receive the grace of forgiveness and new life, renounce the ways of God's enemy, walk the noble

> lowly road shown us by his Son, learn the lessons of humble warfare, and ultimately ascend the thrones prepared for us before the foundation of the world as kings and queens of God's creation. If we squander our high birthright, forget who we are, conform ourselves to the world's dark ways, and despise the promises held out to us, we will forfeit our place in the design of God and end as broken failures.
>
> Here then is the real significance of that potent but often misused word: choice. The ancient battle rages all around us, and the adventure we were born for beckons. Life and death are held out to us and all heaven's bright company is aiding us. Our time on earth is short. Our eternal destiny awaits. The choice is in our hands.[58]

In the gospel of Luke, we read about the first encounter between Jesus and a man named Peter. Peter is a fisherman, in business with his brother, Andrew, and two other brothers, James and John. Together, they run a sort of co-op. As the crowds press in upon Jesus while He preaches, He asks if Peter will let Him get into his boat so He can preach from offshore. When Jesus finishes preaching, He tells Peter, "Put out into the deep and let down your nets for a catch." Peter protests that they had worked all night long and had caught nothing, but perhaps because of the authority in Jesus's voice, he does what he is told. A miraculous catch of fish follows, the likes of which Peter and Andrew have never before seen. There are so many fish, in fact, that they have to call their partners, James and John, to come and help, and still both boats are in danger of sinking under the weight of the huge haul.

Realizing something supernatural has happened at the command of Jesus, Peter is overwhelmed with a sense of his own humanity and falls to his knees before Him. "Depart from me," he says, "for I am a sinful man, O Lord." Ignoring the plea, Jesus tells Peter, "Do not be afraid; from now on you will be catching men" (see Luke 5:1–11).

At least that's how it's usually translated.

Zogron is the Greek word Luke uses that we translate as "catching." It has nothing to do with fishing. It means "to capture alive" or "to spare the life of," but when it's found in the Greek translation of the Old Testament, it is always found in a military context. In the New Testament, we find the word twice and both instances are metaphorical, referring back to that military meaning.

Remembering how the only enemy captured our race way back at the beginning, we could perhaps better understand what Jesus says to Peter this way: "Do not be afraid; from now on you will be going behind enemy lines and rescuing your brothers and sisters who are held captive." This he will be able to do, of course, because of the rescue Jesus accomplishes by His death and resurrection.

During their efforts to bring hope to the German people and defeat National Socialism, the members of the White Rose movement once quipped, I wonder if one day there will be a sign here that reads, "The resistance movement was launched here."[59] As momentous as that movement was, the real resistance started on Good Friday. On that day, Jesus began the ultimate resistance movement, and the Church, with Peter as its head and armed with the Lord's own authority over the enemy, has the ongoing mission, until Jesus returns and makes all things new, of going into enemy-occupied territory and rescuing men and women held captive in the enemy's grip.

Disciples of Jesus are nothing less than rescued people.

Rescued from the power of Sin, the power of Death, the power of the enemy, and from the nightmare that is life apart from God. To them—to us—is now entrusted a most extraordinary mission: to rescue, renew, and transform the human family into the family of God.

Rescued people rescue people.

Will you join?

Let's get to it!

APPENDIX I

HOW THE CHURCH FATHERS SAW THE PASSION

This collection of patristic preaching was gathered by the team at Acts XXIX from a variety of sources and can be found at drive.google.com/drive/folders/1SQp_0yA7PdGtehSp5ZW9QxS5N3Tc6EDe.

Andrew of Crete (d. 740)

Therefore, the cross is something wonderfully great and honorable. It is great because through the cross the many noble acts of Christ found their consummation—very many indeed, for both his miracles and his sufferings were fully rewarded with victory. The cross is honorable because it is both the sign of God's suffering and the trophy of his victory. It stands for his suffering because on it he freely suffered unto death. But it is also his trophy because it was the means by which the devil was wounded and death conquered; the barred gates of hell were smashed, and the cross became the one common salvation of the whole world.

Athanasius (d. 373)

In this way the wicked one, by pouring forth deadly words, frequently ensnares some of those who live a good life, but we must not believe his promises or fear his threats for he always deceives and none of his promises are true. For if everything he says were not a lie, how is it that when he made such infinitely extravagant promises the Lord hooked him like a serpent using the hook of the cross and he was bound with a halter like a beast of burden, and tied up in chains like a runaway slave, his lips pierced by an iron ring, and he was not given the chance to devour any of the faithful at all? Now he is as miserable as a sparrow caught by Christ in the net to be mocked at; now he groans for his companions who have been trodden beneath the Christians' heel like scorpions and serpents. He who took pride in the fact that he had destroyed all the seas, he who promised that he would hold the world in his hand, look at him! You have conquered him and look how he is unable to prevent me arguing with him.

Augustine (d. 430)

It is not difficult, therefore, to see how the devil was conquered when he, who was slain by him, rose again. But there is something greater and more profound of comprehension: to see how the devil was conquered precisely when he was thought to be conquering, namely, when Christ was crucified. For at that moment the blood of him who had no sin at all was shed for the remission of our sins. The devil deservedly held those whom he had bound by sin to the condition of death. So it happened that One who was guilty of no sin freed them justly from this condemnation. The strong man was conquered by this paradoxical justice and bound by this chain, that his vessels might be taken away. Those vessels which had been vessels of wrath were turned into vessels of mercy.

The devil jumped for joy when Christ died; and by the very death of Christ the devil was overcome: he took, as it were, the bait in the mousetrap. He rejoiced at the death, thinking himself death's commander. But that which caused his joy dangled the bait before him. The Lord's cross was the devil's mousetrap: the bait which caught him was the death of the Lord.

The next verse explains something of the reason why so much honor should be paid to him, and why all nations should serve him: He has delivered the needy from the tyrant, that poor person who had no other champion. This needy and poor person is the people that believes in him, and within this people are kings who worship him. They are not too proud to be needy and poor, which means humbly acknowledging that they are sinners and in need of the glory of God, so that the true King, the Son of the King, may free them from the powerful foe. Powerful indeed he is who has been called the accuser. Yet it was not his own strength that brought men and women into subjection to this powerful tyrant, and kept them there in captivity, but human sins. The powerful tyrant is also called in scripture "the strong man," but Christ, who humiliated the accuser, also broke into the strong man's domain to bind him and seize his possessions. Christ is the one who has delivered the needy from the tyrant, that poor person who had no other champion, for no one else had the strength to accomplish that—no righteous person nor even any angel. There was no champion at all, therefore; but Christ came and saved them.

Let us turn to Him who did these things. He is Himself "The Bread which came down from heaven;" but Bread which refresheth the failing, and doth not fail; Bread which can be tasted, cannot be wasted. This Bread did the manna also figure. Wherefore it is said, "He gave them the Bread of heaven, man ate Angels' Bread." Who is the Bread of heaven, but Christ? But in order that man might eat Angels' Bread, the Lord of Angels was made Man. For if He had not been made Man, we should not have His Flesh; if we had not His Flesh, we should not eat the Bread of the Altar. Let us hasten to the inheritance, seeing we have hereby received a great earnest of it. My brethren, let us long for the life of Christ, seeing we hold as an earnest the Death of Christ. How shall He not give us His good things, who hath suffered our evil things? In this our earth, in this evil world, what abounds, but to be born, to labor, and to die? Examine thoroughly man's estate, convict me if I lie: consider all men whether they are in this world for any other end than to be born, to labor, and to die? This is the merchandise of our country: these things here abound. To such merchandize did that Merchantman descend. And forasmuch as every merchant gives and receives; gives what he has, and receives what he has not; when he procures anything, he gives money, and receives what he buys: so Christ too in this His traffic gave and received.

But what received He? That which aboundeth here, to be born, to labor, and to die. And what did He give? To be born again, to rise again, and to reign for ever. O Good Merchant, buy us. Why should I say buy us, when we ought to give Thee thanks that Thou hast bought us? Thou dost deal out our Price to us, we drink Thy Blood; so dost thou deal out to us our Price. And we read the Gospel, our title deed. We are Thy servants, we are Thy creatures: Thou hast made us, Thou hast redeemed us. Any one can buy his servant, create him he cannot; but the Lord hath both created and redeemed His servants; created them, that they might be; redeemed them, that they might not be captives ever. For we fell into the hands of the prince of this world, who seduced Adam, and made him his servant, and began to possess us as his slaves. But the Redeemer came, and the seducer was overcome. And what did our Redeemer to him who held us captive? For our ransom he held out His Cross as a trap; he placed in It as a bait His Blood. He indeed had power to shed His Blood, he did not attain to drink it. And in that he shed the Blood of Him who was no debtor, he was commanded to render up the debtors; he shed the Blood of the Innocent, he was commanded to withdraw from the guilty. He verily shed His Blood to this end, that He might wipe out our sins. That then whereby he held us fast was effaced by the Redeemer's Blood. For he only held us fast by the bonds of our own sins. They were the captive's chains. He came, He bound the strong one with the bonds of His Passion; He entered into his house, into the hearts, that is, of those where he did dwell, and took away his vessels. We are his vessels. He had filled then with his own bitterness. This bitterness too he pledged to our Redeemer in the gall. He had filled us then as his vessels; but our Lord spoiling his vessels, and making them His Own, poured out the bitterness, filled them with sweetness.

The psalm proceeds: It is the Beloved's part also to divide the spoils for the beauty of the house. The word Beloved is repeated for emphasis. But in fact it is not all the codices that have this repetition, and the more exact among them prefix a star to it. Such signs are called asterisks, and they inform us that the passages so marked are present in the Hebrew, but not in the interpretation by the Septuagint. But whether we think Beloved was repeated, or was written once only, I think we must take the words that follow it, to divide the spoils for the beauty of the house, in the sense, it is the Beloved's part also to divide the spoils for the beauty of the house; that is, he was chosen also for the division of the spoils. Undoubtedly the Church which Christ has created is a beautiful house, and he has adorned it by distributing his spoils to it, as a body is made beautiful by the due distribution of its limbs.

Now the word "spoils" is used of goods seized from vanquished enemies, and the gospel throws light on this passage by saying, No one can get into a strong man's house and carry off his implements, unless he has tied up the strong man first (Mt 12:29). Christ tied up the devil with spiritual chains by overcoming death and ascending from the underworld to heaven; he bound the devil by the sacrament of his incarnation, because although the devil found nothing in Christ that deserved death, he was nonetheless allowed to kill him. The consequence was that Christ tied up the devil and took away his belongings as booty. These were the unbelievers through whom the devil worked his will. But the Lord cleansed these tools by forgiving their sins; he left the enemy felled and chained, and sanctified the spoils he had seized. He then assigned them to their due places for the adornment of his own house, appointing some to be apostles, some prophets, some pastors and teachers for the work of ministry, for the building up of the body of Christ.

Bernard of Clairvaux (d. 1153)

He comes as an Infant, and without speech, for the voice of the wailing infant arouses compassion, not terror. If He is terrible to any, yet not to thee. He is become a Little One, His Virgin Mother swathes His tender limbs with bands, and dost thou still tremble with fear? By this weakness thou mayest know that He comes not to destroy, but to save; not to bind, but to unbind. If He shall take up the sword, it will be against thine enemies, and, as the Power and the Wisdom of God, He will trample on the necks of the proud and the mighty.

We have two enemies, sin and death—that is, the death of the soul and the death of the body. Jesus comes to conquer both, and to save us from both. Already He has vanquished sin in His own person by assuming a human nature free from the corruption of sin. For great violence was offered to sin, and it knew itself to be indeed subdued, when that nature which it gloried to have wholly infected and possessed was found in Christ perfectly free from its dominion. Henceforth Christ will pursue our enemies, and will seize them, and will not desist until they are overcome in us. His whole mortal life was a war against sin. He fought against it by word and example. But it was in His passion that He came upon the strong man armed, and bound him, and bore away his spoils.

Jesus Christ also conquers our second enemy, death. He overcomes it first in Himself, when He rises from the dead, the first fruits of them that sleep, and the first-born from the dead. Afterwards He will, in like manner, vanquish death in all of us when He shall raise our mortal bodies from the dust, and destroy this our last enemy. Thus, when He rose from the dead, Jesus was clothed in beauty, not wrapped in swaddling-clothes as at His birth. He that previously overflowed with mercy, "judging no man," girded Himself in His resurrection with the girdle of justice, and in so doing seemed in some degree to restrain His superabundant mercy in order to be thenceforth prepared for the judgment which is to follow our future resurrection.

Bonaventure (d. 1274)

Now that the combat of the passion was over, and the bloody dragon and raging lion thought that he had secured a victory by killing the Lamb, the power of the divinity began to shine forth in his soul as it descended into hell. By this power our strong Lion of the tribe of Judah (Apoc. 5:5), rising against the strong man who was fully armed (Luke 11:21), tore the prey away from him, broke down the gates of hell and bound the serpent. Disarming the Principalities and Powers, he led them away boldly, displaying them openly in triumph in himself (Col. 2:15). Then the Leviathan was led about with a hook (Job 40:25), his jaw pierced by Christ so that he who had no right over the Head which he had attacked, also lost what he had seemed to have over the body. Then the true Samson, as he died, laid prostrate an army of the enemy (cf. Judges 16:30). Then the Lamb without stain by the blood of his Testament led forth the prisoners from the pit in which there was no water (Zach. 9:11). Then the long-awaited brightness of a new light shone upon those that dwelt in the region of the shadow of death (Isa. 9:2).

The Council of Chalcedon (451)

His birth in time in no way subtracts from or adds to that divine and eternal birth of his: but its whole purpose is to restore humanity, who had been deceived, so that it might defeat death and, by its power, destroy the devil who held the power of death. Overcoming the originator of sin and death would be beyond us, had not he whom sin could not defile, nor could death hold down, taken up our nature and made it his own. He was conceived from the Holy Spirit inside the womb of the virgin mother. Her virginity was as untouched in giving him birth as it was in conceiving him.

Cyril of Alexandria (d. 444)

He has conquered the ruler of this world. Having, so to speak, hamstrung him and stripped him of the power he possessed, he has given him over for a prey to his followers. He says, "The strong man, being armed, guards his house; all his goods are in peace. But when one who is stronger than he shall come on him and overcome him, he takes away all his armor wherein he trusted and divides his spoil." This is . . . a plain demonstration and type of the matter depicted after the manner of human affairs. . . .

Before the coming of the Savior, he was in great power, driving and shutting up in his own stall flocks that were not his own but belonging to God over all. He was like some voracious and most insolent robber. Since the Word of God who is above all, the Giver of all might and Lord of powers attacked him, having become man, all his goods have been plundered and his spoil divided. Those of old who had been ensnared by him into ungodliness and error have been called by the holy apostles to the acknowledgment of the truth and been brought near to God the Father by faith in his Son.

Ephrem (d. 373)

Death trampled our Lord underfoot, but he in his turn treated death as a highroad for his own feet. He submitted to it, enduring it willingly, because by this means he would be able to destroy death in spite of itself. Death had its own way when our Lord went out from Jerusalem carrying his cross; but when by a loud cry from that cross he summoned the dead from the underworld, death was powerless to prevent it.

Death slew him by means of the body which he had assumed, but that same body proved to be the weapon with which he conquered death. Concealed beneath the cloak of his manhood, his godhead engaged death in combat; but in slaying our Lord, death itself was slain. It was able to kill natural human life, but was itself killed by the life that is above the nature of man.

Death could not devour our Lord unless he possessed a body, neither could hell swallow him up unless he bore our flesh; and so he came in search of a chariot in which to ride to the underworld. This chariot was the body which he received from the Virgin; in it he invaded death's fortress, broke open its strongroom and scattered all its treasure.

At length he came upon Eve, the mother of all the living. She was that vineyard whose enclosure her own hands had enabled death to violate, so that she could taste its fruit; thus the mother of all the living became the source of death for every living creature.

But in her stead Mary grew up, a new vine in place of the old. Christ, the new life, dwelt within her. When death, with its customary impudence, came foraging for her mortal fruit, it encountered its own destruction in the hidden life that fruit contained. All unsuspecting, it swallowed him up, and in so doing released life itself and set free a multitude of men.

He who was also the carpenter's glorious son set up his cross above death's all-consuming jaws, and led the human race into the dwelling place of life. Since a tree had brought about the downfall of mankind, it was upon a tree that mankind crossed over to the realm of life. Bitter was the branch that had once been grafted upon that ancient tree, but sweet the young shoot that has now been grafted in, the shoot in which we are meant to recognize the Lord whom no creature can resist.

We give glory to you, Lord, who raised up your cross to span the jaws of death like a bridge by which souls might pass from the region of the dead to the land of the living. We give glory to you who put on the body of a single mortal man and made it the source of life for every other mortal man. You are incontestably alive. Your murderers sowed your living body in the earth as farmers sow grain, but it sprang up and yielded an abundant harvest of men raised from the dead.

Come then, my brothers and sisters, let us offer our Lord the great and all-embracing sacrifice of our love, pouring out our treasury of hymns and prayers before him who offered his cross in sacrifice to God for the enrichment of us all.

Gregory of Nazianzus (d. circa 390)

Is it not clear that the Father received the sacrifice, not because He Himself demanded it or needed it, but only on account of the

Divine economy . . . that He Himself might deliver us, in overcoming the tyrants by His power, and by the mediation of His Son bringing us back to himself.

Gregory of Nyssa (d. circa 395)

He was about to engage him who had taken human nature prisoner and was about to loosen death's bonds; by having destroyed the last enemy [cf. 1 Cor. 15:26], he might restore mankind to freedom and peace. . . .

Since the hostile power was not going to enter into relations with a God present unveiled, or endure His appearance in heavenly glory, therefore God, in order to render Himself accessible to him who demanded of Him a ransom for us, concealed Himself under the veil of our nature, in order that, as happens with greedy fishes, together with the bait of the flesh the hook of the Godhead might also be swallowed, and so, through Life passing over into death, and the Light arising in the darkness, that which is opposed to Life and Light might be brought to naught. For darkness cannot endure when the Light shines, nor can death remain in being where Life is active. . . .

Drugs can be mixed with food either by an enemy or by a physician desiring to heal his patient. The one does it to cause death, the other as an antidote; and this method of healing is not inconsistent with a beneficent purpose. For if both drug the food, we must have regard to the motive when we praise the one and blame the other. Therefore it is nothing but just when he who led us astray is paid back in his own coin; for just as he at the beginning beguiled men with the bait of fleshly lust, he is now beguiled through God clothing Himself in the veil of humanity. But the purpose which God sought to attain brings it about that His action must be treated as good and just.

. . . [I]t was not in the nature of the opposing power to come in contact with the undiluted presence of God, and to undergo His unclouded manifestation, therefore, in order to secure that the ransom in our behalf might be easily accepted by him who required it, the Deity was hidden under the veil of our nature, that so, as with ravenous fish, the hook of the Deity might be gulped down along with the bait of flesh, and thus, life being introduced into the house of death, and light shining in darkness, that which is diametrically opposed to light and life might vanish; for it is not in the nature of darkness to remain when light is present, or of death to exist when life is active.

Ignatius of Antioch (d. circa 110)

There was concealed from the ruler of this world the virginity of Mary and the birth of our Lord, and the three renowned mysteries which were done in the tranquility of God from the star. And here, at the manifestation of the Son, magic began to be destroyed, and all bonds were loosed; and the ancient kingdom and the error of evil was destroyed. Henceforward all things were moved together, and the destruction of death was devised, and there was the commencement of that which was perfected in God.

Irenaeus (d. circa 202)

[Why did Christ become man?] That He might destroy sin, overcome death, and give life to man. . . . Man had been created by God that he might have life. If now, having lost life, and having been harmed by the serpent, he were not to return to life, but were to be wholly abandoned to death, then God would have been defeated, and the malice of the serpent would have overcome God's will. But since God is both invincible and magnanimous, He showed His magnanimity in correcting man, and in proving all men, as we have said; but through the Second Man

He bound the strong one, and spoiled his goods, and annihilated death, bringing life to man who had become subject to death. For Adam had become the devil's possession, and the devil held him under his power, by having wrongfully practiced deceit upon him, and by the offer of immortality made him subject to death. For by promising that they should be as gods, which did not lie in his power, he worked death in them. Wherefore he who had taken man captive was himself taken captive by God, and man who had been taken captive was set free from the bondage of condemnation. . . .

The adversary enticed humanity to transgress our maker's law, and thereby got us into his clutches. Yet his power consisted only in tempting the human will toward trespass and apostasy. With these chains he bound up the human will. This is why in the economy of salvation it was necessary that he be bound with the same chains by which he had bound humanity. It would be through a man that humanity would be set free to return to the Lord, leaving the adversary in those bonds by which he himself had been fettered, that is, sin. For when Satan is bound, man is set free; since "none can enter a strong man's house and spoil his goods, unless he first bind the strong man himself." It is in this way that he became exposed as the opposer of the Word who made all things, and subdued by his command. The new man showed him to be a fugitive from the law, and an apostate from God. He then was securely bound as a fugitive, and his goods hauled away. These goods are those who had been in bondage, whom he had unjustly used for his own purposes. So it was a just means by which he was led captive, who had led humanity into captivity unjustly. In this way humanity was rescued from the clutches of its possessor by the tender mercy of God the Father, who had compassion on his own handiwork, and gave to it salvation, restoring it by means of the Word, Christ, in order that humanity might learn from this actual event that they receive incorruptibility not of themselves, but by the free gift of God.

The passion of Christ brought us courage and power. The Lord through His passion ascended up on high, led captivity captive, and gave gifts to men, and gave power to them that believe in Him to tread upon serpents and scorpions and upon all the power of the enemy—that is, the prince of the apostasy. The Lord through His passion destroyed death, brought error to an end, abolished corruption, banished ignorance, manifested life, declared truth, and bestowed incorruption.

The Word of God was made flesh in order that He might destroy death and bring man to life; for we were tied and bound in sin, we were born in sin and live under the dominion of death.

Isidore of Seville (d. 636)

The devil was deluded by the death of the Lord. . . . for through the visible mortality of his flesh, Christ—whom the devil was trying to kill—concealed his divinity, like a snare in which he might entangle him like an unwise bird by a clever trick . . .

The devil, although he attacked the flesh of the humanity in Christ that was evident, was captured as if by the fishhook of his divinity that was lying hidden. For there is in Christ the fishhook of divinity; the food, however, is the flesh; the fishing line is the genealogy that is recited by the Gospel. Holding this fishing line truly is God the Father.

John Chrysostom (d. 407)

Let all pious men and all lovers of God rejoice in the splendor of this feast; let the wise servants blissfully enter into the joy of their Lord; let those who have borne the burden of Lent now receive their pay, and those who have toiled since the first hour, let them now receive their due reward; let any who came after the third hour be grateful to join in the feast, and those who may have come after the sixth, let them not be afraid of being too late; for the Lord is gracious and He receives the last even as the first. He gives rest to him who comes on the eleventh hour as well as to him who has toiled since the first: yes, He has pity on the last and He serves the first; He rewards the one and praises the effort.

Come you all: enter into the joy of your Lord. You the first and you the last, receive alike your reward; you rich and you poor, dance together; you sober and you weaklings, celebrate the day; you who have kept the fast and you who have not, rejoice today. The table is richly loaded: enjoy its royal banquet. The calf is a fatted one: let no one go away hungry. All of you enjoy the banquet of faith; all of you receive the riches of his goodness. Let no one grieve over his poverty, for the universal kingdom has been revealed; let no one weep over his sins, for pardon has shone from the grave; let no one fear death, for the death of our Savior has set us free: He has destroyed it by enduring it, He has despoiled Hades by going down into its kingdom, He has angered it by allowing it to taste of his flesh.

When Isaias foresaw all this, he cried out: "O Hades, you have been angered by encountering Him in the nether world." Hades is angered because frustrated, it is angered because it has been mocked, it is angered because it has been destroyed, it is angered because it has been reduced to naught, it is angered because it is now captive. It seized a body, and, lo! it encountered heaven; it seized the visible, and was overcome by the invisible.

O death, where is your sting? O Hades, where is your victory? Christ is risen and you are abolished. Christ is risen and the demons are cast down. Christ is risen and the angels rejoice. Christ is risen and life is freed. Christ is risen and the tomb is emptied of the dead: for Christ, being risen from the dead, has become the Leader and Reviver of those who had fallen asleep. To Him be glory and power for ever and ever. Amen.

John Damascene (d. 749)

God the Word was made man for this reason: that that very nature which had sinned, fallen, and become corrupt should conquer the tyrant who had deceived it. . . .

Since our Lord Jesus Christ was without sin (for He committed no sin, He Who took away the sin of the world, nor was there any deceit found in His mouth) He was not subject to death, since death came into the world through sin. Rom. 5:12 He dies, therefore, because He took on Himself death on our behalf, and He makes Himself an offering to the Father for our sakes. For we had sinned against Him, and it was meet that He should receive the ransom for us, and that we should thus be delivered from the condemnation. God forbid that the blood of the Lord should have been offered to the tyrant. Wherefore death approaches, and swallowing up the body as a bait is transfixed on the hook of divinity, and after tasting of a sinless and life-giving body, perishes, and brings up again all whom of old he swallowed up. For just as darkness disappears on the introduction of light, so is death repulsed before the assault of life, and brings life to all, but death to the destroyer.

Justin Martyr (d. circa 165)

Christ became man by the Virgin, in order that the disobedience that proceeded from the serpent might receive its destruction in the same manner in which it derived its origin. For Eve, who was a virgin and undefiled, having conceived the word of the serpent, brought forth disobedience and death. But the Virgin Mary received faith and joy when the angel Gabriel announced the good tidings to her that the Spirit of the Lord would come upon her, and the power of the Highest would overshadow her: wherefore also the Holy Thing begotten of her is the Son of God; and she replied, "Be it unto me according to Thy word" (Lk 1:38). And by her has He been born, to Whom we have proved so many Scriptures refer, and by Whom God destroys both the serpent and those angels and men who are like him.

Leo the Great (d. 461)

When, therefore, the merciful and almighty Saviour so arranged the commencement of His human course as to hide the power of His Godhead which was inseparable from His manhood under the veil of our weakness, the crafty foe was taken off his guard and he thought that the nativity of the Child, Who was born for the salvation of mankind, was as much subject to himself as all others are at their birth. For he saw Him crying and weeping, he saw Him wrapped in swaddling clothes, subjected to circumcision, offering the sacrifice which the law required. And then he perceived in Him the usual growth of boyhood, and could have had no doubt of His reaching man's estate by natural steps. Meanwhile, he inflicted insults, multiplied injuries, made use of curses, affronts, blasphemies, abuse, in a word, poured upon Him all the force of his fury and exhausted all the varieties of trial: and knowing how he had poisoned man's nature, had no conception that He had no share in the first transgression Whose mortality he had ascertained by so many proofs. The unscrupulous thief and greedy robber persisted in assaulting Him Who had nothing of His own, and in carrying out the general sentence on original sin, went beyond the bond on which he rested, and required the punishment of iniquity from Him in Whom he found no fault. And thus the malevolent terms of the deadly compact are annulled, and through the injustice of an overcharge the whole debt is canceled. The strong one is bound by his own chains, and every device of the evil one recoils on his own head. When the prince of the world is bound, all that he held in captivity is released. Our nature cleansed from its old contagion regains its honorable estate, death is destroyed by death, nativity is restored by nativity: since at one and the same time redemption does away with slavery, regeneration changes our origin, and faith justifies the sinner.

Maximus the Confessor (d. 662)

His flesh was set before that voracious, gaping dragon as bait to provoke him: flesh that would be deadly for the dragon, for it would utterly destroy him by the power of the Godhead hidden within it. For human nature, however, his flesh was to be a remedy since the power of the Godhead in it would restore human nature to its original grace.

Just as the devil had poisoned the tree of knowledge and spoiled our nature by its taste, so too, in presuming to devour the Lord's flesh he himself is corrupted and is completely destroyed by the power of the Godhead hidden in it.

I am a worm and not a man (Ps. 21:7, LXX). He truly became, and was thus called, a worm because He assumed the flesh without being conceived by human seed. For, just as the worm is not born through copulation or sexual procreation, so too our Lord was not born in the flesh through sexual procreation. Moreover, the Lord mounted His flesh on the fish-hook of His divinity as bait for the devil's deceit, so that, as the insatiable serpent, the devil would take His flesh into his mouth (since its nature is easily overcome) and quiver convulsively on the hook of the Lord's divinity, and, by virtue of the sacred flesh of the Logos, completely vomit the Lord's human nature once he swallowed it. As a result, just as the devil formerly baited man with the hope of divinity, and swallowed him, so too the devil himself would be baited precisely with humanity's fleshly garb; and afterward he would vomit man, who had been deceived by the expectation of becoming divine, the devil himself having been deceived by the expectation of becoming human. The transcendence of God's power would then manifest itself through the weakness of our inferior human nature, which would vanquish the strength of its conqueror. As well, it would be shown that it is God Who, by using the flesh as bait, conquers the devil, rather than the devil conquering man by promising him a divine nature.

Melito of Sardis (d. circa 180)

When the Lord had clothed himself with humanity, and had suffered for the sake of the sufferer, and had been bound for the sake of the imprisoned, and had been judged for the sake of the condemned, and buried for the sake of the one who was buried, he rose up from the dead, and cried aloud with this voice: Who is he who contends with me? Let him stand in opposition to me. I set the condemned man free; I gave the dead man life; I raised up the one who had been entombed. Who is my opponent?

I, he says, am the Christ. I am the one who destroyed death, and triumphed over the enemy, and trampled Hades under foot, and bound the strong one, and carried off man to the heights of heaven, I, he says, am the Christ. Therefore, come, all families of men, you who have been befouled with sins, and receive forgiveness for your sins. I am your forgiveness, I am the passover of your salvation, I am the lamb which was sacrificed for you, I am your ransom, I am your light, I am your savior, I am your resurrection, I am your king, I am leading you up to the heights of heaven, I will show you the eternal Father, I will raise you up by my right hand.

This is the one who made the heavens and the earth, and who in the beginning created man, who was proclaimed through the law and prophets, who became human via the virgin, who was hanged upon a tree, who was buried in the earth, who was resurrected from the dead, and who ascended to the heights of heaven, who sits at the right hand of the Father, who has authority to judge and to save everything, through whom the Father created everything from the beginning of the world to the end of the age.

This is the alpha and the omega. This is the beginning and the end—an indescribable beginning and an incomprehensible end. This is the Christ. This is the king. This is Jesus. This is the general. This is the Lord. This is the one who rose up from the dead. This is the one who sits at the right hand of the Father. He bears the Father and is borne by the Father, to whom be the glory and the power forever. Amen.

Origen (d. circa 253)

But to whom did He give His soul as a ransom for many? Surely not to God. Could it, then, be to the Evil One? For he had us in his power, until the ransom for us should be given to him, even the life of Jesus, since he [the devil] had been deceived, and led to suppose that he was capable of mastering that soul, and he did not see that to hold Him involved a trial of strength greater than he was equal to. Therefore also death, though he thought he had prevailed against Him, no longer lords it over Him, He having become free among the dead and stronger than the power of death, and so much stronger than death that all who will amongst those who are mastered by death may also follow Him, death no longer prevailing against them. For every one who is with Jesus is unassailable by death.

He assumes the dress of those who were under the tyrant, and in appearance he becomes like them in every way until, while placed under the tyrant's sphere of rule, he persuades at least those who were serving him to leave off and turn back to the rightful kingdom. Then at the opportune time he binds the strong man and despoils his powers and principalities and leads away the captives which had been seized and were being held by the tyrant.

It was certainly in this way, then, that Christ also emptied himself voluntarily and took the form of a slave and endured the dominion of the tyrant, having become obedient unto death. Through that death he destroyed him who was holding the power of death, the devil, so that he could liberate those who were being held fast by death.

When [Christ] had bound the strong man and triumphed over him by means of his cross, he even advanced into his house, the house of death in the underworld, and from there he plundered his possessions, that is, he led away the souls which [the devil] was keeping. . . . So then, first he bound him at the cross and thus he entered his house, the underworld, and from there "ascending on high he led captivity captive," namely those who have been raised together with him and have entered the holy city, the heavenly Jerusalem.

(*Comm. on Rom.* 5.10.11–12)

But to whom did He [Christ] give His soul as a ransom for many? Surely not to God. Could it be then to the evil one? For he had us in his power, until the ransom for us should be given to him, even the life of Jesus, since the evil one had been deceived, and led to suppose that he was capable of mastering that soul, and he did not see that to hold Him involved a trial of strength greater than he was equal to. Therefore also death, though he thought he had prevailed against Him, no longer lords it over Him, Christ having become free among the dead, and stronger than the power of death, and so much stronger than death, that all who will amongst those who are mastered by death may also follow Him [out of death's domain], death no longer prevailing against them. For everyone who is with Jesus is unassailable by death.

(*Comm. on Matthew* 16.8)

Rufinus of Assisi (d. circa 411)

If a fish seizes a baited hook, it not only does not take the bait off the hook, but is drawn out of the water to be food for others, so he who had the power of death seized the Body of Jesus in death, not being aware of the hook of Divinity within it, but having swallowed it, he was caught forthwith, and the bars of hell being burst asunder, he was drawn as it were from the abyss to become food for others.

Theodore of Mopsuestia (d. circa 428)

Jesus here [Matthew 12:29] compares the earth with a house and human beings with vessels or possessions. Human beings have become possessions of demons and of the devil, having by evil means been brought under his authority. Thus it was impossible for the demons' own possessions to be taken away unless the demons were first weakened and bound with chains.

Epiphanius of Cyprus (d. 403)

The reading is a sermon of our father among the Saints Epiphanius Archbishop of Cyprus and the burial of the divine body of our Lord and savior Jesus Christ on Joseph of Arimathea and Nicodemus and on the Lord's descent into hell which occurred in wondrous manner after his saving passion.

What is this? Today, great silence in the earth. What is this? Great silence and great stillness. Great silence, for the King sleeps. The earth feared and was still when God fell asleep in the flesh. God died in the flesh, and Hell trembled. God slumbered a short spell, and woke up out of Hell those of times past who were sleeping.

Where now are yesterday's commotions, the cries, the clamourings against Christ, O ye transgressors? Where are the mobs, the riots, the troops, the weapons and the spears? Where the kings, the priests, the judges worthy of judgment? Where the torches, the swords, the unruly shouts? Where the crowds, the jeers, the insolent guards?

Truly in verity and verily in truth, the peoples imagined vain and futile things. They stumbled at the cornerstone Christ and were broken. They crashed themselves against the solid Rock, but their waves scattered into foam. They struck against the indestructible Anvil, but were themselves shattered. They lifted up the Rock upon the Tree, but it fell down and crushed them. They bound the great Samson, Sun, and God, but he loosed the age-old bonds, and destroyed the Philistines and transgressors. The divine Sun set beneath the earth, and brought about deep darkness for the Jews.

Today is salvation for those on earth, and those of ages past beneath the earth. Today is salvation for the world, both seen and unseen. Twofold is the Master's coming today, twofold the dispensation, twofold the love of man, twofold the descent, and likewise the condescension, twofold the visitation unto men—from heaven to earth, and from earth to under the earth.

God draws nigh, Hell's gates open wide. O ye of times past who are fallen asleep, rejoice! Ye that sit in darkness and the shadow of death, receive the great Light! The Master is with his slaves, God with the dead, the Life with mortals, the Guiltless with the guilty, the unwaning Light with those in darkness, the Liberator with the captives, the One far above the heavens with those in the lowest depths.

When Christ was on earth, we believed on him; now that Christ is among the dead, let us go down with him. Let us learn the mysteries there, let us come to know the wonders of the hidden God hid beneath the earth, let us learn how the preaching appeared even to those in Hades. What then? Did God save all without exception when he appeared in Hell? Not so, but there too, only those who believed.

Yesterday, he displayed the things of economy: today, those of sovereignty; yesterday, the things of infirmity: today, those of authority; yesterday, the things of humanity: today, those of divinity. Yesterday, he was slapped: today, he strikes Hell's household with the thunderbolt of his Godhead. Yesterday, he was bound: today, he binds fast the tyrant with unbreakable bonds. Yesterday, he was condemned: today, he grants freedom to the damned. Yesterday, Pilate's minions mocked him: today, Hell's porters shudder to see him.

Come then, listen to the lofty tale of Christ's Passion, listen and praise him, listen and glorify him, listen and proclaim God's great wonders: how the Law retreats, how Grace flourishes; how the types pass away, how the truth is preached; how the shadows recede, how the Sun fills the world; how the Old Covenant expires, how the New Covenant is established; how old things are passed away, how new things blossom forth.

Two peoples were present in Zion at the time of Christ's Passion, that of the Jews and that of the Gentiles; two kings, Pilate and Herod; two high priests, Annas and Caiaphas; that there might likewise be two Passovers—one that was ending, and Christ's, just beginning. Two sacrifices were accomplished that evening, since two salvations were at work—of the living, that is, and of the dead.

The Jew bound a lamb and slew it in sacrifice, while the Gentile sacrificed God in the flesh. The one looked to the shadow, while the other ran to the Sun and God. The Jews bound Christ and sent him away, while the Gentiles eagerly took him in. The one brought in sacrifice an animal victim, while the other offered the body of God; the Jews made remembrance of their passing over from Egypt, while the Gentiles made proclamation of their deliverance from error.

And where did these things take place? In Zion, the city of the great King, where he wrought salvation in the midst of the earth—Jesus, that is, the child of God, known in the midst of two living things: acknowledged to be the Life from Life engendering life in the midst of the Father and the Spirit, the two Living Beings; born in a manger in the midst of angels and men; set as a cornerstone in the midst of the Jews and the Gentiles; preached alike in the midst of the Law and the Prophets; seen on the mountaintop in the midst of Moses and Elias; acknowledged to be God by the wise thief in the midst of two thieves; sitting as eternal Judge in the midst of this life and the next; and working today a twofold life and salvation in the midst of the living and the dead. Twofold life, I repeat; twofold birth, which is to say, rebirth; listen, then, to the facts of the twofold birth, and applaud the wondrous works.

An angel announced the birth of Christ to Mary, Christ's mother, and an angel announced the rebirth of Christ from the tomb to Mary of Magdala. By night was Christ born in Bethlehem, and again by night was he reborn from the dead in Zion. In a cave of stone was Christ born, and in a cave of stone was Christ reborn. He received swaddling-bands when he was born, and he is wrapped in swaddling-bands here as well. He received myrrh at his birth, and he receives myrrh and aloes at his burial. There—Joseph, supposed spouse of Maria; here—Joseph of Arimathea. His birth was in Bethlehem, laid in a manger for his crib, while here, the place where he lay as in a manger, was in a crypt.

Shepherds first preached the glad tidings of Christ's birth, and the shepherds of all men, Christ's disciples, first preached the glad tidings of Christ's rebirth from the dead. There, the angel cried "Hail!" to the Virgin, and here, Christ the Angel of great counsel cried out "All hail!" to the women.

Forty days after his first birth, Christ went up to the earthly Jerusalem, to the temple, and as firstborn, brought a pair of turtledoves to God; and forty days after his rebirth from the dead, Christ ascended to the Jerusalem which is above, whence he had never been parted, into the true Holy of holies, as the incorrupt firstborn from the dead, and brought to God his Father, like two unblemished turtledoves, our soul and our body; and God, the Ancient of days, took him up in his arms, like another aged Simeon, into his uncircumscribed bosom. Now, if thou hearest these things as fables, and not with faith, the unbroken seals of the tomb of Christ's lordly rebirth are thine accusers. For just as Christ was born of a Virgin while keeping sealed the bolts that open the womb, Christ's rebirth took place without breaking open the seals of the tomb. Let us then listen to the sacred oracles concerning how Christ the Life was laid in a tomb, when and by whom.

When the even was come, it says, there came a rich man, named Joseph; the same went in boldly unto Pilate, and asked of him the body of Jesus. Mortal went in unto mortal and asked to receive the God of mortals. Clay asks clay to receive the Fashioner of all, straw from straw seeks to carry off the heavenly Fire, a tiny drop from a drop receives the whole Ocean. Who has ever seen or heard the like? Man grants man the Creator of men. A lawbreaker ventures to hand over the lawful Legislator of laws. An unjust judge sends to burial the Judge of judges as one judged.

When the even was come there came a rich man, named Joseph. Rich indeed, for he carried away the whole compound Person of the Lord. Truly rich, for he received the dual essence of Christ from Pilate. Yea verily rich, for he was vouchsafed to carry off the priceless Pearl. Rich indeed, for he bore off a sack full of the treasure of divinity. How could he not be rich, who acquired the Life and Salvation of the world? How could Joseph not be rich, who received as a gift the Nourisher and Master of all?

When the even was come, for the Sun of righteousness had now set in the grave; wherefore, there came a rich man named Joseph, of Arimathea, which was a disciple secretly for fear of the Jews; and there came also Nicodemus, who once came to Jesus by night. O hidden mystery of mysteries! Two secret disciples come to hide away Jesus in a tomb, teaching by their hiding the hidden mystery of God hid bodily in the grave, each one outdoing the other in their zeal for God—Nicodemus, magnanimous in providing the myrrh and aloes, and Joseph, meritorious for his boldness and daring before Pilate.

You see, this latter, casting off all fear, went in boldly unto Pilate, and asked the body of Jesus. Now when he went in, he dealt very shrewdly, so as to achieve his desired aim. Hence he used not pompous and high-sounding words with Pilate, lest he provoke him to anger and be denied his request; neither did he say, "Give me the body of Jesus, who just a short while ago darkened the sun, rent the rocks, made the earth to quake, opened the graves, and rent in twain the veil of the temple." Nothing of this sort said he to Pilate. What then?

A small request: O judge, I am come to ask a small favour of thee: Give me to bury the dead body of the one condemned by thee, Jesus of Nazareth, Jesus the pauper, Jesus the wanderer, Jesus hanging naked, Jesus the commoner, son of a carpenter, Jesus the prisoner, Jesus bereft of shelter, the stranger, unknown among strangers, who lies hanging, scorned by all and hated. Give me this stranger: for what use to thee is the corpse of this stranger?

Give me this stranger: for he is come here from a far country to save strangers. Give me this stranger: for he is come down into darkness to draw up strangers. Give me this stranger: for he alone is truly a stranger. Give me this stranger, whose country is unknown to us strangers. Give me this stranger, whose father is unknown to us strangers. Give me this stranger, whose place and manners are unknown to us strangers. Give me this stranger, who lived a strange life amidst strangers. Give me this Nazarene stranger, whose birth is unknown to us strangers. Give me this voluntary stranger, who hath not where to lay his head. Give me this stranger, who as a stranger in a strange land was born homeless in a manger. Give me this stranger, who from this same manger fled Herod as a stranger.

Give me this stranger, who from infancy lived in Egypt a stranger, having neither city, nor village, nor house, nor lodging, nor kinsfolk, dwelling in foreign parts with his mother, while yet possessing all things. Give me, O governor, this man crucified and naked, that I may cover him who covered my nature's nakedness. Give me this man, at once dead and God, that I may cover him who covered my sins. Give me to bury this dead man who buried my sin in Jordan. I beseech thee for a dead man, wronged by all, betrayed by a friend, sold by his disciple, persecuted by his brethren, buffeted by his own servants. I entreat thee for a dead man, condemned by those he freed from bondage, given vinegar to drink by those he nursed like babes, wounded by those he healed, abandoned by his disciples, deprived of his own mother. I implore thee, O Pilate, for a dead man hanging on a tree, seeing he has on earth no father at his side, neither any friend, nor disciple, nor kinsman, nor any to bury him, but is all alone in the world—the only-begotten of the only Father—himself God, and no other.

When Joseph had spoken these things to Pilate, Pilate commanded to give him the all-holy body of Jesus. Then he went to Golgotha and took down God incarnate from the Cross; and laid upon the earth God naked in the flesh, yet henceforth naked no more. And so he who draws all men up above is seen lying below; the Life and Breath of all is for a time bereft of breath; the Creator of the many-eyed angels is seen devoid of sight; the Resurrection of all men is laid down to rest; God who raises the dead is dead in the flesh; the thunder of God's Word is silent in the flesh; he who holds the earth in the hollow of his hand is borne about by the hands of men.

Joseph, O Joseph, who didst ask and receive: knowest thou well whom thou hast received? Well? when thou didst draw near the Cross and take down Jesus, didst thou know then whom thou barest? If indeed thou knowest whom thou hast held, now art thou rich. But how then dost thou also prepare for burial that divine and most-fearsome body of Jesus? Laudable is thy purpose, but even more so thy soul's boldness. What? dost thou not tremble to carry in thine arms him who causes the Cherubim to tremble? With what fear dost thou strip off the covering of that divine Flesh? Or with what reverence dost thou steady thy trembling gaze, to look upon and uncover the fleshly nature of the God above all nature? Pray tell me, O Joseph, dost thou bury toward the east as one dead, Jesus, the Sunrise of the east? Or dost thou shut with thy fingers, after the custom of the dead, the eyes of Jesus, who with his immaculate finger opened the eyes of the blind? Dost thou then cover over the mouth of him who opened the mouth of the dumb? Dost thou wrap up the hands of him who stretched out the hands that were withered? Or dost thou bind up, after the custom of the dead, the feet of him who made lame feet to go? Dost thou take up in a bed him who commanded the paralytic, "Take up thy bed and walk"? Dost thou pour out myrrh upon the heavenly Myrrh who poured himself out and sanctified the world? Darest thou to wipe dry the divine and still-bleeding side of Jesus, who as God healed the woman with an issue of blood? Dost thou then wash with water the body of God, who washes all men and grants them cleansing? What lamps dost thou light for the true Light, which lighteth every man? What funeral dirges dost thou sing for him who is ceaselessly praised by all the hosts of heaven? Dost thou indeed shed tears for him, as though dead, who wept and raised up dead Lazarus? Or makest thou lamentation for him who gives joy to all and put an end to Eve's sorrow?

How be it, I bless thy hands, O Joseph, which have tended and handled Jesus' divine and still bleeding hands and feet. I bless thy hands which drew near the gash in God's side even before Thomas, the faithless believer and commendable inquisitor. I bless thy mouth, insatiably sated by and joined to the mouth of Jesus, whence it was filled with the Holy Spirit. I bless thine eyes, which were pressed to the eyes of Jesus, whence they received the true Light. I bless thy face which touched the face of God. I bless thy shoulders, which bore the Bearer of all things. I bless thy head, which came so close to Jesus, the Head of all.

I bless both Joseph and Nicodemus, for they are become Cherubim before the Cherubim, bearing aloft God in their midst; they are become divine ministers before the six-winged Seraphim, covering and reverencing God not with wings, but with a winding-sheet. Joseph and Nicodemus bear upon their shoulders him before whom the Cherubim tremble, just as all the bodiless ranks together bear him; for where Joseph and Nicodemus are, is not the whole divine assembly of angels gathered together as well? The Cherubim go before, and the Seraphim run alongside, the Thrones together bear him, the six-winged cover him, the many-eyed are affrighted to see Jesus sightless in the flesh, the Powers likewise enshroud him, while the Principalities sing hymns. Indeed, all the ranks of angels tremble, astonished and astounded, and they inquire among themselves, saying:

What is this dreadful matter, fearful and frightful in manner? What is this grand and exceptional spectacle? The invisible God who is above us, the bodiless, is seen below as a man among men, naked and lifeless. Joseph and Nicodemus fearlessly give burial to him upon whom the Cherubim attend with reverent fear. When did he descend, who never left the heights? How did he go out, who is ever within? How did he come to earth, who fills all things? How did he depart unnoticed by all, who as God is ever with the Father on high? He who has never appeared to us at any time, has appeared to men as both man and man's friend. How is the Invisible seen? How is the Immaterial incarnate? How did the Passionless suffer the Passion? How was the Judge brought to judgment? How did the Life taste death? How is the Uncontainable contained in a tomb? How does he dwell in a grave, who never left the Father's throne? How does he enter the door of the cave, who opened not the gates of heaven, yet opened the gates of Paradise; who broke not the doors of the Virgin's womb, yet shattered the gates of Hell; who opened not the doors before Thomas, yet opened the gates of the Kingdom to men; who kept unopened the doors and seals of the tomb? How is he numbered among the dead, who is free among the dead? How does the unwaning Light appear in darkness and the shadow of death? Whither does he go, whither does he descend, he who cannot be held by death? What is the reason, what the manner, what the purpose for his descent into Hell? Perhaps he goes down to bring up Adam, our condemned fellow-servant. Yes, surely he goes to seek the first-formed man like a lost sheep. Doubtless he wishes to visit even those who sit in darkness and the shadow of death. Doubtless he goes to loose from their bonds captive Adam and his fellow-prisoner Eve, he who is at once their son and God. So let us descend with him, let us assemble with him, let us hasten, let us skip, let us escort him, let us raise a shout, let us hurry, that we may see God's reconciliation with men, and the gracious Master's release of the condemned.

Indeed, the natural friend of man goes to bring out with his great might and authority the prisoners from ages past who dwell in the tombs, whom the harsh and indomitable tyrant tyrannizes, having spitefully seized and stolen them from God, and filled his infernal lair with those who once dwelt above. There is Adam the prisoner, the first-enchained and first-sentenced to death, lower down than all the rest. There is Abel, the first-slain and first-righteous shepherd, prototype of the unjust slaughter of Christ the Shepherd. There is Noah, the type of Christ, Builder of the great Ark of the Church, who saved all the beastly nations from the flood of ungodliness by the Dove of the Holy Spirit, and expelled from her the dark diabolic Raven. There is Abraham, Christ's forefather, the sacrificer, who with unslain victim and unstained knife offered God propitious sacrifice. There is Isaac in bonds, who was bound of old by Abraham, as a type of Christ. There is Jacob, grieving in Hades below, who once grieved over Joseph above. There is Joseph the prisoner, who was cast into prison in Egypt, as a type of Christ, the imprisoned Potentate. There is Moses, in darkness below, as once in a basket he was in darkness above. There is Daniel in the den of Hell below, who was once in a den of lions above. There is Jeremiah, as in a pit of mire, in the pit of Hell and the decay of death. There in the all-devouring belly of Hell lies Jonah, the type of Christ, the eternal and pre-eternal Jonah, who lives for ever, yea, for ever and evermore. There is David, God's forefather, of whom Christ was descended according to the flesh. But why speak I of David, Jonah, and Solomon? There is the illustrious John himself, greater than all the prophets, who heralds Christ's coming to all those in

Hades, as he did even in the darkness of his mother's womb; the twofold forerunner, the preacher to the living and the dead, who was sent from Herod's prison to Hades, the common prison of those fallen asleep since the world began, righteous and unrighteous alike.

From thence, all the prophets and the righteous secretly sent up ceaseless supplications to God, asking for deliverance from that most dismal place, from the dark and dreary domination of the enemy, and the endless, impenetrable black of night. So one said to God, From the belly of hell cometh my cry: hear thou my voice; while another said, Out of the depths have I cried unto thee, O Lord: Lord, hear my voice. Yet another, Shine thy face that we may be saved. And another, Thou that sittest upon the Cherubim, shine forth. Another, Stir up thy might and come to save us. And another, Let thy tender mercies quickly overtake us, for we are brought very low. Another, Deliver my soul from the nethermost hell. Yet another, Lord, bring my soul out of hell. And another, Abandon not my soul to hades. And another, Raise up my life from corruption, O Lord my God.

Having heard all these pleas, the all-compassionate God determined to extend his love for mankind not only to those living in his day and afterwards, but also to those before his coming held in Hades, sitting in darkness and the shadow of death. Wherefore, just as God the Word visited men in the flesh by means of soul-bearing flesh, so also did he appear to the bodiless souls in Hell by means of his immaculate and God-bearing soul—bereft of his body, but not his divinity.

Let us then make haste and journey in mind to Hades, that we may see how there at last, he masters with masterly might the most mighty master and tyrant, and with his brilliant lightning, as with a whole army, effortlessly subdues the ranks of that immortal infantry; Christ the Door having first burst open the exitless doors in the midst, and shattered the woodless gates of bronze by the wood of the Cross; by the nails having broken and sundered the age-old iron bars, by the bonds of his hands having dissolved the indissoluble bonds like wax, and by the spear in his divine side having pierced through the fleshless heart of the tyrant. There did he break the strength of the bow, when on the bow of the Cross, he stretched out the sinews of his divine arms like bowstrings.

Therefore if thou followest Christ in silence, thou wilt presently see where he bound the tyrant, where he hung his head aloft, how he razed his dungeon and led out the prisoners, how he trampled the serpent, and where he displayed his head, how he freed Adam and raised up Eve, how he broke down the middle wall, where he condemned the cruel dragon, how he set up invincible trophies, where he put Death to death, how he spoiled corruption, and restored man to his primal dignity.

Accordingly, he who yesterday refused the aid of legions of angels in his economy, telling Peter, "I could even now set before me more than twelve legions of angels," today with God-befitting majesty, as both Warrior and Master, goes down by means of death to the depths of death and Hell to oppose the tyrant of death, having with him immortal legions of bodiless soldiers and invisible orders; and not twelve only, but thousands of thousands and ten thousands of ten thousands—Angels, Archangels, Powers, Thrones, six-winged Seraphim, many-eyed Cherubim, and all the host of heaven—escorting, attending, and hymning Christ as their own Master and King; not indeed as fellow-warriors (perish the thought! for what reinforcements could Christ almighty need?), but out of both their duty and longing to stand constantly by God their Master. Among them are loyal spearmen, keen footmen, and swift sceptre-bearers of the Master's divine orders, who at a mere gesture, outrun one another with divine alacrity and zeal, at once putting deed into action at his command, and arraying themselves in triumph against the ranks of the enemy tyrants. Wherefore they then descended, hasting and hurtling to follow after their God and Master, towards the infernal subterranean habitations of those sleeping from past ages hidden deep beneath the earth, to bring out the prisoners and those who had fallen asleep since the world began.

Now when the luminous presence of the Master's divine retinue had arrived at the walled-off, sunless, pitch black habitations of Hades, with its dens and dungeons, caves and caverns, Gabriel the chief-commander went before all—it being his custom to bring glad tidings of joy unto men—and as befits an archangel and general, issued to the hostile powers a mighty, resounding, and lion-like command, saying: Lift up your gates, O ye princes! After him cried Michael, And be ye lift up, ye everlasting gates! Thereafter the Virtues said, "Stand back, ye lawless porters!" Then the Powers said with power, "Be broken, ye unbreakable bonds!" And another, "Be abashed, ye inimical foes!" Yet another, "Be affrighted, ye lawless tyrants!" And just as before the battle array of some terrible and invulnerable, all-powerful, royal, trophy-bearing army, a certain terror and trembling, panic and painful fear seize the enemies of an unconquerable king, just so did it befall those in Hades at Christ's unexpected coming to the netherworld, which occurred like a sudden lightning-flash from above, blinding the eyes of the hostile powers of Hell, as they heard certain thunderous voices bellowing, and angelic hosts commanding, and saying: Lift up your gates, O ye princes! Lift up your gates! Do not simply open them, but lift them up from the foundations, root them out and remove them, that they may never more be shut. Lift up your gates, O ye princes! Not as though the Master here present is unable, even with the doors shut, to enter in at his own bidding, but because as fugitive slaves, he relegates to you the task of raising, removing, and shattering the everlasting gates; on which account he commands not the common lot among you, but those reckoned by you to be princes, saying, Lift up your gates, O ye princes! 'Princes,' and not any other sort among you; for if indeed until now ye have wickedly exercised princedom over those sleeping from the ages, yet henceforth ye shall be their princes no longer, neither of any others, but of yourselves only—yet not even of yourselves. Lift up your gates! for Christ the heavenly Door is at hand. Make way for him that rideth into the dusky regions of Hell—Lord is his name; and to the Lord belong the ways out from the gates of death. Ye indeed made the entryways of death, but he is come to make the ways leading out therefrom; wherefore: Lift up your gates, O ye princes! Lift them up, and do not delay! Lift them up, and make haste! Lift them up, and do not wait! For if ye think to tarry, we shall command the same gates to be lifted up without hands of themselves, saying, Be ye lift up, ye everlasting gates!

No sooner had the hosts of heaven cried out, than at once the gates were lifted up, at once the chains and bars were broken, at once the bolts fell away, at once the foundations of the prison were shaken, at once the hostile forces took flight—one running into another, another tripping over the other, one shouting at the other to flee. They were terrified, shaken, astonished, dismayed, bewildered, stunned and stupefied, confused and quivering. One stood with mouth agape, another hid his head between his knees, another was sprawled out face to the ground, another stood stiff as a corpse, another was seized with terror, another lay petrified and pale faced, while another fled further inside. There did Christ cleave with frenzy the heads of the mighty, there were they shaken by him, there did they gape open their mouths, and say:

Who is this King of glory? Who is this Great One, who with such great numbers, performs here such great wonders? Who is this King of glory, who works now in Hell things never before done in Hell? Who is this that brings out hence the prisoners of all the ages? Who is this that undoes our imperishable power and pride?

Then the Master's forces shouted to them in reply, saying:

Would ye learn who is this King of glory? The Lord strong and mighty, the Lord mighty, and powerful, and invincible in battle. This is he who thrust you out and banished you from the vaults of heaven, O ye miserable, criminal tyrants! This is he who brake the heads of your dragons in the waters of Jordan. This is he who by the Cross openly put you to scorn, triumphed over you, and mortally wounded you. This is he who bound you in chains, and cast you into the dark abyss. This is he who shall expel and destroy you in the eternal fire of Gehenna. So do not dally, do not tarry, but hurry, and send forth those whom until now you have cruelly swallowed up; for your dominion is now abolished, your tyranny is now ceased, your insolence is miserably quashed, your arrogance is brought to an end, your strength is trampled on and destroyed.

When the Master's forces had said these things to the hostile forces, they pressed onwards. Some of them dug up the foundations of the prison, others pursued the hostile powers that fled from the outer chambers further in. Others went about and searched through the crevices, cells, and caverns, while still others carried prisoners to the Master from various places. Some shackled the tyrant, while others unshackled the prisoners of the ages. Some gave orders, while others swiftly carried them out. Some ran before the Master as he went further in, while others stood beside him as their God and victorious King.

While these things, and even more besides, were taking place in Hades and being noised abroad, and as everything was in an uproar and great commotion, since the Master's presence was about to reach the very nethermost of the nether regions; then

Adam, the first-created and first imprisoned of all men, held fast in chains with great security deeper down than all the rest, heard the Master's footsteps coming toward the prisoners, and recognized their sound as he walked about the prison, and turned to all the prisoners with him from former ages, and said:

I hear the sound of someone's footsteps coming toward us; and if he has truly deigned to come unto this place, we are free of our chains: if we should truly see him here with us, we are delivered from Hell.

As Adam spoke these things and others like them to all his fellow-condemned, the Master entered in unto them, wielding the victorious weapon of the Cross. Upon seeing him, Adam the first-formed beat his breast in shock, and cried out to all those sleeping from times past, "My Lord be with you all!" And Christ answering said to Adam, "And with thy spirit." Then he took him by the hand and stood him up, saying: Awake thou that sleepest, and arise from the dead, and Christ shall give thee light. I am thy God, who for thy sake became thy son—for thy sake and thy posterity—who now speak and with authority command the prisoners, 'Go forth,' and them that are in darkness, 'Show yourselves,' and them that sleep, 'Arise.' Again I bid thee, Awake thou that sleepest: for I did not make thee, that thou shouldest be held captive in Hell. Arise from the dead: for I am the Life of mortals. Arise, my creation; arise, my form, made in mine own image.

Arise, let us go hence; for we are one single, inseparable person—thou in me, and I in thee. For thy sake, I thy God became thy son; for thy sake, I the Master took upon me thy servile form; for thy sake, I that am far above the heavens came upon earth, and went under the earth; for thy sake, who art a man, I became as a man without help, free among the dead; for thy sake, who wast exiled from a garden, I was betrayed to the Jews in a garden, and in a garden was crucified.

Behold my face which received spittings, that I might restore to thee thy primal in-breathing. Behold my cheeks which received blows, that I might set right thy marred form according the original image. Behold my back which received scourging, that I might loose the burden of thy sins laid upon thy back. Behold my hands which were nailed to the Tree for good, on behalf of thee who didst stretch forth thy hand to the Tree for evil. Behold my feet which were pierced and nailed to the Tree, on behalf of thee who didst wickedly run to the Tree.

On the sixth day, thine expulsion took place; so on the sixth day, I worked thy restoration and the opening of Paradise. I tasted gall for thee, that I might heal thee from the bitter pleasure of that sweet fruit. I tasted vinegar, that I might neutralise the acrid and unnatural cup of death. I accepted the sponge, that I might blot out the handwriting of thy sins. I accepted the reed, that I might sign the release of the human race. I slept on the Cross and was pierced in the side by a spear, on behalf of thee who didst sleep in Paradise and bring forth Eve from thy side. My side healed the pain of thy side, my sleep shall draw thee out of sleep in the grave, my spear has stopped the sword which turned every way against thee.

Arise then, let us go hence. I drove thee from the land of Paradise, yet I shall return thee no more to Paradise, but to a celestial throne. I barred thee from the archetypal Tree of Life, but lo, I myself, the Life, am now wholly united to thee. I placed Cherubim to keep thee out of Eden as a slave, but now I make Cherubim to bow down before thee as a god. Thou didst hide from God as one naked, but lo, now thou hast hidden within thyself the denuded God. Thou wast clothed in a shameful coat of skins, but I, being God, am clothed in the sanguine coat of thy flesh.

Wherefore arise, all of you, let us go hence, from decay to incorruption, from death unto life. Arise, let us go hence, from darkness to everlasting light. Arise, let us go hence, from grief to joy. Arise, let us go hence, from bondage to liberty, from prison to the Jerusalem above, from bonds to God, from straitness to the bliss of Paradise, from earth to heaven. For to this end, I both died and rose again, that I might be Lord both of the dead and the living.

Wherefore arise, let us go hence; for my heavenly Father awaits the lost sheep; the ninety and nine sheep, the angels, are waiting for the time when Adam their fellow-servant should arise, when he should ascend and return to God. A cherubic throne is set, and those who bear it aloft are ready and waiting, the bridechamber is furnished, the choice foods are made, the everlasting tabernacles and mansions are built, the treasuries of blessings are open, the kingdom of heaven has been prepared before the ages. The good things which eye hath not seen, nor ear heard, neither have entered into the heart of man, are laid up in store for mankind.

When the Master had finished these sayings and others like them, Adam, who was united to him, arose with him; and Eve also arose together with them; and many bodies of the saints which slept from ages past arose, and preached the Master's Resurrection on the third day; the which, let us who believe cheerfully greet, behold, and embrace; dancing with the angels, celebrating with the archangels, and glorifying Christ who raised us up from corruption: to whom be glory and dominion, together with his beginningless Father, and the all-holy, good, and life-giving Spirit, now and ever and unto the ages of ages. Amen.

APPENDIX II

"I THIRST FOR YOU" MEDITATION

"BEHOLD, I STAND AT THE DOOR AND KNOCK" (REV 3:20).

It is true.

I stand at the door of your heart, day and night. Even when you are not listening, even when you doubt it could be me, I am there. I await even the smallest sign of your response, even the slightest hint of invitation that will allow me to enter.

I want you to know that whenever you invite me, I do come. Always, without fail. Silent and unseen I come, but with infinite power and love, bringing the many gifts of my Father. I come with my mercy, with my desire to forgive and heal you, and with a love for you beyond your comprehension—a love every bit as great as the love I myself have received from the Father. *"As the Father has loved me, so I have loved you"* (Jn 15:9). I come longing to console you and give you strength, to lift you up and bind your wounds. I bring you my light, to dispel your darkness and all your doubts. I come with my power, that I might carry you and all of your burdens; with my grace, to touch your heart and transform your life; and my peace I give to still your soul.

I know you through and through. I know everything about you. The very hairs of your head I have numbered. Nothing in your life is unimportant to me. I have followed you through the years, and I have always loved you, even in your wanderings. I know every one of your problems; I know your needs, your fears, and your worries. I hear your every whispered prayer, always. Even when it seems I am silent, I am ever at work in your life to bless you and protect you.

Every movement of your heart I follow, and your every thought. I know all your pain, your struggles and trials, your failures and heartaches. And yes, I know all your sins. But I tell you again that I love you, and not for what you have or haven't done. I love you for you; I love you because you are. I love you for the beauty and the dignity my Father gave you, creating you in his own image. It is a dignity you have often forgotten, a beauty you have tarnished by ego and sin. But I love you as you are, infinitely, completely, without reserve; and I have shed my Blood to win you back. If you only ask me with faith, my grace will touch all that needs changing in your life, and I will give you the strength to free yourself from sin and from all that binds and burdens you, and from all that takes you away from me.

I know what is in your heart. I know your loneliness and all your hurts: the rejections, the judgments, the humiliations. I carried it all before you. And I carried it all *for* you so you might share my strength and my victory. I know especially your need for love—how you thirst to be accepted and appreciated, loved and cherished. But how often have you thirsted in vain, seeking that love outside of me—I who am its Source—striving to fill the emptiness inside you with passing pleasures, and often—with the even greater emptiness of sin. Do you thirst for love? *"If anyone thirst, let him come to me"* (Jn 7:37). I will satisfy your desire for love beyond your dreams. Do you thirst to be appreciated and cherished? I cherish you more than you can imagine—to the point [of] leaving heaven for you, and of dying on a cross to make you one with me.

Don't you realize that your thirst for love is a thirst for me, I who *am* Love? I am myself the answer to your deepest desires.

I THIRST FOR YOU . . . Yes, that is the only way to describe my love for you: I thirst to love you and to be loved by you—that is how precious you are to me.

- Come to me, and I will fill your heart and heal your wounds. I will make you a new creation, and give you peace in all your trials.
- You must never doubt my mercy, my acceptance of you, my desire to forgive, my longing to bless you and live my life in you.
- If you feel unimportant in the eyes of the world, that matters not at all. For me, there is no one more important than you.
- Open to me, come to me, thirst for me, give me your life—and I will prove to you how important you are to my Heart.

Don't you realize that my Father already has a perfect plan to transform your life, beginning from this moment? Trust in me. Ask me every day to enter and take charge of your life—and I will. I promise you before my Father in heaven that I will work miracles in your life. Why would I do this? Because I thirst for you. All I ask of you is that you entrust yourself to me completely. I will do all the rest.

Even now, I behold the place my Father has prepared for you in my kingdom. Remember that you are a pilgrim in this life, on a journey home. The things of this world can never satisfy you, nor bring the peace you seek. All that you have sought outside of me has only left you more empty, so do not cling to material things. Above all, do not run from me when you fall. Come to me without delay. When you give me your sins, you give me the joy of being your Savior. There is nothing I cannot forgive and heal. So come now, and unburden your soul.

No matter how far you may wander, no matter how often you forget me, no matter how many crosses you bear in this life, there is one thing I want you to always remember, one thing that will never change: *I thirst for you*—just as you are. You don't need to change to believe in my love, for it will be your belief in my love that will change you. You forget me, and yet I am seeking you every moment of the day—standing at the door of your heart and knocking. Do you find this hard to believe? The look again at the cross—look at my Heart that was pierced for you. Have you not understood my Cross? Then listen again to the words I spoke there, for they tell you clearly why I endured all this for you: "I thirst . . ." (Jn 19:28). Yes, I thirst for you—as the rest of the psalm-verse I was reciting says of me: "*I looked for pity, but there was none*" (Ps 69:20). All your life I have been looking for your love—I have never stopped seeking to love you and to be loved by you. You have tried many other things in your search for happiness. Why not try opening your heart to me, right now, more than you ever have before?

Whenever you do open the door of your heart, whenever you come close enough, you will then hear me say to you again and again, not in mere human words but in spirit:

No matter what you have done, I love you for your own sake. Come to me with your misery and your sins, with your troubles and needs, and with all your longing to be loved. I stand at the door of your heart and knock. Open to me, for I thirst for you.

—written by Saint Mother Teresa of Calcutta

NOTES

Introduction: Why Stories Matter

1. William Shakespeare, *Macbeth,* act 5, scene 5.

2. Ian Ousby, *Occupation: The Ordeal of France, 1940–1944* (Cooper Square Press, 2000), 170.

3. Annie Murphy Paul, "Your Brain on Fiction," *The New York Times,* March 17, 2012, nytimes.com/2012/03/18/opinion/sunday/the-neuro science-of-your-brain-on-fiction.html.

4. Rod Dreher, *How Dante Can Save Your Life: The Life-Changing Wisdom of History's Greatest Poem* (Regan Arts, 2015), 53.

5. N. T. Wright, *The New Testament and the People of God* (Fortress, 1992), 125, 124: In pages 123–24 of this same work, Wright argues that worldviews do four basic things: 1) They provide the stories through which human beings view reality; 2) from these stories a person can discover how to answer basic questions like who we are, where we are, what's wrong, and what's the solution; 3) "the stories that express the worldview, and the answers which it provides to the questions of identity, environment, evil and eschatology, are expressed . . . in cultural symbols"; and 4) worldviews involve action—a way to live that flows from the earlier question, "What's the solution?"

6. *Oxford Reference,* "worldview," oxfordreference.com/view/10.1093/oi/au thority.20110803124830471.

7. Rajendra Kumar Shah, *Pedagogy in Practice: Theoretical Frameworks, Instructional Strategies, and Contextual Influences* (Deep Science Publishing, 2025), 201.

8. Wright, *The New Testament and the People of God,* 137.

9. Dreher, *How Dante Can Save Your Life,* 54.

10. Dreher, *How Dante Can Save Your Life,* 54.

11. For an excellent examination of these two eras, see James Shea, *From Christendom to Apostolic Mission: Pastoral Strategies for an Apostolic Age* (University of Mary, 2020).
12. Fulton Sheen, "The Fourth Great Crisis in the Church," transcript provided by WQPH, wqphradio.org/2020/11/fulton-sheen-the-fourth-great-crisis-in-the-church.
13. Dreher, *How Dante Can Save Your Life,* 54.
14. Dreher, *How Dante Can Save Your Life,* 54–55.
15. Mitch Albom, "Why Is Living Shorter, Dying Sooner a New Trend?" *Detroit Free Press,* March 31, 2019, freep.com/story/sports/columnists/mitch-albom/2019/03/31/mitch-albom-us-life-expectancy/3319933002.
16. As a point of comparison, the World Health Organization cites that as of December 2023, with a worldwide population of eight billion people, there had been just under seven million deaths due to COVID-19. "COVID-19 epidemiological update—22 December 2023," World Health Organization, who.int/publications/m/item/covid-19-epidemiological-update---22-december-2023.
17. U.S. Department of Health and Human Services, "New Surgeon General Advisory Raises Alarm about the Devastating Impact of the Epidemic of Loneliness and Isolation in the United States," press release, May 3, 2023, hhs.gov/about/news/2023/05/03/new-surgeon-general-advisory-raises-alarm-about-devastating-impact-epidemic-loneliness-isolation-united-states.html.
18. Rikki Schlott, "Number of Teens Who 'Don't Enjoy Life' Has Doubled with Social Media," *New York Post,* June 19, 2023.
19. Michael J. Gorman, *Apostle of the Crucified Lord: A Theological Introduction to Paul and His Letters* (Eerdmans, 2016), 130.
20. Fleming Rutledge, *The Crucifixion: Understanding the Death of Jesus Christ* (Eerdmans, 2015), 6.
21. His Holiness Pope John Paul II, *On Catechesis in Our Time: Apostolic Exhortation (Catechesi Tradendae)* (United States Catholic Conference, 1979), 34.
22. N. T. Wright, *Jesus and the Victory of God* (Fortress, 1996), 176.

Chapter 1: The Splendor of Creation

1. Second Vatican Council, *Dei Verbum* (1965), para. 11–12.
2. Second Vatican Council, *Dei Verbum*, para. 12.

3. Second Vatican Council, *Dei Verbum*, para. 12.
4. *Enuma Elish,* 4:101–4, 129–32, 135–38, 144, in *The Babylonian Genesis: The Story of Creation,* trans. Alexander Heidel, 2nd ed. (University of Chicago Press, 1951).
5. Paraphrased from *Atrahasis,* I.iv, in *Myths from Mesopotamia: Creation, the Flood, Gilgamesh, and Others,* trans. Stephanie Dalley (Oxford University Press, 1989).
6. Elizabeth Howell, "How Many Stars Are in the Milky Way?" Space.com, June 9, 2021, space.com/25959-how-many-stars-are-in-the-milky-way.html.
7. "How Many Earths Can Fit into VY Canis Majoris, the Largest Known Star?" *Vedantu,* vedantu.com/question-answer/earths-can-fit-into-vy-canis-majoris-the-largest-class-6-physics-cbse-5ff2a82946b76d623b35a89b.

Chapter 2: The Only Enemy of the Human Race

1. Robert Spitzer, *Christ Versus Satan in Our Daily Lives: The Cosmic Struggle Between Good and Evil* (Ignatius Press, 2020), 140.
2. C. S. Lewis. *The Screwtape Letters* (1942; HarperCollins edition, 2001), ix.
3. *Catechism of the Catholic Church,* 2nd ed. (Libreria Editrice Vaticana, 1997), para. 391.
4. Sophia Institute, *The Christian Cosmic Narrative: A Deep History of the World* (ACTS XXIX Press, 2021), 23.

Chapter 3: Trafficked

1. *Catechism of the Catholic Church,* 2nd ed. (Libreria Editrice Vaticana, 1997), para. 407.
2. Fleming Rutledge, "Midnight in the Kingdom of Death (The Great Vigil of Easter)," in *The Undoing of Death: Sermons for Holy Week and Easter* (Eerdmans, 2002), 237.
3. William Stringfellow, *Count It All Joy* (Eerdmans, 1967), 52, as quoted in Rutledge, *The Undoing of Death,* 275.
4. Scott Hahn and Curtis Mitch, *Romans: Catholic Commentary on Sacred Scripture* (Baker, 2017), 102.
5. Fleming Rutledge, *The Crucifixion: Understanding the Death of Jesus Christ* (Eerdmans, 2015), 368.

Chapter 4: Rescued

1. This imaginative exercise is inspired in large part by "The Spiritual Exercises of Saint Ignatius," which I described in chapter 3. In the second week of the Exercises, Ignatius invites us to prayerfully consider the Trinity gazing upon fallen and enslaved humanity, saying among themselves, "Let us work the redemption of the human race."
2. See John 12:32.
3. Rutledge, *The Crucifixion,* 369.
4. C. S. Lewis, *Mere Christianity* (1952; Harper Collins, 2001), 46.
5. Words like *nature* and *person* are immensely important for understanding the identity of Jesus. They can also be confusing to many of us. I find it helpful to think of it this way: *Nature* answers the question, "What is it?" *Person* answers the question, "Who is it?" In the case of Jesus, *what He is* is both human and divine. *Who He is* is the second person of the Blessed Trinity.
6. A similar idea is hinted at in J.R.R. Tolkien's The Lord of the Rings series. In a conversation between Gandalf and Aragorn, Gandalf says, "Indeed he [Sauron, a satanic figure] is in great fear, not knowing what mighty one may suddenly appear, wielding the Ring, and assailing him with war, seeking to cast him down and take his place. That we should wish to cast him down and have no one in his place is not a thought that occurs to his mind. *That we should try to destroy the Ring itself has not yet entered into his darkest dream*" (italics mine). *The Two Towers* (Houghton Mifflin, 2002), 500–501. Much as Sauron couldn't imagine the Ring being destroyed—for in his mind, everyone wants power—so Satan couldn't imagine the Creator becoming a humble creature. The sheer humility of God is mind-boggling. Conceived in the womb of a creature He made. Born and raised in a town so insignificant it's not even mentioned in the Old Testament. And then, for some thirty years, hiding like a heavenly "sleeper cell," living an ordinary life as a tradesman.
7. By all means God desires to bring all of us out of slavery, but the key here is that, unlike us, God never sees crowds. He doesn't rescue a generic race but sons and daughters whom He knows personally.
8. Frank Sheed, *To Know Christ Jesus* (Ignatius, 1962), 122.
9. In fact, the Messiah did come to liberate the people from their enemies. The real enemy, though, was not Rome (or Babylon or Assyria or any other nation) but Satan and his legions.

10. Sometimes angels are called sons of God (see Job 38:7; Psalm 29:1). Sometimes the Israelites are called sons of God (Deuteronomy 14:1; Isaiah 63:8). Sometimes the kings of Israel from David's line are called sons of God (2 Samuel 7:14; Psalm 2:7). Sometimes the nation of Israel is collectively designated the son of God (Exodus 4:22; Hosea 11:1).
11. Sheed, *To Know Christ Jesus,* 119.
12. Serge-Thomas Bonino, *Angels and Demons: A Catholic Introduction* (Catholic University Press, 2016), 295.
13. The great Roman orator Cicero (d. 43 B.C.) wrote, "Let the very word 'cross,' be far removed from not only the bodies of Roman citizens, but even from their thoughts, their eyes, and their ears."
14. Rutledge, *The Crucifixion,* 78, 92–93.
15. Asphyxiation is the cause of death in crucifixion.
16. Kenneth Bailey, *The Cross and the Prodigal: Luke 15 Through the Eyes of Middle Eastern Peasants* (InterVarsity, 2005), 67.
17. Bailey, *The Cross and the Prodigal,* 70.
18. Let me state clearly that what follows is not intended as a corrective to the beautiful, vast, and inspiring ways that people often reflect on the Passion of Jesus. I take it somewhat for granted that most people have heard not only of the love of God being revealed on the cross and our sins being forgiven there, but also of such other beautiful themes as the humility and selfless love of Jesus. The writing on these is so vast that it need not be repeated here. What follows, then, is intended to complement this well-known material; it is intended as a retrieval of a dimension of what Jesus was doing that has largely been forgotten and unheard.
19. See Appendix I for various excerpts from early Church leaders preaching on this.
20. From a sermon by Saint Ephrem, "Sermo de Domino Nostro," 3–4. 9: Opera, ed. Thomas Joseph Lamy, 1, 152–58, 166–68, as quoted in *The Liturgy of the Hours,* vol. II (Catholic Book, 1976), 735–36.
21. The entire homily can be found in Appendix I.

Chapter 5: So What?

1. See John 12:32.
2. Mary Healy, *Hebrews: Catholic Commentary on Sacred Scripture* (Baker, 2016), 65.

3. Joseph Ratzinger, Pope Benedict XVI, *Seek That Which Is Above: Meditations Through the Year* (Ignatius, 1986, 2007), 84–85.

Chapter 6: Convince Me

1. For a comprehensive treatment of the credibility of the claim that Jesus bodily rose from the dead and was seen by others, including some who were not His followers, see N. T. Wright's *The Resurrection of the Son of God* (Fortress, 2003). A shorter, more accessible summary of the main argument can also be found in chapter 4, "The Strange Story of Easter" in Wright's *Surprised by Hope: Rethinking Heaven, the Resurrection, and the Mission of the Church* (HarperCollins, 2008).
2. For those who want to go deeper, I highly recommend *The Holy Spirit, Fire of Divine Love* by Wilfrid Stinissen (Ignatius, 2016) and *Sober Intoxication of the Spirit: Filled with the Fullness of God* by Raniero Cantalamessa (Franciscan Media, 2005).
3. There are too many texts to cite, but for examples see Exodus 31:3; 1 Samuel 16:13; and especially Ezekiel 36:25–27.
4. Hahn and Mitch, *Romans,* 126.
5. Thomas Acklin and Boniface Hicks, *Spiritual Direction: A Guide for Sharing the Father's Love* (Emmaus Road, 2017), 78.

Chapter 7: I Give Up

1. See Appendix II for Saint Mother Teresa's "I Thirst for You" meditation.
2. See, for example, Matthew Bates, *Salvation by Allegiance Alone: Rethinking Faith, Works, and the Gospel of Jesus the King* (Baker, 2017).
3. Bates, *Salvation by Allegiance Alone,* 52.
4. For an excellent discussion of the apostles and how their deaths testify to Jesus's resurrection, see N. T. Wright's *The Resurrection of the Son of God: Christian Origins and the Question of God,* vol. 3 (Fortress, 2003). A shorter, more accessible summary of the main argument can also be found in Wright's *Surprised by Hope: Rethinking Heaven, the Resurrection, and the Mission of the Church* (HarperCollins, 2008).
5. Romans 12:2, *The New Testament in Modern English* by J. B. Phillips (Touchstone, 1960, 1972).
6. Aloysius I.A.N. Nwabekee, *Consolation Theology: The African Christian Theological Accent* (Assumpta, 1996), 5.
7. Timothy Keller, *Counterfeit Gods: The Empty Promises of Money, Sex, and Power, and the Only Hope That Matters* (Penguin, 2009), xix–xx.

8. See for example, Arthur C. Brooks, *From Strength to Strength: Finding Success, Happiness, and Deep Purpose in the Second Half of Life* (Portfolio, 2022) and (with Oprah Winfrey) *Build the Life You Want: The Art and Science of Getting Happier* (Portfolio, 2023).
9. Mishnah, *Pesahim* 10:5, as quoted in Brant Pitre, *Jesus and the Jewish Roots of the Eucharist: Unlocking the Secrets of the Last Supper* (Image, 2016), 65.
10. Pitre, *Jesus and the Jewish Roots of the Eucharist,* 65–66.
11. See 1 Peter 3:18–22.
12. For an excellent discussion of this subject, see Jeremy Driscoll, *What Happens at the Mass, rev. ed.* (Liturgy Training, 2011).

Chapter 8: Go, Turn the World Upside Down

1. See for example, Matthew Bates, *Salvation by Allegiance Alone: Rethinking Faith, Works, and the Gospel of Jesus the King* (Baker, 2017) and N. T. Wright, *The Resurrection of the Son of God* (Fortress Press, 2003).
2. John Paul II, "Address to CELAM" (Opening Address of the Nineteenth General Assembly of CELAM, 9 March 1983, Port-au-Prince, Haiti), *L'Osservatore Romano* English Edition 16/780 (18 April 1983), no. 9.
3. See Matthew 5:13–14.
4. See Matthew 13:33 and Luke 13:20–21.
5. N. T. Wright, *Surprised by Hope: Rethinking Heaven, the Resurrection, and the Mission of the Church* (HarperCollins, 2008), 194–201.
6. See Revelation 21:1–5.
7. Lewis, *Mere Christianity,* 46.
8. See Acts 2:38; 22:16; Colossians 1:13–14; Romans 8:14–17; 12:4–5; 1 Corinthians 6:19; 12:12–14; 2 Corinthians 5:17; *Catechism of the Catholic Church,* para. 1262–74.
9. During the Catholic rite of baptism, as the celebrant anoints the child with the sacred chrism, he recites the following: "God the Father of our Lord Jesus Christ has freed you from sin, given you a new birth by water and the Holy Spirit, and welcomed you into his holy people. He now anoints you with the chrism of salvation. As Christ was anointed Priest, Prophet, and King, so may you live always as a member of his body, sharing everlasting life." Quoted from *The Order of Baptism for Children,* 2nd ed. (Liturgical Press, 1986/2020), sec. 62.
10. N. T. Wright, *Into the Heart of Romans: A Deep Dive into Paul's Greatest Letter* (Zondervan Academic, 2023), 148.

11. Wright, *Into the Heart of Romans,* 141.

12. Jeremy Driscoll, "The Mass: Supreme Encounter with God in Jesus," sermon delivered at a parish retreat, Our Lady of Good Counsel Catholic Church, Plymouth, Michigan, February 2018.

13. For just a few examples among many possible verses, see Mark 8:34; Romans 8:17; Philippians 1:29; 1 Peter 4:12–16.

14. *The American Heritage Dictionary of the English Language,* 5th ed. (2022), under "sabotage."

15. Rosa Parks, *Rosa Parks: My Story* (Puffin, 1992), 116.

16. Jeanne Theoharis, *The Rebellious Life of Mrs. Rosa Parks* (Beacon, 2013), 179.

17. Rosa Parks, *Quiet Strength: The Faith, the Hope and the Heart of a Woman Who Changed a Nation* (Zondervan, 1994), 16–17.

18. Parks, *Quiet Strength,* 17–18.

19. Sophie and her brother, Hans, had expressed a desire to be received into the Catholic Church just before their execution, but this did not happen.

20. Sophie Scholl's diary, February 12, 1942, *At the Heart of the White Rose: Letters and Diaries of Hans and Sophie Scholl,* ed. I. Jens, trans. J. Maxwell Brownjohn (Harper & Row, 1987), 191–92, as quoted in Paul Shrimpton, *Conscience Before Conformity: Hans and Sophie Scholl and the White Rose Resistance in Nazi Germany* (Gracewing, 2018), 112–13.

21. Scholl's diary, July 15, 1942, *At the Heart of the White Rose,* 208.

22. Scholl's diary, August 6, 1942, *At the Heart of the White Rose,* 209.

23. As quoted in Shrimpton, *Conscience Before Conformity,* 129.

24. A seventh flier was printed shortly after the execution of Sophie, her brother Hans, and Christoph Probst. Other members of the resistance, notably Hans, also painted anti-Nazi graffiti on the sidewalks and building facades in Munich.

25. Sophie Scholl's statement to the Volksgerichtshof [People's Court] of Judge Roland Freisler, February 22, 1943, as quoted by Jacob G. Hornberger, "Holocaust Resistance: The White Rose—A Lesson in Dissent," Jewish Virtual Library, accessed online at jewishvirtuallibrary.org/the-white-rose-a-lesson-in-dissent.

26. This was shared privately with me by a bishop who was present at the opening of the proceedings for Dorothy Day's canonization.

27. Dorothy Day, "Houses of Hospitality: Peter Maurin's Simple Program," *Commonweal,* April 15, 1938, accessed online at commonwealmagazine.org/houses-hospitality.

28. Day, "Houses of Hospitality."

29. Day, "Houses of Hospitality."

30. It was the same body of Jesus, but it was resurrected, and oftentimes the gospel writers tell us that He kept them from recognizing Him until a certain moment when He chose to reveal Himself.

31. See Genesis 3:8.

32. Charles Colson, interview by Timothy Naftali, Richard Nixon Presidential Library and Museum, Yorba Linda, CA, August 17, 2007, nixonlibrary.gov/sites/default/files/forresearchers/find/histories/colson-2007-08-17.pdf.

33. Colson, interview by Timothy Naftali.

34. Recorded in a taped meeting in the Oval Office, June 17, 1971, and reported in Michael Dobbs, "Charles Colson, Nixon's 'Dirty Tricks' Man, Dies at 80," *Washington Post,* April 21, 2012.

35. Jonathan Aitken, *Charles W. Colson: A Life Redeemed* (Doubleday, 2005), 392.

36. Kathryn Schulz, "From the White House to the Jailhouse to the Pulpit: Chuck Colson on Being Wrong," Slate.com, October 20, 2010, slate.com/news-and-politics/2010/10/from-the-white-house-to-the-jailhouse-to-the-pulpit-chuck-colson-on-being-wrong.html.

37. Chuck Colson, *Born Again* (1976; Hendrickson, 2008), 425.

38. "What We Do," Prison Fellowship, prisonfellowship.org/about.

39. More precisely, it's operating everywhere in the United States except Rhode Island.

40. Aleksandr Solzhenitsyn, "The Bluecaps," chap. 4 in *The Gulag Archipelago* (HarperCollins, 1974), 168.

41. "Inscription Prohibiting Entry to the Temple Mount," City of David.org, accessed online at timeline.cityofdavid.org.il/event/inscription-prohibiting-entry-to-the-temple-mount.

42. *Shoah* is a Hebrew word meaning "catastrophe."

43. Rudolph Höss, *Commandant of Auschwitz: Autobiography* (World, 1959), 35.

44. Rudolf Franz F. Hoess, "Affidavit," May 20, 1946, Nuremberg Military Tribunal II, Case 4, accessed online at nuremberg.law.harvard.edu/documents/4201-affidavit-concerning-the-concentration.

45. Rudolph Höss, "Final Declaration," April 12, 1947, as quoted by Manfred Deselaers, "The Conscience of a Perpetrator–Rudolf Höss,

Commander of Auschwitz," Centre for Dialogue and Prayer in Oświęcim, accessed online at cdim.pl/en/texts/manfred-deselaers-the-conscience-of-a-perpetrator/#:~:text=in%20the%20seclusion%20of%20my%20detainment%20I,enormous%20my%20crime%20against%20humanity%20has%20been.

46. Höss, "Final Declaration."

47. This quote is contested. It was once cited by an abbot who wishes to remain unknown. See James W. Bernauer, ed., *Auschwitz and Absolution: The Case of the Commandant and the Confessor* (Orbis, 2023), xxvii.

48. Rudolf Höss, *Death Dealer: The Memoirs of the SS Commandant at Auschwitz,* ed. Steven Paskuly (Prometheus, 2012), 192.

49. *Diary of Saint Maria Faustina Kowalska: Divine Mercy in My Soul* (Marian Press, 1987), 1059.

50. Marriage is unique among the sacraments. It was instituted way back at the beginning of our race, when God brought the first man and woman together. Jesus, then, didn't institute it but rather elevated it so that marriage now points to Him and His relationship with the Church.

51. To be sure, the married couple *is* a visible sign of the love that Jesus has for His bride. But this is not to the exclusion of the fact that the individual persons are the visible sign to each other of Christ's love, and this comes first.

52. Though this is the name of what the couple receives after the Lord's Prayer in the Catholic Marriage Ritual, it is considered "a kind of consecration" (Gaudium et Spes 48). That is to say, it's more than a mere blessing. Something happens to them—both as individuals and as a couple. They receive something they didn't have before.

53. A glimpse into who my dad was can be found by listening to his funeral homily at watch.actsxxix.org/videos/a-homily-for-his-father-s-funeral-fr-john-riccardo.

54. As told to Andre Frossard and quoted in Jane Barnes and Helen Whitney, "John Paul II: His Life and His Papacy," *Frontline,* PBS, n.d., pbs.org/wgbh/pages/frontline/shows/pope/etc/bio.html.

55. "Homily of His Holiness John Paul II for the Inauguration of His Pontificate," October 22, 1978, accessed online at vatican.va/content/john-paul-ii/en/homilies/1978/documents/hf_jp-ii_hom_19781022_inizio-pontificato.html.

56. "Collect of Mass for the Church, B," *Roman Missal,* as quoted in Barbara Morgan and Athanasius Munroe, *Echoing the Mystery: Unlocking the Deposit of Faith in Catechesis* (Lumen Ecclesiae, 2022), 259.

57. Winston Churchill, "Joan of Arc," *The Birth of Britain: A History of the English-Speaking Peoples* (1956; Bloomsbury, 2015), 260.

58. Sophia Institute, *The Christian Cosmic Narrative,* 155–56.

59. Richard Hanser, *A Noble Treason: The Story of Sophie Scholl and the White Rose Revolt Against Hitler* (Ignatius Press, 2012), 116.

ABOUT THE AUTHOR

FR. JOHN RICCARDO is a Catholic priest, author, syndicated radio host, and executive director of ACTS XXIX—Mobilizing for Mission, a Detroit-based Catholic apostolate. He founded ACTS XXIX in 2019, and its mission is to renew and transform the Church by proclaiming the gospel in attractive and compelling ways. Under Fr. John's leadership, ACTS XXIX and its missionaries are active in dioceses and parishes throughout the United States and in more than twenty other countries. Fr. John Riccardo is a graduate of the University of Michigan, the Pontifical Gregorian University, and the Pontifical John Paul II Institute for Studies on Marriage and Family.

ABOUT THE TYPE

This book was set in Garamond, a typeface originally designed by the Parisian type cutter Claude Garamond (c. 1500–61). This version of Garamond was modeled on a 1592 specimen sheet from the Egenolff-Berner foundry, which was produced from types assumed to have been brought to Frankfurt by the punch cutter Jacques Sabon (c. 1520–80).

Claude Garamond's distinguished romans and italics first appeared in *Opera Ciceronis* in 1543–44. The Garamond types are clear, open, and elegant.